$4

My Three Lives on Earth

MY THREE LIVES ON EARTH

THE LIFE STORY OF AN AFGHAN AMERICAN

TAWAB ASSIFI

To: Elieine

Tawab Assifi

04-09-2016

authorHOUSE®

AuthorHouse™
1663 Liberty Drive
Bloomington, IN 47403
www.authorhouse.com
Phone: 1 (800) 839-8640

Published by AuthorHouse   08/13/2015

ISBN: 978-1-5049-0447-6 (sc)
ISBN: 978-1-5049-0473-5 (hc)
ISBN: 978-1-5049-0472-8 (e)

Library of Congress Control Number: 2015905110

Print information available on the last page.

Acknowledgments

I sincerely appreciate and thank my dear family and friends for their encouragement and help in writing this memoir:

My wife Fariha for her patience in putting up with me during the long hours I spent chugging along the computer keyboard.

Our son Tamim has been a master of solving all my problems that I had with the computer and presentations.

Our daughters Giselle, Madina, Shamila, Somaya, sons-in-law and friends have continously supported me.

I thank Rosanne Klass for editing Part 2 of this book and for providing the explanatory footnotes in the text.

The Life Story of an Afghan American is the true story of the author's *three lives,* depicted in three parts.

In part one, you will read about his early years when he was growing up, going to school, earning a higher education at an Ivy League university in the United States, and returning to his homeland, Afghanistan, to build it. Then, the author returns to America for higher degrees in engineering before returning once more to develop his ancestral homeland. In this part, you will read about how he did all of this work, from scratch to fulfillment, under almost impossible conditions.

In part two, you will read about how hell breaks loose in his homeland, resulting in his imprisonment by Soviet-supported Communists. In addition to being tortured, the author faces the threat of being killed at any moment while hundreds of his people are continuously killed all around him. The writer portrays the true story of life in hell—Afghanistan—and discusses the tragic consequences of the Soviet coup. The author then tells the story of his efforts to extricate himself and ooze out of the human grinding machine run by Communist operatives in Afghanistan.

In part three, you will read about how the author struggles to enter a heaven on earth for a chance at beginning a third life in beautiful America, and then about how this Afghan American tries again to rebuild his destroyed homeland and bring hope and resources to its broken-down people. There is an account of the author's struggles to reach out of the morass of adversities engulfing him in a manmade hell on earth.

What kept the author and his family going was the hope of and promise for a chance at a new life in a place where liberty and justice prevails, that is served by a government made of the people, which runs and is supported by the people—working for the good life and prosperity for all! The author describes his endeavors in trying to make his homeland into a heaven on earth!

This story of the three lives of this Afghan American is absolutely true, exhilarating, and saddening, given the tragic events that the downtrodden people of Afghanistan had to endure. By reading this story, you can envision how a person with an indomitable spirit and with a deep belief in eternal justice and in American founding principles can overcome insurmountable tragedies, all with a glimmer of hope for a new life in heaven on earth—in America.

PART 1

THE BEGINNING

I was born in 1931, to diplomatic parents stationed at the Afghan embassy in Tehran. When I was about nine months old, my parents took me with them to Ankara, where my father, Abdul Wahab Assifi, was appointed as first secretary of the Afghan embassy in Turkey.

I attended kindergarten and then first grade in Ankara. The first language that I learned was Turkish. During this period, the Afghan ambassador stationed in Turkey was Sultan Ahmad Sherzoy, my mother's older brother. He had shown courage and bravery on the side of Turks during the Turkish wars with Bulgaria and Greece. The president of Turkey at the time, Mustafa Kemal Atatürk, remembering this gesture, personally attended the parties given at the embassy celebrating Afghan independence from British rule.

Atatürk was always accompanied by Prime Minister İsmet İnönü, who liked to play chess with my father during the party. My father was a chess champion. He had won all the chess games when he was in Tehran and later when he came to Ankara. İnönü would tell my father, "Come, on Wahab Bey, let Atatürk party. You and I will play chess." İnönü was a very kind person. He would tell me, "Come on, son, watch your father beat me in *shatranj* [chess]." I would stand next to them and watch them play chess.

My Father

Abdul Wahab was nine years old when his father (my grandfather), Mohd Asif Khan, passed away while he was the governor of Andkhoy, Faryab.

Asif Khan was a modest person and served the people of Andkhoy very well. They had him buried in Baba-Wali, a holy shrine. My grandfather was not a rich person. All that he left behind was five camels and very little money. He had married four wives and had left behind five daughters and four sons.

At that time, my father and his ten-year-older brother, Mohd Ishaq, were the men of the family and had to take care of their sisters and younger brothers. The local people and friends of my father's father took most of the things that had to be done into their own hands and arranged for their transport to Mazar-i-Sharif, to the residence of their father's older brother, Mohd Omar Khan.

In Mazar, a friend of my father's father, Akhund Zada Sahib, took care of my father and told him, "I will get you a job as an apprentice in a friend's cloth-selling shop." After he worked for a period at the shop, they told him that he did not have the talent to make a good cloth salesman. Thereafter, he was sent to Kabul to enter a school at Baghban Bashi, a district of Kabul. After graduating from school, he applied for and got a job as an entry-level clerk at the Foreign Ministry. My father was a very intelligent and hardworking person. He excelled at whatever job he was assigned to do.

As a nine- to ten-year-old boy, my father often watched some older gentlemen playing chess. One day, one of the chess partners had not yet arrived. My father asked the other person, "Uncle, could you show me how to play chess?"

The man said, "Come on, kid. Although this is an older people's game, I will show you how it is played." He then showed my father how different pieces moved and how one took pieces and checkmated, etc.

My father then asked, "Uncle, now that I have learned how chess is played, may I play a game with you?"

The man responded, "Okay, my son, let us have some fun," and then proceeded to play. My father really surprised the gentleman when, somehow, he beat him. The man said, "I do not know how that happened, but let me now show you how chess is really played!" So, they played again, and my father beat him the second time. But this time, the man got upset. He picked up his cane, got up, started shaking the cane at my father, and said, "You impertinent kid. Let me show you what beating is really like." Then, he began moving toward my father, who rose and started running away from him. He kept chasing my father around the house and the yard, wielding his cane and shouting, "I will show you a real beating, kid," until he ran out of breath.

Everyone in the house and the yard were watching the scene and laughing at what they were seeing. The next day, the old gentleman sent word around to tell Abdul Wahab-jan. "Come and watch us play chess, and tell the boy that I am sorry. I will not behave like I did the other day."

My father said that pretty soon, word got around that there was a kid who beat older people in chess. Gradually, my father became quite well-known. He beat people in the Foreign Ministry, and then when he got a job as a secretary in Tehran. Later, at his job in Ankara, Turkey, he was finally recognized as a champion chess player.

In later years, when he came back to Kabul, my father organized a chess club, introducing and showing local chess players the rules of European-style chess. At one time, he participated with a team of chess players from Afghanistan, in the International Chess Championship Games held at Tripoli, Libya. I believe that their team placed second in the championship.

One time, I asked my father, "Do I have talent in chess? Could you tutor me to become a player like you?"

He said, "Son, you have seen me spending hours, weeks, and months playing chess. What did it get me?" He then said, "Son, you are were very good at your studies and are good at the work that you do. Keep on doing what you've been doing. It is very good and much better than spending your time playing chess." To this day, I watch others play chess and try to imagine what the best moves are, given the current configuration of pieces on the chessboard.

It was one of my happiest moments when my father and mother came to the United States. However, my father had an asthma problem— and an inability to see and recognize things, because of wet macular degeneration, which did not have a cure at that time.

His old chess friends would come to our home and whisper to each other, saying, "Let us play chess and beat him now that he cannot see." They would ask him, "Sir, how about a game of chess? Would you like to play for old time's sake?"

My father would say, "Yes, boys, I will let you guys beat me now." But the result was still what it had always been before.

Later on, I asked my father, "How are you able to do that when you cannot see?"

His answer was, "Son, I see the chessboard in my mind; I do not need eyes to see the board and play chess!"

In the summer of 1936, when my father was appointed to a new post at the Afghan Foreign Ministry, he and my mother, Bibi Hawa, decided to go to Afghanistan. We traveled first by train to Istanbul, and then by boat through the Black Sea to Odessa, Ukraine. From there, we took a train to Moscow, Russia. After that, we took another train to Termez, Uzbekistan, near the border of Afghanistan. I remember this trip quite well, as it was my first ship ride through a rough sea. My mother was very seasick during our ship ride in the Black Sea.

Moscow

I was fascinated by the locomotives in the Moscow train station. I asked my mother to let me watch one of them. But while I was there, a policeman came and said something in Russian that I could not understand. He did not understand my response in Turkish. Then, he lifted me up on his shoulder and carried me to a room, where some white-coated women would not let go of me. They formed a circle, held hands around me, and squatted down. No matter how much I struggled and kicked them, I could not release myself—not until my mother came and saved me from them.

Also, I remember that in Moscow, the train station was very big, the streets were very wide with not many cars in them, and the buildings looked dark and dreary.

Amu Darya (Oxus River)

Our train trip from Moscow to Termez, Uzbekistan, was long. We went close to Amu Darya (Oxus River) and took a ferryboat across the river. My mother's brother-in-law, Mohd Akhtar Omar (Sher Agha), greeted us on the Afghanistan side. He was the chief officer of the border gendarme units. He took us on a *gawdi,* a two-wheeled horse carriage, from the river post to the village of Siaah-Gird to the command post of the gendarmerie. On our way to the command post, I saw very large sand dunes for the first time. At Siaah-Gird, we were greeted by Aunt Saliha-jon (Bibi gul), my mother's younger sister. My mother, after a long time, was very happy to see her sister. Siaah-Gird was an oasis with sand dunes all around it. I enjoyed running and playing on top of the domes of straw–mud buildings, pretending that I was riding my tree-branch horse in a desert surrounded by dunes.

Mazar-i-Sharif

We did not stay very long with my aunt and her husband. We boarded another gawdi for our trip to the town of Dehdadi in Mazar-i-Sharif, where my father's sister lived with her family. The large Afghan army division was located at this place. My father's uncle Naaeb Saalaar Mohd Omar Khan had built this place and was the chief commander of the whole division. However, staying in Dehdadi was not enjoyable. I did not know it at that time, but after quite some time, my mother told me that my father was very much saddened when he went to meet his sister and learned that she had passed away.

From Mazar-i-Sharif to Kabul, we went by taxi. It took us three days, on gravel roads, to make this trip. We crossed several small rivers and high mountain passes on our way to Kabul.

Kabul

In Kabul, we lived in a two-story stonemasonry house that my grandfather (my mother's father, Sardar Sher Ahmad Khan) had built with the money that my parents had sent from Turkey. My mother, Bibi Hawa-jon, was the oldest daughter. My parents enrolled me in the first grade at İstiklal High School. It was not easy for me, because I had to learn the Dari and Pashto languages. Since we did not have a car or a gawdi and there were no buses at that time, I had to walk about a four-mile distance, going to school and coming back home, every day.

My Mother

My mother was Sardar Shir-Ahmad Khan's oldest daughter. She and my father fell in love and got married when they were both working at the Afghan embassy in Tehran, Iran. She was the sister of the ambassador Sultan Ahmad Shirzoy, who had taken her with him from Kabul to Tehran, because of the tragic event of her first husband's assassination in Kabul. She, many years later, told me that her young husband had been killed. The rumor in the court was that this was done by order of the king during a military exercise, because the king was not happy that one of his sisters had fallen in love with this young, handsome officer who was already married.

My mother had studied in a girls' high school in Kabul, continuing her education in the medical field when she was in Tehran. She took lessons and practical training from a Russian dentist who had migrated to Iran because of the Bolshevik Revolution in Russia. She was an intelligent woman and had learned the Turkish, French, and English languages as the wife of a diplomat.

Later on, when we moved to Kabul, my mother became a nurse to her ailing father, Sher Ahmad Khan, and to our larger family, who were mostly living close by.

When my father and mother came to America, my mother polished her English and had become quite fluent in it. After five years, she applied for citizenship, passed the examination, and became a US citizen. During the swearing-in ceremony at the convention center in Los Angeles, a large number of people were being sworn in to become citizens. Since the walking distance was large, I had taken my mother in a wheelchair. The people who were conducting the ceremony learned that she was one of oldest people in the room who was going to be a citizen. They made an announcement and called her name so that she would come near the podium. She held a small American flag and was waving it, saying, "I am an American. I am an American."

When we were in Kabul, I met my grandfather at the old Qala-i-Yakatoot, which had tall fortification towers and a very large garden with apple, pear, peach, apricot, and plum trees. My grandfather had erected a very tall swing for all his grandchildren to play on and swing very high. I always loved to run in the garden paths and the orchard. My mother told me that my grandfather loved to see me run. He said, "That Tawab runs like a deer."

During King Abdur Rahman's reign, Sher Ahmad Khan was trained as an engineer by British engineers. In his younger years, he had designed several river diversions, intakes, and canals. All the canals that he had designed and constructed he named "Nahr-i-Shahi," meaning "King's Canal." I have seen several of the canals that he designed and constructed. His engineering work was very good, and all the work that he did has lasted to this date.

My grandfather's father, Sardar Abdul Qadir Khan, was a freedom fighter during the British invasion of Afghanistan. In fact, all his family were fighting the British soldiers when they occupied the city of Kabul. The British garrison was in Tapa-i-Bala Hisar. My great-great-grandfather and his freedom fighters would attack the garrison at night and then come back to the fortifications. My great-grandmother would take care of the wounded and prepare food for them while they rested before launching another attack on the British fortifications.

Several times, the British found out where these fighters gathered. They attacked with cannon fire and bombarded the *qala*.[1] I could find cannonballs, heavy and round, on the towers and in some other places in the qala. These cannonballs were very heavy and difficult to play with.

At one time, the British soldiers had attacked the qala while the freedom fighters were gathered. Before the attack, word had gotten to my great-great-grandfather Qadir Khan that the British were attacking. In order to divert the attacking soldiers away from the fighters, Qadir Khan, two of his young sons, and an adjutant had gone on their horses in front of the troops and then started running away, but in a different direction. They had diverted the British cavalry in an easterly direction, away from the qala and the freedom fighters.

The chase lasted for quite a distance. The freedom fighters came to a big canal called Nahr-i-Ajmeer. The four of them jumped their horses over the canal. Qadir Khan's horse was injured during the jump. He had told his young sons, Nadir Khan and Sher Ahmad Shirzoy, and their adjutant to go inside the canal, back toward their own Qala-i-Yakatoot, so the British cavalry could not see them. He himself got ready to fight the British on foot.

Eventually, the British caught up with him. He fired his pistol and then fought the British with his sword. He was killed right in that place. The British could not find the other three riders.

---

[1]   A qala is a fortified residence.

Eventually, my grandfather, his brother, and their adjutant made it back to the qala. Their mother asked them, "Where is your father?"

They responded sadly, saying, "He stayed back to fight the British troops."

My great-great-grandmother and family did not know what had happened to Qadir Khan. They sent some people around to search for him, but they could not find him. At one point, some people in one of the villages had told them, "We saw that the British troops were fighting someone. He fought quite valiantly, but at the end, he was killed. Some of us went from the village, brought his body, and buried him in Ziarat-i-Khwaja Zanburak."

When my great-great-grandmother and some freedom fighters from our qala had gone to that area and dug out the place, they found Qadir Khan's body. There was fresh blood in one of his hands. Some of his long hair had been cut and was sitting in the blood.

Many years later, I went to Khwaja Zanburak and said a few words of prayer for the soul of the brave grandfather I am proud to have had.

I had made it to third grade in Kabul when my father was appointed as Afghan general consul in Bombay, India. My parents took me with them to Bombay.

Bombay

In Bombay, I was enrolled in the second grade of Saint Mary's High School, which was run by the British. Our class teacher was an Englishwoman. I had to learn the English language. My parents hired an English-language tutor to help me catch up and learn English. The school was not very close to the Afghan consulate. I rode the school bus every day. I made it to the third grade in Bombay.

At that time, India was under British rule, and people often heard news of World War II on the radio. The Afghan consulate was located in Malabar Hill, next to the British viceroy's mansion near the bay.

Once, I saw the viceroy coming out of there in his Rolls-Royce. During the time my family was in Bombay, we once went to a park on top of Malabar Hill. We saw the place to which fire-worshipers brought their dead, a huge well that had a platform in the middle where they laid the bodies for vultures to pick on.

Mashhad

When my father was reassigned as Afghan general consul in Mashhad, Iran, my parents took me with them to Mashhad. They called this city Holy Mashhad, because the shrine of Imam Reza-i-Gharib was there.

I was enrolled in the fourth grade of Rezā Shāh-i-Pahlavi Grade School. Here, again, I had to learn a new language—this time, Farsi—and catch up with the school program. My parents hired a tutor to help me in my studies. The Iranian school program was different. I had to relearn the Farsi language and memorize poetry and Iranian history. I did not have difficulty in arithmetic classes because math was not too dependent on languages.

In Mashhad, I begged my mother and father to buy me a bicycle. They agreed and took me to a bicycle shop. In the shop, I became interested in a bicycle that did not have a chain to turn the rear wheel. It had an axle and a gear in the back, very much like automobiles did. I loved this bicycle and brought it with me to other places when we left Mashhad. Since all other bicycles had chains, mine attracted attention when people saw me riding it around.

One of the things that I distinctly remember from our stay in Mashhad was a trip we took to the tomb of the famous poet Ferdowsi Tusi. Ferdowsi had written *Shahnameh,* the epic story of Rustam-i-Dastaan and the history of Seistan, at the behest of the famous king Sultan Mahmud Ghaznavi. My father always liked beautiful scenery. After we visited the shrine of Ferdowsi, he said, "Let us picnic." He drove the car to a nice spot under some willow trees near a small river and spread a blanket. We sat there enjoying the view of Ferdowsi's shrine, while my mother gave us some food that she had brought for us from Mashhad. Mashhad, very much like Afghanistan, has very tasty, sweet grapes and melons.

Maimana

I had made it to the sixth grade in Mashhad when my father was appointed as the governor of Maimana (Faryab) Province. My father was a very intelligent, honest, and hardworking person. This is why he was promoted to higher positions within foreign and interior ministries. We went to Maimana. Around this time, my parents decided that I should continue my schooling in Kabul, the capital of Afghanistan.

Back to Kabul

That decision required that my mother and I go to Kabul and that my father stay in Maimana. My mother and I took a bus from Maimana to Mazar-i-Sharif, and another bus from Mazar-i-Sharif to Kabul. From then on in Kabul, we lived in our own house.

High School

I entered the seventh grade at Habibia High School. The school was about four miles from our home, and I had to walk there and back every day.

My mother made some arrangements to have my grandmother and uncles (my father's brothers) Rafiq Jon and Atiq Jon stay with us in our house. In this way, she could go to Maimana and be with my father. I loved my uncles very much.

Horseback Riding

My uncle Atiq Jon was a lot of fun to be with. During summer vacations, we both went to Maimana to visit my parents. We did a lot of horseback riding there. My father arranged for us to go to several very interesting places in Maimana, like Sari-Houze, a lake formed by the construction of an old masonry dam a hundred years ago, a project initiated by General Ghausuddin Khan. The Sari-Houze Lake was a wildlife refuge with many kinds of migratory and local birds flying around and swimming in it.

Another place that we went to was the mineral water springs, where a lot of water gushed out of mountainside rocks. My father had arranged for us to take many empty bottles and fill them with mineral water before taking them back to Maimana. At the springs, there were several large wooden spoons for people to use when drinking of this water. The local people called it "Chashma-i-Shafa," meaning "Good-Health Spring." When I drank the mineral water, I concluded that it tasted like the carbonated mineral water that we used to buy from a soda shop in a park near the Afghan embassy in Ankara, when my mother took me there to play.

From this time on, in Kabul, I continued my schooling in Habibia High School.

As the son of a diplomat whose job changed every two to three years, I had to change schools and study different languages and systems many times during the grade-school period. While this may have been stressful on me to shift into different modes and channels of learning, it nevertheless had the positive effect of preparing me to cope with difficulties and become resilient and strong in my learning and thinking processes.

Habibia

During the time I was in seventh and eighth grades at Habibia, I caught up with the Dari and Pashto languages. My class advisor and Pashto teacher for three years was Mohd Islam Khan Mayan, who was a person of high moral character and integrity. We students were very fortunate to have him as advisor for this period of our education. Gradually, I realized that I was strong in mathematics and science classes. When I entered the ninth grade, my parents rewarded me by buying me a secondhand bicycle. The old gear bicycle that I had brought with me was broken and too small for me to use anymore.

This bicycle was a regular bike with a chain. From then on, I did not have to walk to school anymore.

American Teachers

At about this time, the school administration was handed over to an American principal. Several of our teachers were also Americans. The class curriculum and teaching of math and sciences was all done in the English language, except some social subjects like theology and Afghan history. Dr. Bushnell became the principal of Habibia High School. Dr. Arnold Fletcher was the English teacher, and Mr. Fluker was my math teacher. There were a number of other teachers, such as Mr. Larson, Mr. Soderberg, and Mr. Thomas. The teacher of physics was an Indian named Mr. Sharma.

The names of my classmates in Habibia that I remember are as follows: Burhanullah, son of Izzuddawlah; Bashir Ludin; Ahmad Moosa, son of Moosa Khan Kandahari; Gharzai Malik Nasery; Rahmatullah Salimi and his brothers; Azizurrahman Samadi and Saifurrahman Samadi; Irfan Raffaat; Ashraf Shuhab, son of Ghobar; and Shirahmad Noor.

The changes to the curriculum provided me with enormous opportunities. I started shining in my class and was the top student from the ninth grade through the twelfth grade. I was about eighteen years old when I graduated from the Habibia High School, in 1949.

My extracurricular activities during this period were bicycling, mountain hiking, track and field, swimming, skiing, volleyball, and soccer. During the last two years in high school, I participated in the school volleyball and soccer teams. Also, with a group of very good friends, I bicycled to all the interesting places and hiked to the top of all the mountains around Kabul.

Tapa-i-Maranjan

Kabul is very cold winter, and school vacations were during the three months in winter. We had a lot of snow and ice, which provided me with an opportunity to ski on a hill and skate in the ponds near our house. Once, during the winter, I saw some dark specks going down the hill that was called Tapa-i-Maranjan. My cousin Hasan-jan and I decided to go to the hill and see what those specks were. When we got closer, we found out that the specks we had seen were actually people skiing down the hill. We decided to go and find out who those people were. When we got close to the bottom of the hill, we saw several security people wearing uniforms. They told us that the king's son Ahmadshah-jan was skiing there. From this time on, we became interested in skiing ourselves. At that time, there were no skis to be found in Kabul, so we did not have skis. Therefore, we said, "Let us make our own skis." From pictures we had seen, we knew that a ski was flat and long and that its front end was curved up. I knew that in one of the old storages, there were old, broken armchairs. Hasan-jan and I took an from a chair and connected a flat, long piece of wood to it. Then we made a place where we could put our boot in and tie it. We both were exited to try our self-made skis at Tapa-i-Maranjan.

We went to the Tapa, climbed partway up, tied a ski to each boot, and came downhill on the skis. But this trial did not last very long. After going ten to fifteen meters, one of the skis broke in two—and I fell down. Hasan-jan and I soon realized that the self-made skis were not going to work. After the ski broke, we tried to go downhill on a lagan, a flat-bottomed tray/pot made of copper. However, going downhill on a lagan was dangerous, because the lagan would go too fast and keep turning around, with no way to control it. We soon realized that the use of lagan without any controls was not a good idea. Next, we began our search in the Kabul bazaar for a ski, but we had no luck.

I found an old ski that belonged to my cousin Walijan. His mother, Modar-jan, told me that there was an old ski in their storage room. She took me there. I was very excited to get it. Hasan-jan found a pair that his father, who was working at the king's palace, had found—an old, discarded set of skis that had once belonged to Prince Ahmadshah-jan.

From then on, my cousin and I frequented Tapa-i-Maranjan after it snowed. After some time, we both learned to ski quite well. In order to ski downhill, we had to go uphill on our skis. There were no ski lifts at that time in Kabul. Now that I think about it, we used to get quite an exercise during these ski times. Gradually, our group of skiers grew, and some of my hiking and bicycling friends, Ziajan Yusuf, Irfan Rafaat, and Murad Ali Khan, joined us. We used to have a good time skiing in Tapa-i-Maranjan.

Music

I was talented in music and had learned to play the tanboor (a string instrument) by myself. Then, I became interested in learning the sitar. My mother's older brother, Sultan Ahmad Khan, who was a progressive-minded and very kind person, had promised to reward me for being in the top of my class at school. When he asked me, I told him that I was interested in learning the sitar. He told me, "Go ahead. Find one, and I will pay for it." When he bought me one, I found out that a sitar was very hard to play. My parents then agreed to have me study under a master of sitar who was in Kabul for that purpose. After a while, I learned to play the sitar under his tutelage.

I Am Awarded a Scholarship

School studies in English and the presence of American teachers made it possible for us schoolchildren to learn the English language well. This also gave us further opportunities to use English textbooks and read other books, which resulted in strengthening the level of our general knowledge and preparing us for the possibilities of entering American colleges and universities after graduation from high school.

At that time in Afghanistan, there was a rule that the top three students graduating from a high school were given academic scholarships by the government for further study in American or European universities. This way, students could earn an advanced degree in a field that was understaffed in the country. The stipulation was that, since this privilege was paid for with government or public funds, those who got their degrees would return and serve their country for a period of time.

A classmate of mine, Mr. Bashir Ludin, and I had the honor of graduating at the top of our class, and so we qualified to get a scholarship. We consulted with Dr. Bushnell and our American teachers, who helped us with the application forms. I chose to apply to three top American universities. These were Cornell, Yale, and CalTech. Both Ludin and I decided to study civil engineering and were introduced to the Ministry of Public Works.

My Internship

Bashir and I met with the minister of public works, whose name was Parwanta. He told us that the acceptance of our applications would take some time. Until we were accepted by a university, he said, the ministry would send us to the Helmand Valley Project for an internship with Morrison-Knudsen (MK), an American company.

We were given a five-month internship with Morrison-Knudsen Company in Helmand. At that time, the company was constructing the Kajakai Dam and Boghra Canal irrigation systems of Helmand Valley, and the Dahla Dam of Arghandab Valley. This was a good opportunity for us to get familiar with the construction of these very big and important projects, as it gave us a chance to do field survey and office engineering work with the company. This experience in the field of surveying later helped us in our civil engineering and survey courses at Cornell.

My parents told me that the Helmand Valley Project was in the southwest deserts of Afghanistan. They gave me some advice on how to cope with the hot climate of that area.

At this time, my father was working as deputy minister of the interior, and the prime minister was Shah Mahmud Khan Ghazi.

Helmand

Bashir and I first went to Kandahar, to the head office of Morrison Knudsen, which was stationed in an old fort called Manzil Bagh.

MK had taken over the whole compound, remodeled it, and built new buildings for their offices, shops, warehouses, and barracks.

We reported to Mr. Shook, who was the superintendent of MK. He introduced us to engineer Shockley, who was working in the engineering office. After staying a day at Manzil Bagh, we were sent off to Chah-i-Anjeer, the MK field office for the Helmand Valley Project.

At Chah-i-Anjeer, we met the engineer Eldon Johnson, who assigned us a room in the barracks/dormitory that was used by staff. The room was nice and clean, with a close bathroom and shower facilities, but we had to prepare our own food.

Field Surveying

Bashir and I were introduced to different field survey parties, which were headed by an American party chief. Each survey party had its own jeep pickup to take to the field for surveying. Very soon, I got acquainted with the survey crew members. Surveyor Baqi Khan Baluch and surveyor Asghar Khan from Girishk were very nice and hospitable people. I honored their acquaintance and friendship for many years in the future. They offered that, from then on, we share expenses. They also said that their cook would prepare our breakfast in the morning and some sandwiches for the field, and we could join them for our supper at night in their living quarters.

During the period of four months when I was in Chah-i-Anjeer, I was assigned to work with a field survey crew team that was surveying the flood drainage basins to the north of Boghra Canal. The crew chief first assigned me as a stake man. Gradually, I was trained and kept going up the ladder, learning to become a rodman, a chain man, and a person who worked with the stadia. Then, I was promoted and learned the use of instruments such as the level and the plane table (for making maps), the transit (for measuring angles), keeping surveying notes, doing calculations, and performing every function that the survey party required.

After I passed all the tests in the survey party, I was assigned to work in the design office, which was headed by Mr. Eldon Johnson. He had me do volume calculations and mass diagrams in his office. Obviously, my school studies and work was paying off, as I was able to learn things fast. The internship with Morrison-Knudsen Company at Helmand gave me an opportunity to visit project construction sites such as Kajakai Dam, the Boghra Canal, the Nadi-Ali irrigation project and farms, the Marja Desert, and the Arghandab (Dahla) Dam in Kandahar.

Trip Back to Kabul

After about four months, Eldon Johnson called Bashir and I to his office and informed us that our applications were accepted. He told us that we had to go back to Kabul to take care of the business needed for our trip to America and for studying at school. He was very impressed that all three very high-level universities had accepted us as students. Mr. Johnson gave us a reference letter, a report, and a certificate stating the work that we had done and the things that we had learned.

Bashir and I thanked all of those with whom we had become acquainted and worked. We went back to Kabul and reported to the Ministry of Public Works. We met the minister, who asked us, "Have all three universities accepted you?" We said yes. He asked, "Which one are you going to?" We could not answer. Bashir and I had not thought of the possibility of making a choice.

After talking about it, we decided to consult Mr. Kabir Ludin, Bashir's older brother, who had studied in America and earned a degree in engineering there. His answer was quick and decisive. He responded, "Of course, Cornell University, which has the best undergraduate engineering school in America." I learned later that he himself had graduated from Cornell!

Cornell, as one of the Ivy League universities, prided itself on accepting only very high-level students for its engineering school. The civil engineering curriculum at Cornell, instead of lasting four years, was a five-year program for the Bachelor of Civil Engineering degree. (Now, it is called Bachelor of Environmental and Civil Engineering.)

Bashir and I proceeded with all the work that was necessary for going to Cornell University in Ithaca, New York. The Afghan embassy in Washington, DC, was informed, and they took care of all that was needed for us to enroll in the university. The Ministry of Public Works took care of everything else that was necessary, such as issuing passports for our travel abroad.

American Visa

Bashir and I had to go to the American consul in Kabul to get our visas to the United States of America. At the embassy, the consul asked me, "What is your last name?" I said that I did not have one. He said, "When you go to America, you need to have a last name. Otherwise, you will have difficulty, and everyone will ask you what your last name is." Then he added, "Why don't you make one?"

Assifi, a Last Name

I thought about this for a while. If I used my father's name as my last name, then it would be Wahhabi. Then, everyone would think that I belonged to the Wahhabi religious sect, making it a misnomer. I thought to go one step higher, to my grandfather, whose name was Mohd Assif Khan. I decided to use Assifi as my last name. Since Abdul is a common prefix to a name, I decided to use it as my first name—and Assifi as my last name. I told the consul that from now on, my name was going to be Abdul Tawab Assifi. From that point forward, I used this name on all the forms, for my passport, and so forth. When I came home, I told my father that I had made a family name for us and that it was Assifi. He said, "Well, from now on, I will also use it, and your father's name will be Abdul Wahhab Assifi.

Trip to America

The Public Works Ministry had gotten our air tickets from Pan American Airways. We were supposed to go by bus to Peshawar, take a plane from there to Karachi, and travel from there to New York. The bus from Kabul to Jalalabad and Peshawar passed quite close (a hundred meters) to my house on the roadway to Jalalabad. I had made arrangements with bus company to stop the bus in front of my house so I could board. I said good-bye to my mother, father, and grandmother, Bobo-jan, and then I boarded the bus.

To this day, I have not forgotten, as I vividly remember, the sight of my grandmother Bobo-jan running after the bus, saying good-bye, and raising her hands in prayer for my safe trip abroad.

It was toward the end of July 1950 when Bashir and I started our trip from Kabul to Jalalabad, going on to Peshawar the next day. Two days later, we boarded a Pan Am plane from Peshawar to Karachi, and from there we flew to the Cairo airport. We stayed one night at the airport guesthouse and then flew to Amsterdam, Holland. The flights from Karachi were on four-engine Super Constellation planes.

Pan American put us in a room-and-board guesthouse in Amsterdam. I was very much impressed with the cleanliness of the city and the number of flowers I saw all over the gardens, backyards, and parks there.

Another thing that amazed me was the number of bicycles in the streets. It seemed that everyone was riding a bicycle. In the streets, one saw a river of bicycles flowing in one direction, and another river flowing in the opposite direction.

After three days in Amsterdam, we boarded a plane on our way to New York. The plane made a stopover at Gander Airport. From there, it flew to New York. I was walking outside in Gander Airport when something fell into my eye. I could not get it out. This thing was irritating my eye, and tears kept coming down my face during the flight—and when we arrived in New York.

Bashir and I took a taxi from the airport to the Afghan consulate in the city, and we met the consul, Mr. Abdul Razaq Ziayii. He told us that we had to take the train from New York to Washington, DC, saying that one of consulate staff would help us get to the train station and buy the tickets.

Washington, DC

We went by train to Washington, DC, and were met at the station by Mohd Ibrahim Khan Nouri, who was the brother of my aunt's husband, Mr. Mohd Chouaib Khan Miskinyar. I called these two men Uncle Ibrahim Jon and Uncle Agha-i-gul (a nickname), respectively.

Uncle Ibrahim was a very kind and fun person. I said, "Uncle, something has gone into my eye in Gander Airport, and it is giving me a lot of trouble."

He looked into my eye and said, "Oh yes! I will take you to the drugstore right away." At the drugstore, the pharmacist turned my eyelid inside out and washed my eye. A piece of coal flake came out.

The Afghan embassy told Bashir and I that we would have us stay in Washington, DC, until school started in mid-September. Then, they would get us train tickets to travel to Ithaca, New York.

My Aunt and Uncle

During this time, we were the guests of my aunt Bibi Maliha, Shahgul Jon, who was my mother's younger sister. My uncle Chouaib-jan was the chargé d'affaires of the Afghan embassy. My aunt and uncle had two children, a lovely daughter, Fariha-jon, who was about nine, and a son, Abdullah, who was about two years old. Bashir and I had a very good time during this period, especially because Uncle Ibrahim took us sightseeing to many places of interest in the Washington, DC, area.

Cornell University

After having a good, fun time in DC, Bashir and I boarded the train and went to Ithaca. Once we made it up the hill to the university campus, we reported to the advisor for foreign students. He was a very nice person and told us what we needed to do to enroll at the university. Cornell University's campus is located on top of a hill overlooking Cayuga Lake. It is probably one of the most beautiful university campuses in America.

The Afghanistan embassy sent us a check in the amount of $210 every month. They told us that the embassy would repay us for the cost of textbooks, notebooks, paper, pencils, etc., which we had to buy for our schoolwork. This amount was sufficient for the costs that we incurred during our school period. For instance, the cost of one cup of coffee was a nickel. It cost twenty-five cents for a hamburger. We paid five cents to ride the bus. I paid fifty or sixty dollars per month for my room.

For a period of time, we rented rooms in a room-and-board place called the Cosmopolitan House. From that time on, Bashir and I were enrolled in different classes and rented rooms in different places, although we both studied civil engineering.

Civil engineering at Cornell was a five-year course, as previously mentioned. Seeing as other schools required four years for graduation, Cornell called our class the Class of 1954 even though we wouldn't graduate until 1955. During my education there, I stayed in many different places. After some time in Cosmopolitan House, I decided to rent a room in College Town.

One semester, I was in Cascadilla Gorge Dormitory, which provided room and board. My roommate was another civil engineering student who was also my classmate. Since we were both hardworking and serious students, we ended up being roommates for several years. His name was Mario D'Aquino. He was from Corning, New York, and was of Italian descent.

Afghan Students at Cornell

The Afghan embassy in Washington, DC, had given me the telephone numbers of some other Afghan students who were studying at Cornell. After a few days, I called them and asked about a time when we could meet and get acquainted. I already knew Mohammed Yaqub Lalee, who was four years my senior at Habibia High School, and Shah Mohammed Naibkhel, who was three years my senior. They were both studying civil engineering. Two other students who were graduates of Ghazi High School, Mir Hussain Sadat, studying architecture, and Abdul Hai Qazi, studying civil engineering, were also three years my senior at Cornell. We were all very busy with our studies and occasionally met during some of the holidays. After two years, Qazi transferred from Cornell to Rensselaer Polytechnic Institute in Westchester, New York. I became very good friends with these students while we were at Cornell, and I continued this friendship later when we became co-workers in the Helmand Valley Project.

I have always had an insatiable thirst for learning and knowledge. While at Cornell, I was very interested in taking as many courses as I could. For me, Cornell was a reservoir of knowledge from which I wanted to gain as much as possible. Therefore, I decided to carry twenty-one credits each semester. Also, during the first and last summer vacations, I took some more courses that were available at the school.

Bashir Ludin

Bashir and I were classmates in Habibia High School. We were also very good friends. Although we were both top students in our class, our friendship never floundered because of student competition.

However, during our second year at Cornell, Bashir confided in me that he was no longer interested in civil engineering. He wanted to change the subject of his studies to either social sciences or pure science, like physics. I said, "Bashir, we have been here more than a year, and you have done a good job at your studies. Why do you want to change now? You have never told me about this before. What made you change now?"

He said, "I was never interested in engineering, but I went along because my older brother, Kabir, wanted me to study civil engineering.

I could not make a decision against his wishes. You know how much I respect him and his wishes!"

At this time, the Afghan ambassador in Washington was Sardar Mohammad Naim Khan. Once Bashir submitted his request to him, Naim said that he could not make a decision without the approval of Bashir's older brother, the engineer Kabir Ludin, who was also the Afghan ambassador in London, England. When Ambassador Kabir Ludin was asked about it, he very strongly refused to accept Bashir's request, saying that Bashir had started and should finish his studies in civil engineering.

Now this thing became, as the saying goes, the clash of the Titans, what with Bashir Ludin's unwavering decision and Kabir Khan Ludin's adamant refusal. At this point, I was caught in between the two wills and made some calls to the people I knew at the embassy, but it was no use. Everyone honored Kabir Khan Ludin's decision, who had himself studied at and gotten his bachelor's and master's degrees from Cornell University. He was the one who had advised both Bashir and me to attend Cornell instead of Yale and CalTech. But he was still of the old school of strong family hierarchic relationships that existed in Afghan culture at that time.

Bashir, on the other hand, having been exposed to freedom of speech, free will, and decision making in the United States—and especially at a university such as Cornell, which was at the forefront of, and later played a great exhibition in, the ethno-libertarian movements—was no longer predisposed to accept the hierarchical dictate of an older brother, no matter how much he loved and respected him. This whole affair resulted in delaying Bashir's further studies at Cornell. It compelled him to go to Washington, DC, to meet with the embassy staff and the ambassador himself.

At about that time, Kabir Khan Ludin was appointed as Afghan ambassador to the United States of America in place of Sardar Naim Khan. This change of ambassadorial positions finally resulted in Bashir's going to George Washington University to complete his

24

studies in civil engineering. From there, he went to Princeton University to get a master's degree in soil engineering.

Lifeguarding

I was very interested in learning the techniques to become a lifeguard, so I took lifesaving, water rescue, and CPR classes for a whole semester. Afterward, I applied for lifeguard duty at Cornell University's Beebe Lake. I got this job during my second summer vacation at Cornell. It was very interesting and, in a way, enjoyable work for me. The lifeguard sat on a high stool so that he could see the entire area where people were swimming. When I got the job, I asked the instructor who had hired me for the job what it entailed. I also asked, "What if some football players came and did things that they were not supposed to do." I was instructed to call on them and inform them that they were doing things or swimming in an area that was not allowed. I wanted to know what to do if they did not follow the rule and disregarded what I told them.

The man who hired me showed me the telephone that was on the table at my side. He said, "You call campus security and the university police, who will immediately come and help you in the matter. Remember that you are the boss while you are on duty at this post."

Well, it happened only once. A bunch of football players came and started going into the gorge, where swimmers were not allowed. I called on them. When they did not pay any attention, I blew the whistle. They swam back and shook their hands in a gesture of salute and submission. I had no further problems with them.

During the whole summer when I was on lifeguard duty, I used my skills on only two occasions. One was when a boy of about eight years old went into the water from the sandy beach at the side of the lake and disappeared. When he came up again, I could see his hands making panicky motions, indicating that he was in trouble. I jumped into the water, swam to him, dove under, grabbed him from the back, and brought him out on the side of the lake. He was a little bit shaken but had not swallowed much water.

Another time, as I was looking in the way that lifeguards are supposed to look, at all the possible areas where people could have trouble, I noticed that a young girl went into the water and walked with her feet touching the bottom. She went farther in, lost her balance, and panicked. I could see that she needed help to keep her head above the water so she was able to breathe. I jumped into the water, swam where she had gone under, dove, grabbed her from the back, and swam with her back to the shore, holding her head above the water so she could breathe. She tried to struggle, but I would not let her go. I brought her out of the water and helped her regain her composure. She sat up and looked at me with an expression that indicated, "Thank you." I was proud of myself for the good job I had done. On top of this, she was a beautiful girl with light brown hair. I helped her stand up. Some other girls came to her aid and then helped her walk back to the benches on the grass.

Diamond Lake, Oregon

The Afghan embassy at Washington, DC, informed me that, if I was interested, they could help me get an internship in construction during my summer vacations. They told me that I could work with Morrison-Knudsen Company, doing powerhouse construction work in Diamond Lake, Oregon. I took this job and worked with the company during one summer vacation. This was very nice, because there were two other Afghan students from Cornell, Mir Hussein Sadat (who was studying architecture) and Shah Mohammad Naebkhel, who worked with me on the same project. We rented rooms at a motel at the side of Diamond Lake. This was a beautiful place, with ice-cold water, pine forests all around, and a panoramic view of Mount Wilson to the north and Mount Thielsen to the south. Several times, I enjoyed swimming in the exhilaratingly cold water of Diamond Lake.

Climbing Mount Thielsen

At one time, when we were discussing what we could do during the weekends, Shah, Sadat, and I thought that it would be very interesting to go and climb one of the mountains that we could see from where we were. They agreed to go with me and climb Mount Thielsen

26

that next weekend. However, when I tried to wake them early in the morning that day, they made all sorts of excuses and did not want to go. So, I decided to go by myself.

The manager of the motel told me that I should first go to the forest ranger's station and inform them of my idea. I wore my heavy walking boots, wore a hat, put sunscreen on myself, and took a lunch box and a rope. I walked to the forest ranger's station and told the ranger about my idea. He said that climbers didn't usually go alone. There were always several climbers going together.

When I told him about my plight of lazy friends, he gave me some matches and said, "If you get in trouble or break a leg or something, you pile some dry wood and set fire to it. We are constantly watching from our towers, and as soon as we see smoke, we will get to you and help." He also said, "If you see any bears, just stay put and don't bother them—and hope that they don't bother you. But in this area, we have not had any problem with bears." The ranger gave a map with all the paths and trails marked that showed where the ranger stations and towers were located. He told me, "You should come back before it gets dark."

So, there I was, the lonely mountain climber, trekking up the paths to the top of the mountain. I kept on climbing until I came to an area that had no trees beyond it. Mount Thielsen keeps getting rockier as one goes up. The last portion is like the top of a conical tower, with flat rocks sloping up sharply, and the top peak is like a needle top. Gradually, as I was climbing, the section with boulders became rockier. I saw flat, steep rocks all around me.

I came to the back of the steep, rocky section, the bottom of the needle. I looked up and saw that it was vertical. There was no possibility to go up any more. I sat down and enjoyed looking at the view. It was very beautiful. However, the vertical rock had a crack that went straight up it. And this is when my stupidity took over my smarts and kept on needling me to go up the crack. And that is what I did: I wedged myself in the crack and kept on climbing. Eventually, I came to the top and climbed onto it.

27

Unfortunately, there was not very much room on the top, as it was maybe about fifteen by fifteen feet of solid rock. On both sides, it was a sheer vertical drop. When I saw it, I froze. I could not stand up and so just sat there looking all around, stupefied by the scenery, realizing that I was stuck. There was no tree branches, bushes, or anything that I could set fire to and use to signal the rangers of my predicament.

I stayed there for some time, not knowing what to do. Then, I noticed a metallic box tied to a chain that was attached to a pin that was driven into a crack in the rock. I went close to it, picked it up, opened the lid, and looked inside. There were many notes and identification cards in there. I thought that I should put something in there, also. I looked into my wallet and found an old Cornell University ID card. I took it out of my wallet, put it in the box, and closed the lid. I thought to myself that somebody would read it someday and know that an amateur climber was there.

Some time passed. I realized that I would freeze to death when the cold descended at night. I slowly made it back to the place from which I had started my climb. But the crack in the rock looked awfully long. I thought to myself, *Why did I bring this rope with me? Let me see if I can use it.* I tied the rope to a protrusion in the rock face. Then, I lay facedown on the flat rock and started lowering my legs down toward the crack while holding onto the rope. Slowly, my legs found the crack. I wedged myself into it and kept on lowering myself slowly. When I got into the crack, I felt more confidence in myself and kept going farther down and down, until I reached the bottom where there was flat rock.

All this time, I had my lunch box tied to my belt. When up top, I did not have any desire for food, but now I could eat. After eating, I got up and went downhill on the footpath until I came to the treeline. I followed the trail from which I had come and kept on going until I reached the paved road. I reported in at the forest ranger's station and briefly told him about what had happened at the top of Mount Thielsen. He said, "I know. That is why we do not recommend that people go alone. When I spoke to you this morning, you were confident and did not tell me that you were planning to go to the top of the rock."

I said, "You are right. At that time, I was not planning to do that. I made the decision when I got up there. Actually, I could not visualize the real conditions and the difficulty of getting down. Climbing up was easy, but climbing down was not the same."

He laughed and said, "I know, and I am glad that you made it back."

Back to Cornell

A week before the end of my summer vacation, MK pickups took Naebkhel, Sadat, and I from Diamond Lake to Eugene, Oregon, and from there we took the train to go back to Ithaca, New York, and Cornell.

Cornell University had a semester system. The courses for the first year were general sciences, physics, chemistry, and mathematics such as calculus. In the second year, the subjects became more advanced, such as physical chemistry, more-advanced math, and engineering courses such as surveying. Each year, the level of courses that I took became more advanced. More stress was given to engineering and technical subjects. Also, the school required that students take courses in finance, accounting, and some social sciences. I had chosen my major in hydraulics and my minor studies in structures.

However, I felt that I needed not take courses in fields such as accounting. I met my advisor, Professor Gephardt, and told him that I wanted to study engineering and technical subjects. "Why should I take accounting?" I asked.

Professor Gephardt told me, "Mr. Assifi, courses in accounting and finance are mandatory. If you want to get your degree from Cornell, you must take these courses. Here at Cornell, we teach you with the objective that one day you will be not only an engineer, but also an executive. As such, you should know these subjects. Otherwise, you will not be able to do a good job."

That did it. I took all the finance and accounting courses that were mandatory at Cornell. Later on in my engineering work, I found out that Cornell University was correct in this respect. These courses were very useful for me in the successful management of administrative and executive jobs that I held later on in my professional career.

Chief Joseph Dam, State of Washington

During my third summer vacation, the Afghan embassy informed me that I could go for an internship with Morrison-Knudsen, working at a construction job they had at Chief Joseph Dam powerhouse, which they were building on Columbia River in the state of Washington. This was a very big job.

I reported to company headquarters at the job site and found out that three other Afghan students, Mir Sadat, Shah Naebkhel, and Mohd Aman, were also going to be working there. The four of us got together and decided to rent an apartment at a motel not very far from the construction site. We divided the duties for each one of us in the apartment. Mir volunteered for cooking duty. I volunteered for dish washing, and Shah and Aman volunteered to clean the apartment.

At the job, each one of us was assigned to different survey party chiefs. By this time, I had a lot of experience and knowledge in surveying, having taken the survey courses at Cornell. When I reported to my survey party chief, he told me that his crew was responsible for controlling elevations and alignment of concrete structures, steel penstocks, and turbine spiral housings.

On the first day, he told me that my job was to climb to the top of the sidewall of the powerhouse with a transit instrument and determine control lines for the installation of penstocks. The sidewall of the powerhouse was fifty to sixty feet high, and there was a wooden ladder on the side for climbing to the top. At the time when I was at this job, there were no safety belts or any other means to guarantee the safety of the surveyors and workers. I think that the survey party chief, knowing that I was a third-year engineering student at an Ivy League university, wanted to test my capability to perform this tough job.

He told me that I had to climb up the ladder, holding the transit instrument and its tripod on my shoulder, walk to the end of the wall, which was about fifty feet away, set and plumb the transit on a reference pin on the concrete wall, back-sight another reference, and then give the center-line control for the installation of the power turbine penstock. I could not make any excuses for not going up and doing this job. After all, I had conquered Mount Thielsen one year ago!

So, taking the transit, its tripod, and a survey notebook with me, I, without any hesitation, climbed up the vertical ladder with the transit instrument and tripod on my shoulder. When I got to the top, I noticed that the top of the concrete wall was maybe four to five feet wide. I hesitated for a few seconds and then proceeded to walk to the end of the wall, trying not to look down on the two vertical sides. At the end, I found the reference pin with a cross mark on top, set my transit, tied the plumb bob to the center pin, plumbed and leveled it, took a back sight, turned it to the given degree that was given in the notebook, and then signaled the other survey guy, who was going to mark the center line of the penstock. After all the work was done and we gave the necessary signals to each other, I picked up the transit, walked back to where the ladder was, laid the transit down, got onto the ladder, picked up the transit, and climbed down the wooden ladder with a triumphant smile on my face.

The survey party chief greeted me with a genuine smile and said, "Good job!" He continued and said, "I was not sure that you could do it. They must be teaching you guys real good at the school." From then on, the chief was my friend. He consulted me with problems that we encountered during our survey work. After about a month and a half, he told me that the construction superintendent had a job for me. I should go see him at his office. I do not remember his name. Mr. Ed Sukup, perhaps.

The superintendent said, "I hear you guys from the university are really sharp."

"Well," I said, "I am just a student and do not know whether I am sharp or not."

The superintendent said, "We have a problem in the steel plates for the construction of the penstock that the manufacturer had sent us. There is a discrepancy, and the plates do not fit. There is about two to three inches' error when we try to weld the plates at the spiral housing section of the turbine penstock. I will give you all the drawings. See if you can recalculate so that our welders can cut and weld for the correct alignment. We have been talking to the manufacturer. They are telling us to send the plates back, and they'll correct the error. If we do that, then we will lose a lot of time and will miss the project completion date." With this, the superintendent showed me a desk and said that I could use it.

At that time, there were no computers or electronic calculators, even. There was the Friden calculator, which was good for adding and subtracting. Engineers used slide rules and logarithmic tables for calculations. I have always liked to solve difficult problems in math and geometry, so this challenge was very interesting for me, as the diameter of the spiral penstock housing for the turbine changed. By using three-dimensional trigonometry, I found a way to recalculate and determine the correct plate sizes. The manufacturer had made a mistake in calculation, or else their welders cut the plates erroneously.

During this time, people at the company told me that I could eat my lunch with their staff at the mess hall. Eating lunch with them was quite interesting for me. I had to get used to the language, as they spoke many curse words, at least two or three in each sentence. It seemed that without curse words, they could not speak at all! My internship with Morrison-Knudsen during the construction of Chief Joseph Dam powerhouse was fascinating and quite an experience, and it gave me a lot of curse words to remember.

Southern California

One of the Afghan students, Mohd Aman Khan, who was with us at Chief Joseph offered us the chance to ride with him to San Francisco in his old Chevy car. My friends and I would share in the gas cost and meet some other Afghan students once we got to San Francisco. My friends and I thought that this was a good idea, figuring that we would save some money on train ticket costs to Ithaca, New York. So, we went with Aman to San Francisco. There, we met Karim Nasraty, who was going to Stanford, and Nasrat Malikyar, who was going to USC with Aman, in Los Angeles.

In San Francisco, we had a good time seeing some interesting places, like the Golden Gate Bridge, the San Francisco ship docks, and the San Francisco Museum. After about three days, we rode with Aman to Los Angeles, visiting the campus of USC and then going with him to San Diego to see the zoo. Finally, after all that interesting sightseeing, we took the train back to Ithaca, New York, and then made our way to the beautiful campus of Cornell University.

During the period when I was a student at Cornell, I went two times to the West Coast. Every time, I took the train, but I always made a four- or five-day stop in Chicago. There were two things of interest to me in Chicago. One was the Museum of Science and Industry, and the other was that I could visit an old classmate from Habibia, Ashraf Shuhab Ghobar, who was studying there. I have visited the Chicago Museum of Science and Industry twice. Every time, I spent at least two days, as it fascinated me very much. When I was in Chicago, I stayed at International House, visited Ashraf, and, of course, saw the museum. I always ate at the International House. One time there, I met a student from India who told me that he liked to play the sitar. I told him that I also liked to play the sitar. He said, "If you have time, I will take you to the city, where I know an Indian who loves music and has a collection of musical instruments."

So, he called this gentleman. The day after, we went to his apartment, which was in a multistory building. The Indian fellow greeted us and invited us to play the sitar. He himself played tabla. To me, it was a chance to play sitar in America, which I never dreamed could be done at all. We had a nice jam session, with us and playing the sitar, and he the tabla. I thanked our host afterward and said good-bye. But before I left, he told me, "You are a good sitar player, and you should have a sitar. You can take the sitar that you were playing and return it to me when you decide to go back to your country." Well, this was a very surprising offer, one that I could not refuse. I had his sitar for the last two years at Cornell, and I gave music concerts in the student music hall when an international music or cultural program was performed.

When I graduated from Cornell and was on my way to Santa Fe, New Mexico, I made a special trip to Chicago. I went to this man's apartment again, and he was very happy to meet me. He asked me to sit down and play the sitar while he played the tabla. We had a very good jam session. Afterward, I thanked him for the use of the sitar and said good-bye. Before leaving Chicago, I met Ashraf, telling him that I had finished my studies and was going back to Afghanistan. What he said surprised me. "You are stupid for going back to that backward country that does not have much opportunity for anyone to work." He told me that he would not go back and would stay in the United States to later write a book on the philosophy of mathematics.

I was not happy with his attitude and told him that our poor country had paid for our expenses to study in America. I said that, morally speaking, we owed our country and should go back and work for it, for at least the same amount of time that we studied, thanks to the scholarship funds Afghanistan allotted us. I told Ashraf, "Look, you were good in social subjects in school, but not very good in mathematics and science courses. How are you going to write a philosophy book about a subject that you do not know much about it?" Well, I said good-bye to him and was no longer very proud of our acquaintanceship as classmates in school. From then on, I did not go to Chicago, and I never contacted Ashraf again. He appeared to be a selfish person, one whom I no longer respected.

Soccer

When I was in Kabul during my high school years, my mother often advised me not to play soccer. She would say, "Tawab, do not play soccer, as you will get hurt." Nevertheless, when I entered Cornell University, I was on my own volition. One of my ambitions was to play soccer with the Cornell soccer team. The school informed me that I had to take all the physical education courses before I could play soccer with the team. I ended up taking physical education classes for a whole year before I passed the physical tests.

Finally, I qualified to join the soccer team in the second year. However, I told my coach, Mr. Jim Smith, that I was an engineering student and had laboratory classes in the afternoons. I said that I'd be able to come to practice after I had done my laboratory work. Coach Smith agreed to this arrangement and told me that it was okay for me to come for practice after I did my lab work.

Knee Injury

I continued playing with the Cornell varsity soccer team. One day, we had a game against the University of Pennsylvania. After I came from one of my laboratory classes and walked to the field, Coach Jim Smith told me to go to the center forward position and try to make a goal. In my eagerness to play, I did not tell the coach that I had not yet warmed up. I remember that after playing for a while in this position, I received a high pass, jumped high, and made a goal. I regularly played at the halfback position. I was not very tall, but I could run very fast and jump high. My teammates were very happy with me for just coming in and making a goal. As you can guess, I was elated at this and tried to make another goal. Soon after, I was successful in making another goal. After I jumped high and headed the ball into the goal, I was coming down when one of the backs, who were much taller and stronger than I, slid and scissor-kicked my right leg. I felt a pain in my right knee, dropped, and rolled on the ground. When I tried to get up, my knee would not hold my weight. I kept on falling. Two teammates got under my arms and helped me to the sideline. The coach came and called for the stretcher. I said, "It is not necessary. I can go by myself." He told me to go to a physical therapist and let a doctor take care of me. I continued pretending that I did not need a stretcher. From the soccer field to the gymnasium, I walked by jumping on one leg. This demonstrates the vigor of youth. Even though I was hurt, I pretended not to be. I did not want the coach to know that I could not walk.

When the doctor examined my knee, he asked, "How did you do it? I have not seen you with the football team before."

I said, "I am a soccer player, and today I made two goals against the University of Pennsylvania."

"Well," he said, "those were probably the last two goals that you will ever make. You can't play soccer anymore, as you have torn up your knee badly." By this time, my knee was severely swollen. He inserted a big needle and took a lot of fluid from it. He then proceeded and plastered my leg, from the groin to the ankle, saying that the cast had to stay on for at least two months. I should report to him every week, he advised. During the first few days of using crutches, my armpits became sore. By the end of the week, I had learned to go around the campus quite fast on my crutches.

After the physical therapist/doctor took the plaster away, I found out that my knee was frozen and I could not bend it. Every day, I had to go for therapy, putting my knee in a tank with swirling hot water and continuing to exercise the knee. Actually, after some time, my right knee became very strong. The doctor then told me that I could walk and run, provided that I did not zigzag. Later on, when Beebe Lake iced over and the skating rink was open, I would go there and ice-skate to the music they played there. When I told the physical-therapy doctor about this, he nearly threw me out of his office! I kept on telling him that one does not stress the knee in ice-skating, as it is the ankles that are stressed. He would not listen and told me not to come to therapy anymore! From then on, soccer was out for me. I even had trouble playing volleyball, because I could not jump very high. The only sport that I could do without any trouble was swimming. After many years, my right knee was totally replaced with a mechanical knee joint. It always rings the bells at airport security checkpoints.

A question that comes to mind from all this is, which way is better—Mother's wisdom or the vigor of youth? I think the correct answer is, "Both." But one thing that is sure from my own experiences in sports, especially competitive sports that require extreme exertion, is that one should *always warm up* before entering a competition or vigorous workout.

Back to School

Before I went on my vacation, Mario and I made the necessary arrangements for our apartment at Cook Street, near the campus. I bought a secondhand bicycle to commute to campus and to ride in between classes.

The curriculum for civil engineering at Cornell, as expected, was more advanced in the third and fourth years. Like always, it required a lot of hard work. Mario and I were competing as to who could get higher grades. We were both "A" students. Mario would ask, "How come I study so hard and your grades are as good as mine?"

Jokingly, I would say, "It is because you snore at night!" After the final exams at the end of each semester, we would both celebrate our success, going downtown to an Italian restaurant and ordering spaghetti. Mario, after he finished the first plate, always ordered a second plate of spaghetti. Then, with stomachs full, we would go to the movies. For the cost of twenty-five cents, we saw double features. This constituted our celebration for the end of a semester.

Speed-Reading

As I mentioned before, Cornell University required its students to take nontechnical subjects like economics, finance, accounting, history, and so forth. Some of the courses in social sciences required a lot of reading. The volume of reading took a lot of time to complete. I would study day and night and on weekends, but it was still insufficient to cover all the given assignments.

I made an appointment with my advisor, Professor Gephardt, and told him about this problem. After he heard about it, he said, "I know what your problem may be." He made an appointment for me to visit the Speech and Reading Improvement Center, telling me to go there to be tested for my reading rate.

When I took the tests, the people at the center told me that my reading speed was very slow, about sixty words per minute. I needed to enroll in therapy classes to increase my reading speed. The methods and facilities at this place were amazing. They had projection machines that were calibrated for the number of words at different speeds. First, they started me with numbers. They would project a number on the screen and then turn it off. They increased the digits in the number and then shortened the time of exposure. As time went on, they did this with words, also. First, one word, then two words, and so on. By increasing the number of words and shortening the period of exposure, they helped me increase my reading speed. From the first test that they gave me, they told me that my reading method was all wrong. I was reading aloud, the way that I had been trained in the lower grades. The teachers had always told me to read aloud, so that was the way I was reading.

The center told me that I should not read out loud, saying that, first, the eye sees the word, before the image goes to the brain. After the word is comprehended, the brain sends a message to the mouth that reads it aloud, and then this goes through the hearing process to the brain for comprehension. This method required that my brain work twice as hard for the process of comprehension. All that was necessary, though, was that the eye see the word before it goes directly to the brain for full comprehension. With this help to change my comprehension process, i.e., directly from eye to brain, I realized that the speed of my reading was increasing day by day. At the end of semester, I was reading 350 words per minute, with 90 percent to 100 percent comprehension. My slow reading problem was solved. I was finishing all of my reading assignments and had some spare time to go to sleep earlier at night. I could even go and play Ping-Pong in the game room.

Mr. Adams

The person in charge of the game room was Mr. Adams, a very nice gentleman. One day he asked me, "Do you know how to play billiards?" I said no. He said, "Okay, let me show you how to play billiards." There were two kinds of tables. One type had holes on the sides; he called it the pool table. The other kind did not have any holes, and he called it the billiards table. He then proceeded to show me how to play billiards, which did not take me very long to learn. To play the three-cushion billiards table was not easy, but it was very interesting, because I could use my knowledge of geometry and angles, and I could change the kinetic energy of a spin, directing the movement of the ball. I learned this quite well, but I could never beat Mr. Adams, as he was too good for me.

One day when I played a good billiard game, Mr. Adams told me that he had talked to his wife. He wanted me to come to their home, as she was going to cook some American food. I said "Okay, but I want to bring something with me."

Mr. Adams said that this was not necessary. However, seeing that I was a bit uncomfortable, he said, "Well, maybe you can cook some Afghan food for us."

I said, "Okay. Will do."

I had seen my mother and father cook food back home, but I had never done it myself. There was a dilemma. I knew that Mir Sadat was a good cook, so I asked him how to cook Afghan rice. He told me how to cook rice the Afghan way.

So, the day when I went to the Adams' home, I got some rice from the grocery store and took it with me. Mrs. Adams asked, "How are you going to cook your rice?"

"Well, I will put it in the pot, put some water in, and then heat it. After the rice begins to soften, I'll take it out of the pot, drain the water, and then put the rice in another pot, putting it for a few minutes in the oven to bake."

Mrs. Adams gave me a pot. I did what I had described: I put some water in the pot and then put it on the stove to heat up.

At about this time, Mr. Adams asked me if I was interested in seeing his gun collection downstairs in the basement. I said, "Oh, I am fascinated to see your collection." But when we went down into the basement, I never expected to see such a collection of guns and pistols of all kinds and from all time periods. I became engrossed in seeing the collection and forgot about my pot of rice.

After some time, the Adams' seven- or eight-year-old daughter came down and said, "Mr. Assifi, my mother says to come up and look at what you are cooking."

I suddenly realized that I had something cooking, so I ran up the stairs, opened the top of the pot, and found out that the rice had become a paste and was almost to the top of the pot. I had earlier boasted to the family that Afghans called this rice "chalow" and said that it was unique in that each grain of rice was separate and did not stick to the others. But now I had a paste! Mrs. Adams knew what had happened. A very polite lady, she said, "Maybe we can have some of your paste."

I said, "Yes. I told you that I was cooking chalow, but now we will have the rice that we Afghans call 'batta.'"

Everyone, out of politeness, put a little bit of it on their plates. To make me feel at ease, they commented, "Well, it is very tasty." I had even forgotten to put in some salt, so we had unsalted sweet batta, which was not very tasty.

From then on, whenever Mr. Adams beat me in billiards, I would say, "I will cook you some batta as restitution for my lousy billiards playing." I came to the conclusion that I would never make a good cook or a good billiards player. During the five years that I was at Cornell, I never cooked again.

Student Life at Cornell

While I was staying at Cosmopolitan House and Cascadilla Gorge Dormitory, I ate food at their dining rooms. At other times, I ate at a small drugstore that was close to the place wherein I rented a room to stay.

I always liked to mix different foods that were on the table for eating. I thought that food tasted better that way. One time, I went to a restaurant near campus and ordered vanilla ice cream. When the waitress brought me the ice cream, I asked her to bring me a glass of Coke. Then, I went ahead and put the ice cream in the Coke and started drinking it. I realized that it tasted very good. Since the waitress was standing and watching me, I told her, "Ma'am, this tastes very good! Maybe you should call this ice-cream-Coke and put it on your menu—and thank me for the discovery."

She said "Oh! We already do this, and we call it a Coke float."

Well, that put an end to my belief of having innovative talent. My ego deflated!

Christmastime at Cornell

During summer vacations, the embassy always had interesting programs for me. I could work at construction sites as an engineering surveyor or do some other engineering work. On two summer vacations, I took additional courses at the university.

The worst time at Cornell was during the two weeks of winter vacation at Christmas. Ithaca is very cold and full of snow and ice during the winter. Suddenly, the university campus would become empty. Most of the students went to their homes, and no one was there anymore. So, foreign students were left at the campus to tend to their homesickness. However, some of my Christmas vacations I enjoyed very much.

The office of the foreign student advisor had arranged for some Cornell students to spend their Christmas vacations with families who had volunteered to have students stay with them during that period. These people were older and/or retired. They would invite a student to come to their home as their guest and spend the vacation with them. The program provided me with an opportunity to live with an American family for two weeks. At one time, I was a guest of Dr. and Mrs. Loomis and family. On another vacation, I stayed with the Jacksons. Mr. Jackson had a butcher shop behind his house. He showed me how he did the work. He would sell the meat to grocery stores in town, making some money from it.

These families lived in towns not too far from the Cornell University campus. And this was a wonderful program. It made me feel welcome as a member of a guest family; I could enjoy their hospitality and kindness. I have always cherished the memory of staying as a member of an American family during these periods. It gave me the best picture of the American way of living. I felt quite at home during these periods and saw how good Americans really are.

My Stay in Syracuse

Visiting American homes with my friends' families was the best part of my student life at Cornell. One of the people whom I came to know at Cornell was Mr. Bob Bohm. He was the manager of several dormitories, and quite a nice person. Before one of the shorter vacations, he told me that he would like me to go with him and visit with his family in Syracuse. I told him that it was a very good idea, but that I would like to pay for all my expenses during that period. He said that we could talk about that at a later time. We went in his car to Syracuse, which is not very far from Ithaca. Bob was very intelligent, and I enjoyed talking to him a lot. On the way, before we got to Syracuse, he told me that when I met his family, I should not be too surprised to learn that they could neither hear nor speak. In fact, he said, most of his family communicated in sign language.

Well, the Bohms gave me a room and bed all to myself. Visiting with the family during dinner and at other times was a very pleasant experience for me, one that I will always remember. Bob's parents, brothers, and sisters were all very gentle and kind. They communicated in sign language, but one of them would always translate for me so I could understand what they were discussing.

The Bowditches

Since my classes were all at the university campus, I ate my lunches during the noon break, in the cafeteria of Willard Straight Hall.

There, I always met one of the students who was working in the cafeteria as a dishwasher. As time went on, I became acquainted with him. His name was Pete Bowditch. For some reason, *Nat* sounded better than *Pete,* so I always called him Nat. Nat was very intelligent and liked to talk about international matters. I think that he was taking business and finance classes at the university and was working to pay the expenses of room, board, and tuition. He used to wear an apron. His face was full of sweat and showed signs of working in a hot environment.

Gradually, my lunch hour became an occasion to eat lunch and meet Nat at the same time. I always felt a kind of guilty that I was getting $210 per month for my expenses through my scholarship funds, when here was this guy who was working so hard to pay for his expenses to go to school. But on second thought, I guessed that he may have gotten his lunch for free from the cafeteria because he worked there.

So, before one of the longer school days off, Nat suggested that I go with him to his home in Cambridge, Massachusetts, meet his family, and see some interesting places. I told him that it was a very good idea, provided that I paid for all my expenses during the trip. Nat and I made the trip from Ithaca to Cambridge in his old car, which, I believe, was an old Studebaker. As agreed, we shared the expenses of gas and oil on the way to our destination. Before we were close to Cambridge, Nat told me that his parents had a big house, where I could stay with them. I said, "Okay. I will pay for the cost of the room." Finally, we arrived at the house which was a big two-story gray edifice in what looked to be a very good neighborhood of Cambridge.

We were received at the entrance by a handsome and dignified lady with gray hair. She was wearing an apron, and Nat called her Mother. He introduced me to his mother. She greeted me very pleasantly and then told Nat to take me to an upstairs bedroom. She said, "After you two are washed up, come downstairs for dinner." Nat took me up to my bedroom, which had an attached bathroom. I took a shower and then put on clean clothes—a shirt, a tie, and my Cornell blazer. By the way, in those years it was customary that students at Cornell wear a shirt, a tie, and the Cornell blazer to classes and lectures.

I went downstairs to one of the rooms adjacent to the dining room, where some members of the family were gathering. I was still wondering, *Why does Mrs. Bowditch have an apron on? Is she working here?* My wandering mind came to rest when we went in and sat down at the dinner table. Nat's father, Mr. Bowditch, who was a very handsome and dignified person, came in and sat at the head of the table. And then Nat's mother came in and invited me to dinner, showing me where to sit at the table. Nat's older brother, Pete (Nat), came in, and we were introduced. Then, a maid wearing an apron came in with some food and served us around the table. It was a very pleasant dinner.

Afterward, we went into the next room. I had some coffee and spoke with the Bowditch family about different things. I found out that they were quite well-to-do. Mr. Bowditch was the head of the merchant marine and owned the Sylvania television company. He told my friend to show me around Cambridge and Boston and then take me to their property, a clubhouse and a lake, in the state of Maine, where I could enjoy boat riding on the lake and in the sea.

I had a fantastic time with Nat, who took me to that place. I asked him to tell me why he was working so hard at the cafeteria to make money to pay for his tuition and other expenses when his family was so rich. In fact, I had always felt sorry for him for working so hard at the cafeteria.

Well, he then told me that it was a tradition in their family. All the kids worked to pay their way through school until they finished their studies and stood on their own feet. He said that since the time he was a young boy in high school, he worked to pay for his expenses. He said that he scrubbed the boards on top of boats and ships during summer vacations to earn money to pay for his expenses. The Bowditch tradition was that the young boys and girls worked to pay their own way, stand on their own feet, and then make their own business. He said that he would not take any money from his father.

He would make his own business and life without depending on his father's money. He said, "Later on, maybe, if I have succeeded, I may take some of my share from my father's property to make a bigger and better business."

My trip to Cambridge and visiting with the Bowditches was very pleasant and mind-opening. I have always told my family and friends about it, citing it as a good example of how to raise children, so that they stand on their own feet to make their own life and business in the future.

Foreign Students at Cornell

Cornell University is one of the most prestigious schools in America. As such, it attracts many students from different countries of the world. When Bashir and I arrived at Cornell, we chose to live in the Cosmopolitan House in the university's College Town. This was a room-and-board place, and all the tenants were foreign students who were doing graduate studies at Cornell. Most of the students who stayed there were very hardworking, especially the Chinese students. There were two Arab students, Shawwaf and Sahl Kabbani, and an Iraqi named Haddad. An Iranian graduate student named Jamshid Amuzgar who was working for his PhD in civil engineering was also staying there.

I met Jamshid Amuzgar many years later, when I visited Iran as the minister of mines and industries. He was the prime minister of Iran.

When I was a freshman at Cornell and resided at Cosmopolitan House, Amuzgar told me that if I needed any help in my studies, he would take some time and help.

After a semester or two, I left the Cosmopolitan House and moved to Cascadilla Dormitories. However, later on, I met Sahl Kabbani, a Saudi Arabian, at the campus. Sahl knew one of my Afghan student friends, Yaqub Lalee. Sahl was a very nice and fun person. He was a graduate student in mechanical engineering. He had also moved out of the Cosmopolitan. Lalee and I would sometimes visit him in an apartment that he rented. We talked about his invention for snow tires. The tires he had invented had springed nails that protruded from the tires and gripped the snow and ice on the ground. He was trying to sell his invention to tire companies, but he did not have much luck.

Sahl's Wedding and the Nikah

After a year or two, Sahl informed Lalee and me that he was engaged to an American woman whose parents lived in Worcestershire, New York, which is a city east of Ithaca, toward Massachusetts. He insisted that Lalee, I, and several other Afghan students travel to Worcestershire and attend his wedding. Sahl associated more with Afghan students than with Arab students at the university. Since his wedding was going to be on a day when we were off from school, we promised to attend. Sahl, who was a Sunni Muslim, asked Lalee and me to perform a Muslim Nikah for him. He said that unless a Nikah was performed, he would not consider his marriage vows complete.

Since Lalee was my senior and much more versed in religious matters, I thought that he was the best among us to do this job. But Lalee refused and insisted that I do the Nikah. No matter how much I argued, Lalee would not listen. He argued that he would teach me the whole procedure and the quotations from the Holy Quran, but he would not do the Nikah himself. At that time, he did not tell me the reason, but later on, I figured that Lalee, who was a very honest person, thought that it was not proper for him to do the Nikah due to the slight differences in procedures between the Islamic sect to which he belonged and the sect to which Sahl Kabbani and I belonged. So, I was elected to be the person for this job.

The Islam religion is very simple in these matters. Actually, there are no clergy or priests in Islam. For prayers and religious procedures, the one who is more knowledgeable and trustworthy is chosen by a congregation or a group to lead the prayers or ceremonies. We have to do what we have to do. Sahl's marriage was going to be in another month. This gave me enough time to study the Nikah and become fully versed in all that was needed to be done to make it a proper

Islamic Nikah, one done in the correct way so as to be acceptable to an Arab Muslim. Lalee and Sahl Kabbani were my two honored teachers.

When the time came, Lalee, some other Afghan students, and I went to Worcestershire. The wedding organizer had designated a special room for the Nikah. The bride, the groom, and their families and friends gathered in this room. Lalee and one of the other Afghan students were the two witnesses. I as the Mullah took our places, and the Nikah was performed per the edicts and rules of the religion of Islam. I recited the verses from the Holy Quran and said the prayers at the end. I congratulated the bride and groom, and their families and friends, as part of the Nikah. Sahl Kabbani was very happy with the whole performance and with his Afghan student friends. May God Almighty bless us all for a pious deed. After the Nikah, we all went to the church for a Christian marriage and the wedding party.

Ivy League

Cornell is an Ivy League university. Other Ivy League schools in the USA are Harvard, Yale, Colgate, Dartmouth, Columbia, and Princeton. These universities take pride in their high standard of teaching and learning, and they accept only students who earned a very high grade-point average in their respective high school studies. Some of my classmates had attended prep schools to prepare themselves to be accepted to Cornell.

I was very fortunate in having attended Habibia High School in Kabul at a time when it had an American principal and American teachers. Also, I was a hardworking student and in the top of my class, not to mention class captain from the ninth grade through the twelfth grade. With the advice of my American teachers and Dr. Bushnell, the principal, I applied for admission to three top universities in the United States, namely, Cornell, Yale, and CalTech, as mentioned previously. As it happened, given the high grade average that I had, all three universities accepted me. As a result, I ended up in one of the best universities in America, one that had a top-quality civil engineering school.

During my freshman year at Cornell, the courses were general in math and sciences. To me, it was a repetition of what I had learned at Habibia. When some of my classmates looked at my examination grades, they told each other, "This guy is a little genius from Africa." They did not know that I had already taken these subjects in Afghanistan, which was not in Africa. After the freshman year, when engineering courses became more technical and included a lot of laboratory work, I was just a regular student and not a genius anymore.

I think that there were about 220 of us when we started civil engineering classes. However, at graduation, there were only about 60 of us remaining. This showed how tough the school of engineering was in sticking to their high-standard reputation, which they were very proud to maintain. Let me now tell you about some of the interesting experiences that I had in school.

In my freshman year, I took the required courses in science, such as physics and chemistry, and in mathematics. In physics class, the teacher was Dr. Grantham, a well-known Ivy League professor. His lectures were very interesting. He was one of the best lecturers. It was a lot of fun to attend his classes.

In the American education system, one sees regular homework, weekly quizzes, monthly preliminary examinations (prelims), and then final examinations at the end of the semester, which is a standard. I was very good in my studies, and the material was easy for me. In my first prelim, I knew how to solve each question, so I proceeded to solve each one. However, I noticed that the time allotted for the examination was not sufficient for me to complete the work on all the questions. Once the professor asked us to stop working, he proceeded to collect the exam papers. When I got my examination booklet back, I saw that Professor Grantham had deducted points from all my answers. I was very proud of myself for being a very good student and knowing all the answers to the questions on the examination. I was disappointed and did not know why my professor had made the deductions. Before leaving the class, Professor Grantham told me that he wanted to see me in his office.

When I went to his office, he said, "Why didn't you provide the answers to the questions? It appeared that you knew all the answers but did not do the calculations." He then added, "I also noticed that you had done the calculations in longhand. We do not allow that much time in the exam for longhand calculations, as it takes too much time."

I asked, "How else could I do them, sir?"

He asked me, "Don't you have a slide rule?"

I said, "No, sir."

He said, "Well, I saw your longhand calculations scribbled on the paper and wondered why. You had done all the multiplications, divisions, and square-root and cube-root calculations longhand." He then said, "Mr. Assifi, I am going to give you a makeup exam next week, but this time you better buy a slide rule and use it for the exam."

I said "Thank you, Professor."

I went straight from Grantham's office to the shop in the student union and bought myself a slide rule. It came with an instruction manual. I started learning the slide rule whenever I found time, in between classes and at night. The next week, I went for the makeup exam with my slide rule. Again, I knew the answers to all the questions. I wrote down the equations, solved them, and did the calculations with the help of the slide rule. However, I was not sure about the answers that I got, so I proceeded to recalculate by longhand to make sure the answers were correct. Again, the same problem appeared. I could not finish the calcs for all the problems and had to give my exam paper to one of the instructors who had been assigned to proctor the test.

Afterward, Professor Grantham asked me to see him in his office. He was curious and said, "I saw that you did your calcs by longhand. Why?"

"Sir, I had to do the calcs by hand also, because I was not sure about the calcs I had done with the slide rule."

He laughed and said, "Assifi, I am not going to give you another makeup; you got seventy-five out of one hundred on the exam, which is not too bad. But if you want to get better grades, you should learn your slide rule really well." Well, from then on, I became an expert in the use of the slide rule, which was needed for all my other examinations, too.

A Computer

As I discussed before, civil engineering at Cornell University was a five-year course. At the end of the fourth year, all of my classmates except for those in engineering had graduated and left the school. Although engineering students had to study one more year to complete the requirements for graduation in engineering, everyone still called us the Class of '54. In a way, a student who graduated from this program was actually at the level of a student in a master's degree program, compared to four-year civil engineering programs at other universities.

I had chosen to earn course credits to major in hydraulics and to minor in structures, as I've mentioned previously. One of the requirements for completing the structures program was to do a complete design project, with plan drawings and project specifications. Mario and I decided to work together on a design project that involved the complete structural analysis of a highway bridge. We got carried away by our eagerness for this project and decided that the bridge would have aesthetically curved supports close to the end abutment. Of course, this was, architecturally speaking, a very beautiful bridge, but when we tried to analyze moments and compressive and shear stresses, we realized that they were indeterminate. This meant that by using the methods that we had already learned in the structures classes, we needed to solve indeterminate simultaneous equations. The calculations would take us a lot of time. I would like to remind you that at that time, we had only slide rules and Friden calculator machines, which could only do addition, subtraction, and multiplication. Electronic calculators and computers were not available at that time.

We took our project to Dr. George F. Winter, who was our structures professor. In our structures classes, we actually used a textbook that he had written. When Dr. Winter looked at our project, he immediately said, "I know what your problem is, boys. You guys do not have enough time to solve all these simultaneous equations to calculate the stresses."

We said, "Yes, Dr. Winter."

He said, "I have a solution for your problem. Take your equations to [he gave us an address that was outside the university campus]. There, you will find a computer. The operator will put your equations into the computer and then give you the answers in a very short time. It may cost you about five dollars for his time and the use of the machines."

So, we went to the address that Dr. Winter had given us. It was a building as big as a residential house. There were machines that stood up like closets and had wheels turning tapes. Lights were blinking all over the outfit. The operator took our equations, entered the data by using a keypad that punched holes in cards, entered the cards into the computer machine, and, after about five minutes, handed us our finished calculations. We were privileged to have seen *one of the first computers* near Cornell University. We knew about the invention of the computer, but we did not know that we could use one to get the answers to the calculations of stresses in the project we were doing. Mario and I got an A+ on our final project in structures.

Graduation

I was at the end of my education at Cornell. However, the graduation ceremony was not much fun for me as a foreign student. The people I knew at the ceremony consisted of my classmates and some professors. Caps and gowns were there for show, but there were not many people to show off for. Nevertheless, the whole thing gave me a sense of accomplishment regarding a phase my our life that I had worked so hard for. During the last days of the semester, when we engineering students had completed all the requirements for getting our BCE degrees from the School of Civil Engineering of Cornell University, we had the honor of hearing a speech by Dr. Christensen, the dean of engineering. The whole class of 1954–1955 went to one of the lecture halls at the School of Civil Engineering to attend this final lecture.

Dr. Christensen was a tall, impressive person with graying hair. He congratulated us for our hard work and for being able to meet the high standard of the School of Civil Engineering. He told us that out of 220 students who had enrolled as freshmen in civil engineering, only 60 of us had been able to complete the requirements for the civil engineering degree at Cornell.

He then said, "After five years of hard work, now you all think that you are engineers."

All of us who were in attendance and who felt quite proud of our accomplishment said, "Yes!" in unison.

Dr. Christensen then went on and said, "You *are not really engineers yet!*" This caused some of us to hiss and boo, given the disappointing comment by the dean of engineering.

The dean then commented, "You will be engineers after you have worked in engineering for a period of ten years. Then, you can call yourselves engineers!" He went on to say, "We have prepared you to become an engineer, but you need practical engineering work to really be an engineer. School prepares you, and real professional work and experience makes you become what you have aspired to be all along: a civil engineer. Later on, when some of you decide to pass the state professional engineering examinations, then you can call yourselves professional engineers."

We applauded the dean of engineering for his very honest and candid lecture, in which he told us what the engineering profession's requirements really were. To us, he represented a caring father figure who told his young ones what professional engineering work really involved.

I had a very good impression of Dr. Christensen. Later on, during my work in engineering, I always remembered his remarks and tried to live up to the standards that he had envisioned for us for the future.

In my life, I have always been proud to have been able to successfully graduate from Cornell University and earn my bachelor's degree in civil engineering from that institution. The diploma that I got from Cornell has always adorned my work offices, wherever I have worked. In my library, I have the yearbooks for the Classes of '54 and '55.

Postgraduate Work

The Afghan embassy in Washington, DC, informed me that they had made the necessary arrangements for me to participate in a four-month program working with the Bureau of Public Roads in the state of New Mexico. The Afghan ambassador at this time was engineer Kabir Ludin, who had a degree in civil engineering from Cornell University himself.

Bureau of Public Roads

In Santa Fe, I temporarily registered at a hotel. In the morning, I reported to the engineering department of the Bureau of Public Roads. The chief engineer told me that they had made a program for me. I would first work about a month and a half in the field, and then come back and work in the engineering office, designing roads and bridges.

My fieldwork was in an area halfway between Santa Fe and Albuquerque. I got a room in a motel. Every morning, I went to the field with field surveying crews to survey and map cross-drainage areas for the estimation of floods and for determining the best locations, size of bridges, and types of bridges for the new highway that was slated to be built between the two cities. The motel was in the desert area, close to several American Indian reservations. The field supervisor had advised me not to invite the Indians for drinks, since, he said, they drank too much and passed out. I told him not to worry, because I didn't drink myself and there would not be any problem.

The sunsets in this area were always very beautiful. I took many color pictures to show my friends later. I also visited several Indian reservations, especially enjoying the Indian artwork, which was very interesting.

As scheduled, I reported to the engineering office of the Bureau of Public Roads (BPR) in Santa Fe. The BPR's engineering office was located in the downtown area of Santa Fe. The building was a more modern architectural type of a structure, which was actually not allowed according to Santa Fe city code, which mandated adobe-type buildings. The chief engineer was a nice person. He told me to report to the road design office and get experience in calculating mass diagrams, determining and designing highways, and choosing the location for all structures related to cross-traffic and drainage. He told me that after a month in that section, I would be assigned to design bridge superstructures, abutments, pillars, columns, and foundations.

After the period in the highway location and design section, I reported to the chief engineer. Later, he assigned me to the bridge design section.

Since I had chosen structures as a minor in my studies, working in this section was very interesting for me. The chief of structural design assigned me to work in bridge superstructures, support systems, pavement slab design, columns, abutments, and all the rest: structural design, plans, and specification of bridges. After I worked for a while in these sections, the chief saw that I was pretty good at this work. He then asked me to structurally design column base piling supports and to calculate stresses in bunch piles that were going to be driven at different angles. He informed me of a location that needed this type of piling configuration for the foundation of bridge footings. I was assigned to calculate compression, shear, and bending moment stresses for the each pile, at different angles of penetration into the ground.

I set the equations that were needed for the calculation of stresses. These were indeterminate to seventh degree, so I soon realized that we had a situation. I would have to spend more than a month's time calculating stresses for the different angles of piles that were to be driven into the ground. I showed all these sketches and equations to the chief and reported the amount of time that I needed to get the answers. He smiled and said, "Yes, I know. Several other guys told me the same thing. I thought that since you are fresh out of university, you might solve this problem in a different way." He then said, "Why don't you go think some more and see if you can figure a different method for the solution of stresses?"

I went back to my desk, scratched my head, and tried to find some other way to solve the problem. At that time, as I mentioned before, we did not have computers or other electronic means to shorten the time that it would take to get the answers. I had to use the standard traditional methods that all engineers were trained to use at that time. The chief knew that getting into Cornell University was not easy. One had to be a bright student with very good grades to be admitted to that school. Also, these Ivy League schools raised their standards very high and gave diplomas to those students who worked very hard. It was a plus that Cornell students had the best of professors and used the latest advancements in engineering science and technology.

I started to look at the problem from different points of view, trying to get myself away from the regular structural engineering methods that were used by all engineers at that time. After about two days, I realized that I could set mathematical and trigonometric formulas that would benefit from graphical methods. Since I could easily calculate the stresses for the extreme boundary conditions, I could expand the formulas for the different angles at which bunch piles needed to be driven into the ground. Then, I proceeded to test the formulas that I had developed by using intermediate situations and calculating the stresses from there. I summarized all the sketches for different angles and prepared tables of stresses for the different situations of the piles to be driven into the ground. I asked the chief to schedule a meeting so I could present my results. He proceeded to check the results and was happy with my calculations and stress values. He agreed to schedule a meeting for my presentation of the new method and my results to the other engineers. Well, there is wisdom in the saying that goes like this: "There is more than one way to skin a cat."

My stay in Santa Fe was very pleasant. I enjoyed the atmosphere of the city and the nice people who lived in that area. I rented a room in a room-and-board house. It was not very far from the office where I worked.

Santa Fe is a city where many artists, painters, sculptors, et al., come to exhibit their art and creations. These people were fascinating to me.

Fly-Fishing with Dr. Renkoff

At one point during my stay in Santa Fe, I had to go to an eye doctor to examine my eyeglasses, which were not very good. The eye doctor was a very good man. His name was Herman Renkoff. Dr. Renkoff was not only a very good doctor; he was also a very nice person. He invited me to his home, where his wife made delicious dinner.

Dr. Renkoff asked me if I liked fishing. I told him that I did, but I said that I'd never had time to do any fishing since I had come to America. He invited me to go fly-fishing with him the next weekend. I said that I did not have a fishing rod and did not know how to fly-fish. He said, "You can use one of my rods, and I will teach you how to fly-fish." After that, I was a regular guest at Renkoff's. He taught me how to handle a rod, put fly hooks on, and then how to wave the rod and land the fly hook in a location that offered more of a chance of catching fish. Dr. Renkoff became like an older brother to me. I tremendously enjoyed going out fishing with him and keeping his company. By the way, Dr. Renkoff very much resembled Groucho Marx. I have very fond memories of Dr. Renkoff and his gracious wife. They made my stay in Santa Fe ten times more pleasant.

*　　*　　*

After my work with the Bureau of Public Works in New Mexico, I took the train back to Washington, DC, and reported to the Afghan embassy for permission to return to Afghanistan.

Trip from America to Afghanistan

My father was the governor of Mazar-i-Sharif (Balkh) Province at this time. Instead of flying to Kabul, my hometown, I decided to cross the Atlantic by way of cargo ship to Beirut, Lebanon; take the land route by bus to Herat, Afghanistan; and from there, go on to Mazar-i-Sharif, where my father and mother were. This trip proved to be very interesting and informative. I visited several countries and important cities like Beirut in Lebanon, Damascus in Syria, Baghdad in Iraq, and Tehran and Mashhad in Iran. It took me a little more than two months to travel from New York to Mazar-i-Sharif. On the way, I visited my uncle, who was the police chief of Faryab, and my parents in Mazar-i-Sharif. From there, I and my mother took a bus to Kabul, Afghanistan, where I had lived as a young boy.

Coming back to my hometown, I was full of anticipation and excitement for beginning the new and very productive chapter of my life that awaited me. My excitement was twofold. The first facet was about meeting my fiancée; the second was the prospect of getting married. These two prospects were so powerful that I had no room left to think of the job that was in front of me, and the beginning of my professional career.

My Work with the Helmand and Arghandab Valley Authority

The Ministry of Public Works had informed me that I was assigned as an engineer for the Helmand Valley Project. Since I knew that this was a very big responsibility, I requested two months' leave before going to the job site.

After I married, my employer provided me with a vehicle for the trip to Helmand, where I was to report to Helmand and Arghandab Valley Authority (HAVA) and begin working on the job that was assigned to me. It was about mid-June 1956. Helmand deserts are very hot and dry during the summer months. My new bride, Fariha, told me that she would accompany me wherever I went, whether it was hot or cold.

My engagement and later marriage was arranged by our two closely related families. As one would say, it was an arranged marriage. My Afghan wife, Fariha, both at that time and later on, proved to be an extraordinary, courageous, and devoted partner in my life.

The president of HAVA, Mr. Abdullah Malikyar, had said during my interview that HAVA had started work on project housing with professional cadres who were assigned to different responsibilities. He also told me that they had already built a clubhouse in Lashkargah, a new town, where I and my newly married wife could stay until a house was assigned to us. At this time, some other young Afghan professionals who had studied in America were working in Lashkargah. Mr. Hashim Safi and his wife, Mahboba, were staying there, and they told Fariha and I that we could stay with them. They said that they had two bedrooms and that we could use the spare bedroom until a house was assigned to us. I knew Hashim Safi, as he was the biology teacher while I was at Habibia High School. He had been a student in the College of Sciences and would fill in when Habibia High was in need of teachers. Both Hashim Safi and his wife, Mahboba, were very nice and wonderful people. Mr. Safi had a master's degree in microbiology from American universities. He was the head and organizer of the department of public health and education for the Helmand Valley Project.

Also, there were young graduates from American and European universities who were assigned to head the different departments of HAVA. These young and highly educated people, under the advice of some top-notch American advisors, did a fantastic job of organizing, directing, and training other staff members who were employed to work with HAVA. For instance, Yaqub Lalee, who was my senior at Habibia and then at Cornell University and who had a master's degree from the latter, together with Hai Qazi, a graduate of Rensselaer Polytechnic Institute, and Mohd Aman, who was my senior at Habibia and got his engineering degree from the University of Southern California (USC) and a master's degree in highways from Purdue, organized and established a construction unit in Helmand that took over for Morrison-Knudsen and continued all construction works in Helmand and Arghandab Valleys from that point forward.

HAVA Engineering Department

HAVA had organized an engineering department before; however, it did not have many engineering staff. Engineer Mir Akbar Reza, who had a master's degree from MIT, had become busy assisting engineer Kabir Ludin in the formulation of a very important work, which was the Helmand Water Treaty between Iran and Afghanistan.

HAVA Agricultural Department

The main person who was instrumental in achieving high levels of agricultural production and solving the problems of land settlement by nomads and farmers from all over Afghanistan was Dr. Wakil. He organized the agricultural department of HAVA and its different offices to tackle the very difficult job of making the Helmand Valley Project a success. In this work, he had several young assistants with degrees from American universities. Included were Mr. Hakim Khan, deputy director of the agricultural department, from Tajkurghan, and Mahboob Khan from Wardak, who assisted Dr. Wakil with many different responsibilities in agricultural production and issues of farm settlement.

HAVA Department of Agricultural Research

This department was responsible for finding out which plants gave higher yields in the environment of Helmand. Mr. Painda was a person who was assigned by Dr. Wakil. Painda succeeded with this work by using scientific, insect-control, and economic principles. The department was successful in developing plants and a variety of wheat that would give higher yields and be resistant to rust and other common plant diseases in the locality. The people of this department distributed improved seeds to farmers and settlers so they got higher yields and better production.

The Animal Husbandry Section

This section of the agricultural department was headed by Musa Khan and was responsible for selective breeding between Brown Swiss cows, which gave large quantities of milk, and local cows, which were resistant to local diseases and adaptive to the local environment. The results of their work was successful. People from all over the Helmand area came to buy calves that had been selectively bred by this department.

Agricultural Extension Department

As part of the agricultural department, Dr. Wakil had organized the extension department, which was headed by Mr. Shah Mohamad, a graduate of Wyoming University, who did an exemplary work in this job. Methods for seed selection, planting, insect protection, and other things that the farmers needed to know were tested at the research farm, and the results were made available to the farmers and settlers through extension workers. The work of this department benefited all farmers and settlers in Helmand, as well as in the Kandahar and Tarnak areas.

Production Statistics

As part of the agricultural department, Dr. Wakil had organized this department as well, which was necessary to record all production, farm settlements, and the number of settlers, and to measure the performance of different departments. Their reports were very valuable for any person who wanted to study the performance and production data of the Helmand Valley Project.

Soil Classification Department

This department was a part of the engineering and technical department. Its head was Mr. Formuli, who had a master's degree in soil chemistry from the University of Wisconsin. Before we built and developed the canals, drainage systems, and farm units, people from the soil classification department went to the field, examined the physical features of the soils, and then followed performed laboratory and chemical analysis of the soils to determine which areas were more productive and suitable for agricultural development. On the basis of their classification, our engineering designed the irrigation, drainage, roads, land leveling, and farm units that were given to settlers from all over the country.

Coordination between Agricultural, Irrigation, and Operation Departments

In this department, I was assisted by Mr. Hakim Parwana, who had a degree in irrigation from the United States. He and his assistant, Mr. Ghafar Shuja, were instrumental in training the water-masters to install water measuring devices in canals and farm ditches to make sure that irrigation water would judiciously be applied to the farmland to achieve higher yields and prevent waste of irrigation water.

This was a very important phase of developing HAVA's agricultural production objectives. The control of the quantity of irrigation water applied to the land was one of the reasons for the success of the Helmand Valley Project.

The coordination between these departments resulted in getting rid of the accumulation of salt on the surface of the farmlands, which brought a return of higher productivity of agricultural produce, one of the successes of the Helmand Valley Project.

It was these departments' hard work and devotion that resulted in the eventual success of the Helmand Valley Project, as it became a highly productive agricultural and land settlement project in southwest Afghanistan.

Architectural Division

This office was headed by architect Mir Husein Sadat, who had a degree from Cornell University. He was responsible for the design of residential areas, offices, schools, health clinics, hospitals, and various buildings, including plans for farmhouses, villages, and parts of the city of Lashkargah.

Power

A small hydropower plant was built downstream from the head works of Baghra Canal. This provided power for the base of the Afghan construction unit in the Chah-i-Anjeer, Nad-i-Ali, and Marja areas, which were the agricultural base of these projects, and for the city of Lashkargah. The capacity of this power plant was about three thousand kVA. However, later on, another hydroelectric-generation unit was constructed in Kajakai Dam that also provided some power to the city of Kandahar.

The Cotton Gin and Press

These devices, built with British assistance, assisted with the production of cotton in Helmand. Cotton was introduced to Helmand farmers. The Helmand extension department, under the direction of Dr. Wakil, helped show the farmers the techniques for growing cotton as a new crop. In later years when the production of cotton increased beyond the capacity of the gin and press, the Ministry of Mines and Industries planned to expand the capacity of this factory to twenty thousand tons per year in order to meet increased cotton production in Helmand.

The Alabaster Factory

Helmand has one of the world's best alabaster mines. It is located south of Khan Nishin Mountain, close to the Pakistani border. A graduate of Stanford University, Mr. Karim Nasraty, who had studied in the finance field, was in charge of this industry. The factory mined the alabaster and brought the slabs from the mines, cutting, polishing, and making various items from it. These products met very good markets in Afghanistan and in the outside world.

*   *   *

That is how my professional life and career as an engineer began. Being educated at a very good American university had prepared me to tackle the enormous responsibilities that were assigned to me as an organizer, administrator, and engineer in the very difficult setting of a developing country where most things were being started from scratch.

*   *   *

The Helmand Valley Project had been organized to develop the Helmand Valley lands and some of the desert in between the Helmand and Farah Rivers. The desert lands that were developed were distributed to nomadic settlers and landless farmers from all over Afghanistan.

Water reservoirs, roads, canals, and irrigation systems were constructed, but the budget for the construction of drains and drainage systems was not approved by the central government. The lack of drainage and the nomads' unfamiliarity with farming and irrigation resulted in the salinization of the flat desert lands.

Nomad representatives at this time were complaining to the central government of Afghanistan, saying that with all the promises made to them, the government should have solved the problem of landless nomads who were forced to roam the country to find pasture for their sheep, cattle, and other animals. Now, they were given nonproductive salty lands in Helmand that could not support them and their livestock.

Adverse publicity regarding the failure of Helmand Valley Project, which was built and assisted by the Americans, was heating up more in Kabul because of the fuel thrown by the Soviet Russian propaganda machine to fan the flames of public misunderstanding regarding the Helmand Valley Project.

At that time, the prime minister of Afghanistan was Sardar Daoud Khan. He and King Zahir Shah were very much concerned that this project, which the Afghan government had considered to be a solution to the drought and flood problems of the people and farmers in

Helmand River Valley and the settlement of about a million nomads in Afghanistan, was not succeeding!

To address this issue, Prime Minister Daoud made a special trip to Helmand and met with Afghan and American specialists and advisors. I, as the head of operations and maintenance of Helmand Valley Authority, was present at this meeting.

Prime Minister Daoud asked two questions:

1) Is salinization truly affecting the farmland? And if so, why?
2) Nomads are complaining and do not want to be settlers in Helmand. What is the solution to this problem?

The questions that the prime minister asked were discussed in detail. Regarding the first question, it was explained that by digging the drainage canals, the problem of salinity would be solved. The PM asked, "Why was this not done at the beginning?" The reason for this was discussed.

At one point, I stood up and said, "Sir, the problem was created by the wrong decisions made by politicians in Kabul."

The PM said, "What do you mean, wrong decisions made by politicians in Kabul?"

I responded, "Sir, when the project plans and budget requests were submitted to the government for approval, they included the construction of irrigation canals, roads, and drainage systems. The government approved the budgets for canals and roads, but asked, 'Who ever builds drainage canals in Afghanistan?' Because of this, they cut the budget for drainage systems."

The PM asked, "If we give you the budget for drains, will the problem of salinity be solved?"

The answer to this question was a unanimous yes!

The PM ordered the president of HAVA to submit a request for government approval of a budget for the construction of drainage systems in Helmand.

The second question, regarding the nomads, was answered by Dr. Wakil, the head of the agricultural department. He explained that nomads did not know how to farm. They thought that by putting more water on land, they could get a higher crop yield. Actually, added water, more than is required for irrigation, will destroy and salinize farmland. Wakil explained that in order to have successful farming, we needed settlers who had had past experience with farming.

The PM proceeded further and said that those nomads who did not have experience and did not want to learn farming could go back to being sheepherders. The project lands, he said, should be given to settlers who had past experiences with farming.

Later on the same day, the PM visited the site of the Nad-i-Ali Project. In a big meeting with nomads, he announced that those who did not want to stay as settlers should return to HAVA the parcels of land that were given to them so that these could be redistributed to landless farmers who wanted to be settlers and were willing to learn good farming techniques such as irrigation for better crop yield and settlement of the farms that were developed by the Helmand and Arghandab Valley Projects.

With the application of these two principles, the salinity of the farmland was gradually improved. Giving the farmland to those who had irrigation and farming experience in the past, receiving approval for the budgets, constructing drainage systems, and achieving better water delivery and application of irrigation water to farmlands, the Helmand and Arghandab Valley Project became *a productive oasis in the desert,* as was originally envisioned.

The Helmand and Arghandab Valley Project covers an area of approximately 260,000 square kilometers in southwest Afghanistan. Eventually, this land settlement and agricultural development in an historic and very important part of Afghanistan led some people to call the area "Little America." In any event, the project came to realization.

Through the collaborative efforts of a number of American- and European-educated young Afghan specialists, and with US assistance, the success of the Helmand Valley Project was achieved. Also, the appointment of Mr. Abdullah Malikyar as the head, Dr. Kayeum as his assistant, and Dr. Wakil as the head of the agricultural department of Helmand and Arghandab Valley Authority was another factor that contributed to HAVA's success.

Later on, when more graduates from the College of Engineering became available, and when some were assigned to HAVA, a team of design engineer-advisors from the United States Bureau of Reclamation (USBR) assisted in the training of engineers.

The job involved capacity building, training, and supervision of engineers and staff in the technical and engineering, operation and maintenance, and land classification departments of HAVA. Young engineering staff and graduates of the College of Engineering of Kabul University were hired for training purposes and for the preparation and implementation of plans and projects related to the development of Helmand and Arghandab Valleys. American engineers from USBR assisted the HAVA technical and engineering department in this important work.

For the first time, a fully functional department with Afghan graduates from Kabul University and other colleges were trained to do engineering work at the level of work done in the United States and by other world organizations.

Land classification and preparation of farmland for settlement; design and construction of irrigation canals and drainage systems; land leveling and roads for the establishment of villages and farmhouses; and the settlement of landless farmers and settlers from all over the country was one of the objectives of the department. Also, development of urban areas, including design and construction of towns, transportation systems, roads, and bridges, was part of my responsibility and that of my colleagues at HAVA. The project also included the construction of hydropower facilities, large storage dams and river diversion dams, and rural and urban water supply systems.

The Helmand Valley Project included research programs for finding crops and farm animals better suited to the climate and the area.

It was determined that the coordination of better agricultural crops and better farm management by using irrigation and efficient water application resulted in the elimination of salinized farmland and an increased production of crops. It was necessary to install water flow measuring devices in canals and irrigation systems and to train *mirabs* (water-masters) and ditch-riders to achieve efficient water management. I was successful in programming and supervising water control systems, and in training and managing personnel for the delivery and control of irrigation water to the farmland. I also organized staff and introduced extensive and intensive capacity building, training, and development of human resources for this purpose, which resulted in increased farm production and the success of the Helmand Valley Project.

The following is a very brief description, and the dates of, some of the jobs that I held early in my career.

Operation and Maintenance Department, 1956 to 1965

My first job was to organize and establish an operation and maintenance department for HAVA. The objective was to take over, operate, and maintain the facilities newly constructed by Morrison-Knudsen Company—and to achieve success in this very important undertaking initiated by the government of Afghanistan.

The facilities were two large storage dams, Kajakai on Helmand River and Dahla on the Arghandab River, for a total of 3.3 billion cubic meters' capacity. There were three major river irrigation diversion dams—Boghra Canal diversion dam at Girishk; Darweshan Canal diversion dam at Darweshan; and Zahir Shahi (Babawali) Canal diversion dam in Arghandab, Kandahar—for a total capacity of two hundred cubic meters per second. These facilities' irrigation and drainage systems collectively spanned more than fifteen hundred kilometers.

Staff, managers, and engineers were hired and trained on the job before attending specially established courses for the purpose of building their capacity to carry out the various functions of the operation and maintenance department.

My responsibilities for this project involved the operation and maintenance of storage dams, diversion dams, extensive irrigation systems, canals, drainage systems, and road systems. The job also involved flood forecasting, reservoir operation, riverbank protection against erosion, and modification and rehabilitation of hydraulic structures, spillways, and outlet works.

In order to help farmers and settlers achieve higher agricultural production from the newly developed land that was allotted to them, the government of Afghanistan sent a number of agricultural specialists who had studied in American and European universities to work on the Helmand Valley Project.

In my capacity of overseeing the operation of the water system, I worked closely with specialists and Dr. Wakil, the head of the agricultural department. Dr. Wakil, who had a master's degree in agriculture from a university in India and a doctorate degree in horticulture from London University, was a person of high integrity and professional capability in the field of agriculture.

The collaborative effort between agriculturists and engineers, coupled with advice from American specialists, resulted in the success of the Helmand Valley Project. A number of methods and measures to ameliorate waterlogging and salinity of farmland were developed and implemented. Better agricultural productivity was achieved through more-efficient water use and better water control and irrigation management, thanks to trained water-masters, ditch-riders, and mirabs. Better coordination of operation and maintenance programs and activities vis-à-vis agricultural needs and farm practices also contributed to increased agricultural production.

Cadastral Survey Department

After about five years, the president of HAVA asked me if I would also take over the responsibility of establishing a new project for recruiting and training a number of young people from different levels of education for the establishment of a new cadastral organization (department) to survey land ownership, determine the area and location of ownership, and prepare maps and documents for the recording of ownership deeds of the people living in the rural areas of the country. The United States was prepared to aid this project by hiring Professor Harding of Michigan University, a well-known international authority in cadastral surveys, and providing assistance through PSA, a firm that had already been hired by the United States Agency for International Development (USAID) to help the Ministry of Finance in Afghanistan with financial and accounting improvements.

To accomplish this objective, I was appointed as the president of the new Cadastral Survey Department of Afghanistan, simultaneous with my responsibilities that were part of directing the operation and maintenance (O&M) department at HAVA. The objective was to organize and establish a new Cadastral Survey Department for Afghanistan within a period of three years, from 1960 to 1963. It involved all phases of development, from inception to a fully operational and productive Cadastral Survey Department, including the preparation of laws and regulations to facilitate the survey and establishment of land ownership processes in the country.

First, we needed a facility for the training of about fifteen hundred trainees. The old Kandahar Airport was rehabilitated and turned into a school. Included in the remodeling were plans for administrative and management offices, classrooms, and dormitories.

Second, training staff and instructors were hired from outside the country. Office personnel and managerial staff were hired from various government offices and businesses inside the country.

Third, during the first three years of the project, about fifteen hundred students for training purposes were chosen and recruited from among graduates (at different educational levels) from high schools and colleges in the country. The objective of the project was accomplished within the planned period of three years.

Pilot Project

In order to test the work of the Cadastral Survey Department's teams under actual conditions and learn how to prepare the department for work all over the country, I made a proposal to the government to start cadastral surveys, land ownership determination, and preparation of ownership deeds in a small area as part of a cadastral pilot project. This concept was approved, and the Babajee area near the city of Lashkargah was chosen for the application of the pilot project.

From the application of this concept, the following problems were identified:

1) The finalization of ownership was delayed in local courts.
2) Ownership was fragmented. Six or seven, and up to eleven, parcels owned by the same person were scattered in several villages.
3) Ownership charts were made showing the size and location of these parcels for each owner.
4) When the areas of these parcels were added, the final ownership sizes averaged less than ten jeribs (five acres).
5) Existing laws and regulations needed to be modified to allow the legal process of ownership determination and deeds.

Regarding the first problem, the Cadastral Survey Department made a proposal to the Ministry of Justice and the central government to appoint mobile courts for cadastral processes only. This was approved.

For the second, third, and fourth problems, it was decided to show all the parcels of ownership for each owner in the maps that were given to them when the ownership deeds were done.

For the fifth problem, laws and regulations for facilitating cadastral surveys, determining ownership, and preparing land ownership plots and deeds were enacted.

After a period of three years, a fully functional Cadastral Survey Department, under the Ministry of Finance, began cadastral surveys for the determination of land ownership and the issuance of ownership deeds to landowners in all provinces of Afghanistan.

After both the O&M department of HAVA and the Cadastral Survey Department of Afghanistan were fully established and operational, I was granted an academic scholarship.

Colorado State University

With the experience I had gained through my work in Helmand Valley, I decided to do more research and get a master's degree in the hydraulics of rivers. I applied for a master's degree program in engineering at Colorado State University (CSU) in Fort Collins. My application was accepted. I entered CSU in 1965.

During this trip, I was accompanied by my wife, Fariha Assifi, who enrolled in English literature courses at CSU.

In 1966, the Graduate School at Colorado State University accepted this writer's master's thesis, which was on the hydraulics and geometry of rivers, for the requirement of a PhD dissertation (ATA 7, Colorado State University, Fort Collins, Colorado).

Below, I provide a brief description of how this happened.

Hydraulics Research

Dr. D. B. Simons, the head of the hydraulics and river mechanics department at the School of Engineering, was my main professor, and Drs. Richardson and Maurice Albertson were my secondary professors during this project.

Dr. Simons assigned the Mississippi River study data that had been surveyed and gathered by the US Navy to me and another student, who was also working on his master's degree. Simons told us that the volume of this data was very large and would require that the two of us work on it as a team.

I and my teammate started vigorously analyzing the data. However, after working on it for about two months, we realized that we were not getting anywhere. It was too voluminous and too complex to allow us to make a reasonable analysis and see satisfactory results.

We met with Dr. Simons. My teammate requested to be excused from the project and asked if he might be given another, smaller project that he could finish in time for his master's degree requirement. Dr. Simons asked me, "Mr. Assifi, what is your decision?"

I responded, "Sir, I come from a backward country. One characteristic of our people is that we are very stubborn! I will continue working on the data. If I get some satisfactory result in my further analyses, okay, but if I do not, then I will take the comprehensive examination for the requirement of the master's degree."

He said, "Okay. If you have any questions, you can drop by my office, or after the courses that you attend at the school."

One thing I knew was that Dr. Simons was an international-level authority in river mechanics. He had been asked to be a consultant for the Nile Aswan Dam Project and some other projects in Russia and China. One time I said to him, "Sir, I see you are working on so many projects and studies and make a lot of trips. You do not sleep more than two to three hours in a day, but you are never sleepy. How do you do it?"

He smiled and said, "I have trained myself, and sometimes I catch up on my sleep during the trips and whenever I find a little free time!"

I had a room in the Foothill Lab with blackboards and lots of chalk. The security guards and night janitors were my good friends. My wife worked as a waitress at Billotti's Pizza Restaurant, and later on as the treasurer of the Fort Collins General Hospital until ten or eleven o'clock at night, at which time I drove my old Oldsmobile and took her to our room at the faculty apartments on campus.

My objective was to find criteria and a formula to predict stable Mississippi River channel sections for the Navy to construct ports for their ships.

I reanalyzed the data using a completely new approach, one that was not in the textbooks. After three or four months, I kept seeing that the formulas that were coming from my analysis bore some resemblance, in a complex way, to the formulas that had been developed for pressurized flow in curving pipes. The complexity was a result of so many variables that affected the flow and riverbank conditions in meandering rivers like Ole Miss.

A Breakthrough

I reported my findings to Dr. Simons. He was very impressed and said, "Mr. Assifi, keep on working on it. In the meantime, I am going to ask the Navy to check your findings in the field."

After a week or ten days, he called me to his office and said, "I have good news for you, Mr. Assifi. You have a breakthrough here. Please, keep working on your ideas." His secretary informed me of the date and place of my examination and the presentation of my thesis to my professors' committee.

Defense and Presentation of My Thesis

When I went to the assigned room, I found that it was full of people. I left, thinking that I had made a mistake and entered the wrong room. However, when I was out in the corridor, searching for another room, I heard Dr. Simons' voice from behind me. "Mr. Assifi, you were in the right place. Come on back, but do not be alarmed by the number of people in there; they have heard and are interested to know about your analyses." I followed him back into one of the lecture halls. I was really surprised to see so many students and professors there.

Dr. Simons introduced me and said, "Mr. Assifi will present his findings to you. And by the way, he knows more about this subject than I do!" Then, he told me that I could take as much as two hours for my presentation, at the end of which the audience and professors who were present would ask me their questions.

This was a lot fun for me, presenting the result of the hard work that I had done. Actually, I was quite at ease when making the presentation. I assumed the position of a lecturer, standing in front of the blackboards that I was very familiar with.

At first, I said, "This is a good opportunity for me to contradict my own professor! As students, we do not get that much chance for it!" There was laughter in the hall. I said, "The reality is that Dr. Simons knows a lot more than I could ever learn." Then, I continued with my presentation and used the blackboard as much as needed.

My presentation took a bit more than an hour and half.

I stopped and waited for questions. Some graduate students and professors asked questions. After that, my graduate-program professors asked questions. The last question was from Dr. Simons, who congratulated me for my work. The audience applauded! Gradually, all came down from their places, shook my hand, and individually congratulated me. Dr. Simons gave me a copy of my thesis and said, "I will see you in my office."

I was very happy. The defense of my thesis went very well. I showed the thesis to my wife and told her that the school had printed more than a thousand copies for distribution to engineering departments and other universities. When I opened the thesis, I found that the certification sheet was not signed by my professors. I told myself, *Oh my God. I did all those things, but they have not even signed and approved my thesis yet!*

The next day, I went to Dr. Simons' office. As soon as I entered the room, he said, "Do not be alarmed. I did not sign it because I need to tell you something!"

An Amazing Offer

Dr. Simons continued, saying, "I have discussed your thesis with the university's Graduate School. They have agreed to accept your thesis as the requirement of a dissertation for the PhD degree. The school has agreed that you may work as an associate professor. After a year's residency requirement, you will get your PhD degree. What do you think?"

I said, "Dr. Simons, I request that you allow me some time to think about this important matter."

He said, "Okay, but do not delay too much!"

I consulted with my father and with the president of HAVA. After a few days, HAVA's response was that they needed me to head the engineering and technical department and could not afford to allow me the stay one more year at the university.

I met Dr. Simons after about ten days. When I told him that I could not accept his proposal, he was very much upset with me, even using the word *stupid.*

But when I explained the reasons for my decision, he apologized and told me to register my thesis at the Graduate School without delay. "Otherwise," he said, "your findings could be used by others who are working on their master's theses or PhD dissertations."

One of the rewards of my studies at Colorado State University was that I had become famous overnight. People stopped me in school corridors and even on the campus walkways, congratulating me and asking, "Are you that graduate student from Afghanistan?"

I would say, "Yes. Thank you!"

Head of Engineering and Technical Department of HAVA, and Chief Engineer

Since the Helmand and Arghandab Valley Authority had requested that I return to head the technical and engineering department, I returned to Helmand Valley. From 1966 to 1972, I was responsible, as chief engineer and president of the technical and engineering department, for the organization and upgrading of the HAVA engineering and planning department.

Other Missions

On several occasions, I was assigned by the central government of Afghanistan to provide expert assistance in solving the problems that arose in the South Helmand, Nimroz (Seistan), area. I was also requested to participate as an expert member of the commissions that were delegated to resolve critical cross-boundary issues between Iran and Afghanistan. Some of these assignments are discussed below.

Location of Iran–Afghanistan Border Pillars

An Afghan delegation was assigned to negotiate and discuss with a delegation from the Iranian side, and to find a solution for the relocation and reinstallation of three border pillars that were destroyed by Helmand River's meandering and changing of its course.

The Afghan delegation was led by two men: Mr. Habib Karzai from the Afghan Ministry of Foreign Affairs, and General Rahim Nawabi from the Afghan Ministry of the Interior's gendarme section. I was assigned as an expert member to help the delegation reestablish the location of washed-away pillars so that they could be reinstalled.

The Afghan delegation flew from Kabul to Lashkargah on a Russian-built military helicopter, picking me up on the way to Zaranj, the capital of Nimroz Province in southwest Afghanistan. The copter had to be refueled halfway to Zaranj. This was done by adding spare fuel that had been hauled in oil barrels. The copter pilot's name was Asadullah Sarwari.

The delegations from the two sides met alternately in Zabul, Iran, and in Zaranj, Afghanistan.

The boundary pillar files that the delegations had brought with them contained the necessary specifications for the pillars in question. A review of these documents showed that earlier, in the 1980s, British engineers led by Mr. McMahon had specified the location of the pillars by way of two methods:

a) descriptive features on the two sides of the river channel
b) geographical coordinates

However, the change to the river channel had washed away the unique land features on the two sides that had been used as references for defining the location of the pillars, so their reestablishment by descriptive methods was almost impossible.

At that time, in the mid-sixties, today's computers and GPS systems were not available.

I and a cartographer, Mr. Ghafoor, were able to determine the location of the destroyed pillars by shooting the North Star and calculating the position of the pillars by the methods that I had learned in advanced survey courses during my studies at Cornell University. We made use of logarithmic tables for calculations. I verified our results by using triangulation systems that had been established earlier in some areas in the region.

Destroyed Border Pillars Found

By going to the calculated site, the delegation found the remnants of the mortared-brick pillar foundations that had not been totally washed away by the river. The Afghan delegation's finding the location of the destroyed pillars was quite a surprise to the Iranian delegation, who were arguing that the pillars be relocated by the descriptive specifications given in the Iran–Afghanistan border pillar files, which were in the possession of both delegations. This method would have moved the pillar locations almost a kilometer's distance into the Afghan side.

At the meeting, I explained how I had done the calculations and requested that the Iranian gendarme engineer who was present review and check my calculations for accuracy. Then, I suggested that both delegations go to the calculated site and see if they could find any traces of the old pillars.

When the person leading the Iranian delegation asked his engineer if this could be done, the engineer said yes. However, at this juncture, the Iranian delegation excused themselves and said that they had to go back to Tehran and rest for the twenty days before the New Year (Nawroz) holidays. They said that they'd come back afterward for the completion of the work. *I understand that they never came back.*

Band-i-Kamal Khan

Earlier, it had been determined that a flood control diversion at Kamal Khan was needed to protect downstream agricultural farmland and villages in Afghanistan and Iran from damage caused by extreme flooding during high Helmand flow years. During these years, Helmand River discharges eventually flowed into Gowdizereh, the largest and deepest depression in the chain of interlinked *hamuns* (seasonal desert lakes) in Afghanistan and Iran.

By constructing the Kohak Dam in Helmand's river channel, Iran had, to some degree, reduced damage from the flooding on their side. However, with the construction of the Kamal Khan diversion, flood discharges would have been diverted directly into Gowdizereh through the Rudibyaban Channel, reducing flood damage in both Iran and Afghanistan.

I, together with Hugh Brown of Harza Engineering Company, spent about four months in Zaranj. Brown was retrained to do a feasibility study and make a preliminary design for the Kamal Khan diversion structures.

Several years later, the construction unit of HAVA began work on this project. However, the project was not completed because Soviet forces subsequently invaded Afghanistan.

Dealing with Severe Droughts

The Helmand is a perennial river. Its watershed begins at the Paghman Mountains near Kabul and then flows west and southwest until it discharges into the inland lakes in the Nimroz (Seistan) area. The Arghandab River begins at the mountains near Naawur Ghazni and is a tributary of Helmand River, which joins it at Bost, six kilometers southwest of the city of Lashkargah. Both rivers are snow-fed, and rainwater floods from washes at the two sides contribute to high discharges downstream, causing heavy flooding at certain times during the year. Conversely, during low flows and drought periods, the flow from these rivers is drastically reduced. To reduce the severity of these high and low flows, the government of Afghanistan, after the repeated petition of downstream farmers, decided to construct Kajakai Dam on Helmand River and to build Dahla Dam on Arghandab River. Toward the end of World War II, Morrison-Knudsen Company of Boise, Idaho, was hired for this purpose.

As the chief engineer of HAVA, I was in charge of the operation of reservoirs and irrigation canal systems. Analysis of river-head-area snow cover at Naawur Ghazni, and hydrologic data of river flows and precipitation records during the years around 1972, had indicated a period of severe drought in the forthcoming years, which would dry up the Helmand and Arghandab Rivers.

I presented my prognosis of the forthcoming years and submitted a special report to the central government of Afghanistan, with my recommendations for water conservation measures and assistance to landowners and farmers during this severe drought period. On the basis of my recommendations, a special program was set up in several provinces that were going to be affected. Eventually, these measures proved quite beneficial in reducing damage to agricultural crops and fruit trees owned by farmers, landowners, and other people living in these two river valleys.

Saving Kandahar Fruit Trees

Analysis of hydrological records, Arghandab River flow data, and measurements of snow cover at the head works of the river showed that, even with optimum operation of the Dahla storage dam to conserve water, the Arghandab River would completely dry out in the forthcoming season, endangering Kandahar pomegranates, which are known to be the best in the world. Drying of Arghandab Valley orchards and fruit trees would have inflicted a severe blow to the economy of Kandahar Province and the people living there. Our responsibility at HAVA included agricultural, engineering, and operational plans for both Helmand Valley and Arghandab Valley. Since I was familiar with land and water resources in the Kandahar area, I made a full analysis of the problem that was soon to befall that area. I proposed something unique to the central government to save the fruit trees from drying out during the severe drought period.

We knew from previous land and soil surveys that the groundwater depth in the areas that were going to be affected was no deeper than ten meters. I proposed the following: (1) that the government (a) subsidize the purchase of low-head irrigation pumps by authorizing the Agricultural Development Bank and other banks to lend money at low interest for the purchase of these pumps and (b) encourage tradespeople and businesses to import pumps from neighboring countries for this purpose; (2) that the government authorize low-interest loans to landowners, orchard owners, and horticulturists to dig open wells for the installation of pumps from which to water the trees when the river and irrigation canals dried up; (3) similarly, that the government authorize the purchase of fuel at subsidized prices for the operation of pumps during the drought period.

When my proposal went to the central government, they immediately issued their approval and ordered the related ministries and banks to make the necessary arrangements for implementing the facets of the proposals. The governor of Kandahar Province, Honorable Sidiq, called me and said, "Mr. Engineer, what have you done? You created a big problem for us. You know the people of Kandahar. How can we convince them to do all the things that you have proposed?"

I responded, "Convene a big meeting with the people's representatives and landowners. I will come and speak to them. And do not worry. They know me."

A big meeting was held at the governor's mansion. The governor did not have to introduce me, because all those who were present already knew me, either personally or by reputation. They told the governor that they knew engineer Assifi and trusted what he said and recommended. They even said that this was not the first time that this was happening. Some of them said that they had heard, from their fathers or grandfathers, that the Kandahar and Arghandab Valley orchards and fruit trees had totally dried out during severe droughts in the past, bringing heavy economic losses to the area and to Kandahar Province.

Our proposals were enacted and implemented. They saved Kandahar and Arghandab Valley fruit trees from drying out. Several years later, one of the senators from Kandahar told me that he was present during that meeting. He added, "Engineer Assifi, you should receive one of the highest medals for saving Kandahar from great economic losses during that severe drought period." He went on to say, "The measures that you had proposed are still being used in Kandahar area to this day. Those wells have become a permanent feature of fruit-tree orchards, for supplemental water and water needed during the years that we have water shortages in Arghandab Valley and Kandahar Province."

The Kajakai storage reservoir and lower canal systems were managed on conservation principles and according to the articles of the Helmand Water Treaty between Afghanistan and Iran. An operational program was set up to deliver sufficient water to the Iranian Kohak Dam and the downstream area of Chakhansur in Nimroz Province in

Lower Helmand. However, the people of Nimroz and of the villages in Chakhansur were still experiencing severe water shortages and requested government help.

Water Shortage Study Mission

A fact-finding mission was sent from the central government to study the Nimroz and Chakhansur water shortage problem, and I was appointed as technical consultant for this mission. The survey of the areas that were affected by water shortages showed that although water releases from Kajakai Dam provided sufficient water for Iranian needs as well as irrigation for the downstream villages in Afghanistan, Iranian operators were taking all the water in that section of the river by diverting Helmand flows to Kohak Dam and installing additional pumps in the lower section of the river. This did not leave any water downstream from that location for the village of Chakhansur, and it resulted in the total drying of the Chakhansur area. It also forced the migration of about sixty thousand people from their homes and caused the loss of a large number of livestock in that area of Afghanistan. *A human and environmental crisis had developed.*

The mission prepared a report of their findings and recommended three alternative solutions to the problem.

1) Immediate discussion with the Iranian government to instruct their operators to operate the Kohak Dam properly and remove the additional pumps that were installed below the dam, so as to allow sufficient water to reach the villages in Chakhansur.
2) If the Iranian operators did not do as requested, then the people of Nimroz and Chakhansur threatened to take the law in their own hands and forcefully destroy the Iranian pumps below the Kohak Dam. This was actually a no-no solution, as it constituted an act of war between the two countries.
3) A long-term solution was recommended for the construction of a bypass canal from a location in Helmand River above the Iranian Kohak Dam, to bring water for the downstream Chakhansur and Nimroz areas that had totally dried up. The

first phase of work suggested in the recommendation had to be done as soon as possible and under a food-for-work program, in order to allow the people who had been forced to leave the Chakhansur area to return. This would impede the total migration of the Nimroz population from their homes and farmland, and prevent starvation of the remaining people and livestock in the area.

The Report

The report of the findings and recommendations of the mission was submitted to the Office of the Prime Minister. The government's resolution was that the engineer consultant was to prepare a feasibility report regarding the commission's third recommendation and submit it to the government for its decision before beginning work on the permanent canal.

Alternative Alignment and Its Feasibility

I was fully aware of the plight of the people and the criticality of the situation in the Chakhansur and Nimroz areas. This was, indeed, a very difficult and tough assignment.

In order to arrive at a solution for the best alignment of the bypass canal, the following things needed to be done:

1) Locate the intake, on the basis of canal hydraulics, and a stable section of the river, after establishing horizontal and vertical survey reference points.
2) Survey three alternative alignments, calculate volume and cost, and determine the most feasible alignment.
3) Recommend construction methods, time schedules, and maintenance.

Given the criticality of the situation, the shortness of time, and the fact that this job required high-level expertise, I decided to do the work myself. Therefore, I went back to Helmand, organized the workforce, and immediately proceeded to Nimroz to begin the work.

The workforce consisted of two fully equipped survey crews with jeeps and a logistics support crew that handled the setting up of tents in the desert and prepared food for the crews when they returned from fieldwork at night. This group also brought water in empty oil barrels from a deep well in Kang Nad-i-Ali, the only well in the area that had sweet water.

Survey crews were at the field location of work early in the morning before sunrise. They worked until after sunset when they could no longer see the survey instruments.

Survey Activities

We washed up after work and ate whatever our cook prepared. We had brought field drafting tables with us. After supper, we calculated, plotted, and transposed the day's survey data, thereafter preparing plans and profiles of the canal alignment. Next, we made the necessary calculations for the volume of excavation for that section. We then rested in our sleeping beds, which were cots, and awoke for morning prayers followed by a brief breakfast of tea and field-cooked flat bread (*nan-i-tawagi*), after which we proceeded to the survey location before sunrise.

We continued the fieldwork without stopping, including working on weekends, for a total of twenty-three days and nights. At this time, we knew and could make comparisons of the volume of excavation on the three alignments. We proceeded to prepare maps, plans, profiles, and a preliminary design for each alignment, thereafter discerning the area that would benefit from each alternative. On this basis, an alternative alignment analysis and feasibility report was prepared.

Lashkari Alignment

One of the very interesting discoveries that we made was the coincidence of our best alternative with the alignment and profile of an historic canal (nine hundred to a thousand years old). Our canal alignment and profile coincided with this old canal for about six kilometers. We asked the people living in the vicinity what the name of this old canal was. They told us that it was called Lashkari Canal, saying that it was built during the time of the Seistan civilization. On this basis, we named our new alignment the Lashkari Canal alignment, which was actually the best alignment out of the three that we had surveyed.

This was an interesting addition to our soup!

One night when we came back from the field and were getting ready for supper, a jeep came close to our tents, and several border patrol officers and their commandant got out, came toward us, and said hello. They were curious to know what we were doing walking all the day in the desert, coming into the tents at night, and then going back into the desert the next day. Obviously, they had been observing us. I told one of them that we were doing a field survey to determine the best alignment for a bypass canal, as he knew that the Lower Helmand and Chakansur area had completely dried out. He said, "We have been observing you for the last few days, and it appears you must be doing important work, as you never rest!"

I said, "Now we are going to have our supper. We will do calculations and office work, sleep on our cots, and then, after morning prayers, go out to the field again." I told him that he had come at about the right time, as we were ready to go eat the soup that our cook had prepared. "We will be honored if you could join us for supper," I said.

He accepted the invitation and came into the tent. We all sat on the floor, around the food-cloth. I invited the commandant to sit next to me. Our cook brought a large pot full of soup, giving each one of us a small bowl and a flat piece of bread. We proceeded to eat, cutting the bread into smaller pieces and putting soup into our bowls.

For lighting, we used gaslights and kerosene lanterns inside the tent. The opening to the tent was closed so that insects would not come in. However, on this night, we may not have closed the opening. So, when we started getting soup from the large bowl, a tarantula (*ghundell*) fell from the top of the tent, where we had the bright gaslight, and into a bowl. It was an odd sight to see the big spider trying to swim around and get out of the bowl. I reached out with a large spoon, scooped up the swimming tarantula along with some soup, went out of the tent, and tossed the spider outside. When I came back, I sat and apologized to our guest for the interruption. "Let us eat our soup," I said.

At this time, the commandant excused himself, stood up, and said, "You know, I had already eaten before I came, so, if you will excuse me, I will say good night and go back to my duties." I said that that was okay. I walked him to the entrance of the tent, said good-bye, came back, sat down, and proceeded to eat my soup with the rest of the company!

Needless to say, at this juncture, all of us who were sitting around the food-cloth kept saying, "Now, let us eat the tarantula soup!" After that, a chorus of great laughter came from our tent and reverberated into the desert.

Later on, when I've told this story to friends and acquaintances, their reaction has always been quite mixed. Each one reacted quite differently. None were sure how they themselves may have reacted to the tarantula soup incident. I believe that big laughter was an appropriate response to this unique occurrence.

After the fieldwork, I and the survey party returned to Lashkargah and finalized the feasibility report, recommending the best alignment of the bypass canal. The report was submitted to the Office of the Prime Minister for government decision.

Proposal and Recommendation

In the submitted proposal, in order to attract the people who had left the area and to prevent further starvation of the local population, we had recommended manual workforce for the first phase of excavating the canal. Payments for excavators were to be made under a food-for-work program, which had been successful with other jobs in the country.

I was called in to a cabinet meeting to present the report. After a lengthy discussion, including questions and answers, the cabinet approved the Lashkari Canal alternative and gave the necessary orders to various ministries and the Helmand and Arghandab Valley Authority to proceed with the construction of the canal, under a food-for-work program.

Lashkari Canal Excavation Begins

Soon after the announcement of the work, the people who had left the area began arriving at the job site with their families. The excavation of Lashkari Canal was begun by the people themselves.

One of our survey groups was assigned to the job, to give "slope-stakes" for the excavation of the canal.

More than half of the canal excavation was completed under the food-for-work program.

Later on, President Daoud instructed me to take the commandant of the Ministry of Public Works' mechanized unit to the job site, familiarize him and the relevant workforces with the canal construction plans, and assign a construction survey group from HAVA to assist in completing the Lashkari Canal work according to the construction plans that I had earlier prepared for this purpose.

The rest of Lashkari Canal excavation was done by the Ministry of Public Works' mechanized unit.

Later, with the Communist coup and the Soviet Union's invasion of Afghanistan, most work in Afghanistan stopped, including the construction of the Lashkari Canal intake and spillway structures.

Helmand Valley Project—Farming and Agricultural Production

A large number of settlers composed of landless farmers from all over the country were allotted farm plots to settle for a "new life" in the Helmand's newly developed and improved farmland. Agricultural production after the Helmand and Arghandab Valley Projects was very successful. Wheat silos from Herat and other provinces all the way to Kabul were filled with the wheat grown in the Helmand Valley Project. The production of cotton, which had been introduced to the farmers in Helmand as a new crop, exceeded the capacity of the cotton gin and press in Lashkargah, and plans were being made to enlarge the existing gin and press to meet the increase in cotton production.

A New Assignment for Me

The central government of Afghanistan wanted the rural areas and farmland in the country to be developed as modeled by the Helmand Valley Project. For this purpose, it was decided to reorganize the existing Rural Development Department in the model of HAVA. I was asked to take on this job. Consequently, in 1972, I was appointed as the president and chief engineer of the Rural Development Department of Afghanistan.

After accepting this job, I and my family moved to Kabul. I took on the responsibility of reorganizing and expanding the Rural Development Department of Afghanistan (RDDA).

I began this job by introducing better planning and design methods, and preparing preapproved plans for various sizes and situations to speed up the design period for construction. Training of personnel for the development of projects in rural areas was begun. Projects were for farm roads, bridges, water supply systems, and irrigation canals and facilities, including diversion dams and flood protection structures. Also included was riverbank protection against erosion and projects for the construction of village schools and health clinics in rural areas in Afghanistan.

In order to achieve this objective, I was responsible for introducing a new, four-tier project feasibility system for the evaluation and approval of new projects at RDDA. The four tiers were technical aspects, economic aspects, financial aspects, and social feasibility.

During this period, the staff was reorganized and trained to do all the survey and technical work, including distributing questionnaires and securing agreements for community participation in planning, survey, construction, and future maintenance of the facilities.

The new system of evaluation and approval guaranteed that public funds were used for projects that benefited the economy and well-being of the communities, and prevented misuse of public funds for personal purposes.

Before doing any work on job appointments, I made a detailed survey and inventory of all the personnel and staff that were already part of RDDA. The inventory took into account level of education, experience in office and fieldwork, past performance, honesty, integrity, and reputation, and how each staff member was known with respect to these items. I ranked all personnel on this basis.

Then, on the basis of this survey and the rankings, I proceeded and did the reorganization and made new job appointments at RDDA. For instance, engineer Sediq Aishan got a very high ranking among the engineering staff, so I made him the director of the engineering department. Mr. Mawlana Zada was made the director of RDDA administration, finance, and management.

These assignments proved to be very valuable in making the RDDA one of the most successful departments in the newly formed Republic of Afghanistan.

In my work as the president of RDDA, I was very fortunate to have two very competent American advisors, David Garner and Lou Mitchel. Their role was instrumental in the success of the newly organized Rural Development Department. When I was with RDDA, I was grateful for their help and advice. The same was true later, with my other assignments in Afghanistan. Lou could not continue in his role because an ailment befell him in later years. However, David always benefited me with his wisdom and forethought regarding many important issues during the war against the Soviets and later on in my work with USAID, and subsequently as the technical advisor to the president of Afghanistan.

For instance, David and I were members of the mission that was organized by Development Alternatives, Inc. (DAI), and USAID to make an assessment of the irrigation sector in Afghanistan and recommend strategy for its countrywide rehabilitation after the Taliban were driven from their controlling role in the country.

Without pay, David continued being an advisor to me even after I became an advisor to the president. One of his important contributions in this nonpaying role was his idea for me to continue working on the drought problem in Afghanistan and to prepare reports and make recommendations for remedial measures for an impending famine brought about by drought in the country.

I continued working on this idea during the period that I worked for USAID, and later on as a technical advisor.

I report on this work later, in part three of these memoirs.

Within a few months, my efforts paid off. The RDDA had been reorganized and transformed into an efficient and productive department, much to the appreciation of the beneficiaries and people in the rural communities.

A Major Political Change in Afghanistan: The Establishment of the Republic of Afghanistan

On July 17, 1973, there was a major political change in the country. The former prime minister, Sardar Daoud Khan, made a so-called bloodless coup that drastically changed the political and governmental administration of Afghanistan from a constitutional monarchy to a republic. As a result, King Zahir Shah, who had, for health reasons, gone to Europe, announced his abdication as the king of Afghanistan in favor of the newly formed Republic of Afghanistan. Sardar Daoud Khan became the president of Afghanistan.

Since the new government had announced that all government offices should continue their work as before, I continued my job, without any hesitation, as the president and chief engineer of RDDA. However, after about ten days, I was summoned to meet the president.

The meeting with President Daoud was quite extraordinary. At first, the president praised me for the work that I had done in Helmand, Arghandab, Lower Helmand, and Nimroz. He told me that while he himself was retired and at home, he followed all the work that went on in the country. He knew of the work that I had done, considered me to be a person of high integrity and honesty, and admired my hard work and accomplishments as an engineer.

Then, President Daoud went on and praised my father, Abdul Wahab Khan Assifi. He said, "Mr. Assifi was one of our best governors in the country. His honesty and integrity were exemplary. Your father resigned from the governor's post of Mazar-i-Sharif." He continued, saying, "Actually, it was my fault!" Then, he added, "The people of Mazar-i-Sharif, in recognition of his services, later on elected him as their senator, representing them in the then-Parliament of Afghanistan."

President Daoud then said, "We will be appointing you to a higher post."

To this, my response, was, "Sir, I will be proud to serve my country in work that is within my profession as an engineer, but I am not a political person."

President Daoud responded by saying, "We shall discuss that later." He then stood up halfway, shook my hand, and said, "See you later."

A few days later, President Daoud instructed me to take Wahab Khan, the commandant of the Ministry of Public Works' mechanized unit, to the Lashkari Canal job site and acquaint him with the canal construction plans so that the mechanized unit could complete the remaining work on the canal. Accordingly, I took Commandant Wahab Khan to Nimroz and the Lashkari Canal job site. On the way back, we drove to the old city of Farah. When we were preparing to rest for the night in our tents, an announcement on Kabul Radio broadcast my appointment as the new governor of Herat Province.

When I came back to Kabul, met President Daoud, and reminded him of my earlier statement that I was not a political person, I mentioned that the appointment for the job in Herat was political. The president responded, "The reason I have appointed you as governor of Herat is that representatives from the people of Herat are asking the government to do as we have done in the development of Helmand Valley Project. That is why you were chosen for this job. Go to Herat and begin plans, programs, and the work for the development of Herat, as you did in Helmand."

Governor of Herat Province, 1973 to 1975

As governor of Herat Province in Afghanistan, I was responsible for supervision and management of all government departments, agencies, and institutions. I had to oversee the development and expansion of the economy and all sectors of the province of Herat, including agriculture, public works, water and land resources, mines and industries, public health, education, and cultural, legal, and security sectors. *It was a very tough assignment!*

In my past work, I had learned and was convinced that firsthand, direct contact with the people of the province was essential. I was certain that my success as the governor of Herat depended on this, too. Therefore, I instructed my office manager to open all the doors of a large conference hall next to the governor's office. The hall had room for two to three hundred people and doors on all sides, with one door connecting to the governor's office. Free access was provided to all who wanted to speak to the governor personally.

I told my secretary to gather all the written petitions that people had submitted to the governor's office, saying that I would handle them on a first-come, first-served basis. I said, "Put them on the table that I will be sitting behind, facing the people who come in and seat themselves on the available chairs. Tell the rest to sit on the carpeted floor. Again, I will handle them on a first-come, first-served basis.

At about five o'clock in the afternoon, after finishing all the work in the office, I, the governor, came into the hall. I greeted the people who had stood in respect, and then I sat down beside the secretary and behind a long coffee table, which had the stack of petitions and a telephone on it. The people who had come in would rise when their name was called by the secretary. They usually came in groups— men and women alike, and some with their children.

These sessions took about two hours' time. At the end of it, I would rise and go to governor's residence, wash up, eat, and rest for some time before getting up and going to visit different places of business in the city. I even went to the border posts. I visited prisons and detention centers belonging to police and gendarmerie, hospitals, and other locations that were sensitive as far as the public was concerned. For all of these visits, only the driver of the car and a security person accompanied me.

During the days, I would visit schools, attend sports and public events, and encourage dialogue with students and the younger generation.

After some time, the people of Herat became used to the governor as a modest person who cared about them and went to many places to make sure that people were safe and taken care of. In return, the people would share direct information with me that they thought was pertinent to the well-being of the community.

I organized special meetings with elders and representatives of the community, and I encouraged the exchange of ideas and discussion of what was needed for the province and the people of Herat. I helped people to organize themselves to take care of certain public works that were needed for the preservation of historical places and archeological sites.

This was a heavy and time-consuming workload for a governor. I could not sleep more than three to four hours a night. But I was of young age and carried this load without much difficulty. In fact, I enjoyed working with the people and helping them come up with ideas and do good things for themselves and the community.

For example, the following projects were planned and started for developing Herat Province and raising the economy and living standard for its people:

- Helping the cotton gin and press company expand its capacity to meet the increasing cotton production in Herat.
- Planning and building a new textile factory to utilize the increase in cotton production and provide additional jobs for the people in the city of Herat.
- Increasing the capacity and modernizing the extraction of coal in Herat mines.
- Finalizing studies and planning for and building a new cement factory to provide cement for construction of new development projects in Herat and other provinces in west and southwest Afghanistan.
- Since traditional sheep exports to Iran suffered heavy losses due to the lack of necessary export facilities, I decided to build a modern slaughterhouse to slaughter the sheep, process the meat according to modern sanitary standards, and thereby prevent heavy losses to sheepherders before the meat made it to the markets in the region. My request for funding of this project was approved by the World Bank, and the construction of a modern slaughterhouse started. Before I left Herat, it was completed and operational.

Salma Dam

Hari River water was uncontrolled. As a result, a lot of the floodwater was wasted and not stored for future use. A similar problem was solved in the Helmand River area by constructing the Kajakai Dam and on the Arghandab River by constructing the Dahla Dam. Subsequently, those two dams proved to be very beneficial to the downstream farmers in Afghanistan and Iran.

An Indian company was hired to study and recommend a solution to this problem in Hari-rud. Their studies showed that a dam could be constructed in Salma to provide a reservoir for floodwater storage. It could then be used when water was badly needed in the later months of the year.

On this basis, the Salma Dam Project construction began. Before I left Herat for a new job in Kabul, the construction of Salma Dam was about 20 percent done.

While in Herat, the following things transpired:

- The extension and paving of roads that connected Herat to other provinces was begun, and much work was done during this period.
- The preservation and repair of historical monuments and archeological treasures for which Herat is very well-known.

    a. The Herat's famous minarets. This project began with help from UNESCO.
    b. Preservation and restoration of historical monuments all over Herat Province.

The Great Mosque of Herat

The yard of the Great Mosque of Herat was to be paved with marble. One of the mosque's elders of Herat Province, Abdul Ghani Khan, gave me this idea. I consulted the representatives of the people of Herat and discussed this concept with them. They expressed their willingness to fund this big project by way of their own contributions.

I helped to organize and provided necessary guidance for the election of people's representatives for fund raising, managing, supervision, construction, and laying of imported marble from the marble mines in Wardak Province.

The original pavement was made of baked clay tiles that were gouged and broken. About 20 percent of the work was completed by the time that I, then the governor, was appointed as the minister of mines and industries.

Since people and their representatives were doing this project, the work continued throughout several regime changes. Many years later when I visited Herat, I was very pleased to see that it was 100 percent complete. This example demonstrates my belief that *sustainability and success of any work (project) can be achieved if the work is planned and done with the people's participation and it is for the benefit of the people.*

Another example of how this concept benefited the community can be seen in the following story.

A Gang of Robbers

One day, during the general public hearing meeting in the great hall, a person who had a petition came close to the governor (me) and told me that he would like to talk to me privately. I told this person that he could come to the governor's residence at about eight o'clock the same evening, at which time I would talk to him. When I went home, I told the security guard at the entrance gate to let me know when this person came to talk to the governor. When the person arrived, I told the guards that I would talk to him in one of the rooms close to the side gate of the residence.

The man, who was wearing a qarakul-skin (the skin of qarakul lamb) cap, popular in Afghanistan, said, "Sir, I am a taxi driver. Late last night, I was called in to help haul some things in my taxi. It was past midnight. The people who had called took me close to one of the residential compounds that is close to the minarets. There were several other cars and pickups parked on a side alley. Later on, maybe about fifteen to twenty people who were fully armed and covering their faces with their turbans came out of the compound. They brought with them lots of goods, like carpets, big sacks full of material and items, suitcases, and other things. They loaded all these things in the vehicles, including my taxi. Apparently, these items were from a big heist at the compound. Then, we all drove to another compound in Herat's Old Town area and unloaded all the stuff. The robbers all went inside with the goods. It was about three or four in the morning. They paid my taxi fare and some more money as a tip. But, sir, they did not know that the compound that they had robbed belonged to one of my relatives."

I asked the taxi driver, "Can you find the place that the robbers went in, now? And do you think that they might be still there?"

"Yes, sir. I know the place, and I think they may still be there."

I asked, "Do you have your taxi here?"

He said, "Yes."

I said, "I am going to go to the central police station now. You will follow me. I will tell the guards to let you in. Wait in your taxi. Don't be afraid. I will call you into the office. I want you to tell this story once again, and then I will ask you to show the police the place that the robbers entered. Afterward, I will let you go on your own business, okay?"

He responded, "Yes, sir."

I called the driver for the governor's car and asked one of the security guys to accompany me to the police station. On the way out, I called the police commandant and asked him to be in his office. After a few minutes, I was on my way. The taxi driver was following, as I had told him to do. By the time I got to the police station, it was past eight at night. The commandant was waiting. He rose, saluted, and stood at attention. I told him that I had an interesting story for him to act upon. Once I asked him to call the taxi driver into the office, the driver appeared. I asked him to tell his story. When the driver finished, I asked the commandant, "What is going to be your plan of action?"

He said, "Sir, I will send some people and apprehend these people in the morning."

I asked, "How many reserve and standby police officers do you have here?"

He said, "We have two hundred here."

Then I told him, "Your action plan should be as follows. First, immediately order the police officers to get ready for action, with full uniform and arms. Second, go to the place where the robbers are, and have it surrounded by your police officers. Third, ask the owner of the compound, where the robbers are staying, to allow the police in for an inspection. Fourth, any of the robbers who try to run away should be apprehended by the police that are already on location, surrounding the area. Fifth, apprehend the robbers and bring them all, along with the stolen goods, to the police station. I will not accompany you, but I will be there to observe. But no one will be able to see me."

The commandant said, "Sir, it is dark now. We can't see much. It is better to do this in the morning."

I responded, "You are right, but in the morning we will have lost the element of surprise that we have now. Besides, your police have flashlights and floodlights that could be used, if necessary. Now, get on moving without any waste of time. Remember that I will be there to observe, but no one will be able to see me. Now give me your night code!"

The action plan started. I stayed in the commandant's office for a while, and then I followed the police trucks to the location of action. The night was not totally dark. There was the light of a half-moon, making the whole area look somewhat eerie. I told my driver to go behind the compound and park somewhere dark, from where I would observe all the action.

The police did not surround the compound as was discussed. Two truckloads of policemen went directly to the entrance gate of the compound and summoned the owner of the guesthouse. He opened the door and cooperated with the police, taking them to the rooms where the robbers were relaxing and playing cards.

Nine robbers, and all the goods that they had stolen, were brought into the police station.

Police officers began taking the robbers' statements, and the stolen goods were inventoried. I, the governor, asked the taxi driver to go see his relative who had been robbed and ask him if he would come to the police station. After this man came in, he was asked to check the inventory of all the goods and the money that were taken from the compound.

Investigation showed that, actually, the gang consisted of fifteen people who took part in the robbery. It also came to light that some goods were still missing. The robbers admitted that six robbers had gone directly to another village on the outskirts of Herat and had taken some of the goods with them. This group was headed by one of the robbers who was called Pahlawaan Sarwar. He was very strong and was the one who had broken the big outdoor wooden gates. I asked the commandant when he was going to apprehend the remaining six. The commandant again said that he was going to do it in the morning.

I said that by the time the police got to this outside village, the robbers would have already heard about the story and dispersed to hide themselves in different places. I told the commandant not to lose the element of surprise and to go to the village that night. I added, "Remember that you should surround the compound before you go in the front gates. You did not do this in the first attempt, as I had told you. You were lucky in that case, but you may not be as lucky this time. Again, I will be there to observe, but you may not be able to see me. And remember to turn off your headlights two kilometers before you get to the village. You can drive your vehicles in the moonlight; there is enough for you to see."

The commandant said, "Sir, it is close to eleven at night now."

I responded, "Yes, I know. If you do it right, you will succeed this time, too."

The village in question was about ten kilometers to the east of the city of Herat. The police got ready, boarded their trucks, and started moving toward this village. Some distance behind, I, my driver, and one security person were following in a car.

When we were close to the village, my driver stopped the car. I got out and started walking toward the village. Before I could get any closer, I was called upon by the police sentries, who asked me the night code. I then changed my course and started walking another route. I was again stopped by police sentries asking the night code. Then, I went back to the car and sat in it, waiting for the result of police action.

This time, it took longer to apprehend the robbers. They did not open the gates of the compound. When they climbed down at the back and started to escape, they were confronted by the police sentries. The robbers were forced to go back to their compound. Pahlawaan Sarwar challenged the police and said, "No one should dare to come in!"

The police then woke the village Malik. The old man came, went into the compound, and talked to Pahlawaan Sarwar. He told Sarwar that it was no use, that the whole place was surrounded and he should give himself up.

Then, Pahlawaan Sarwar and his accomplices came out with the stolen goods and gave themselves up to the police. I was informed about this. The whole group of robbers with the stolen goods was taken to the police station.

At this point, I asked the commandant to complete the file and take all the stolen goods back to the owner and get a receipt from him. I instructed the district attorney to complete the robbers' files and take their case to the courts so they would be apprehended according to the law. I instructed the DA to seek whatever the law permitted as punishment for the robbers' forceful entry into and burglary of private property.

These same robbers admitted that their gang had robbed another compound two weeks prior. Later, most of the goods that they had stolen were returned to the rightful owners.

After several days, the people whose goods were robbed came to the governor's audience room. They brought a box of candy and officially thanked me for catching the robbers. In response, I said, "Don't thank me. Thank your relative, the taxi driver, as he is the one who initiated the police action and helped in the apprehension of the robbers."

Then, I asked, "By the way, did you get all the stolen goods back?"

They said, "Yes, sir, everything except a pistol and a Russian alarm clock, the round one that we kept on the mantel. It has a bell on top that rings at the set time. One of the robbers must have liked these two things. Since they are small items, he probably hid them from the rest of the gang."

"Well," I said, "it looks like *thieves steal from thieves, and robbers from robbers!*"

Thus the province of Herat got rid of the gang of robbers with the help of its own courageous people. With this, I had won the confidence of the people of the province and the city of Herat.

Preservation of law and order, justice, and people's rights requires great care and compassion. That is why the job of a governor under the existing legal system in Afghanistan was not an easy job and almost akin to impossible! I, as an engineer, was put to the most difficult test of my life.

At the time when I was the governor, many difficult situations existed. Apprehension of a gang of robbers was easy; however, how could we keep the society clean of corruption, or curb the illegal flow of goods through the borders and stop smuggling and drug trafficking from and to the neighboring countries?

A lot of planning, organization, and careful handling were needed to catch the other kind of thieves and robbers that were the scourge of peace and a healthy society.

I worked against corruption by catching the wrongdoers red-handed and submitting their files to the courts for legal action and punishment. I believe there were about forty-two cases of those who worked in the government, including sub-subgovernors as well as an important police chief. All were caught red-handed.

In the same way, in order to curb smuggling and cross-border drug trafficking, I had to work very hard. As a result, I suffered many sleepless nights.

The following is an example of preserving justice and people's rights.

Arab Boy (Chieftain)

I cite the case of Arab Boy. He was a rich, powerful, influential, sixty-year-old man in one of the villages. Arab Boy liked the beautiful wife of one of his farmers. He made a plan, had the young farmer killed, and usurped the farmer's wife, taking her to his own household. The village people and the young farmer's mother and father brought this case to the attention of the governor. The case was investigated. Arab Boy was found guilty by the courts and was put in jail.

As a matter of routine, I often visited hospitals, detention centers, and prisons after work hours. When I was inspecting the main prison in the city, the commandant told me, "Sir, let me show you where we keep Arab Boy." He then took me to the prison yard and showed me a chicken coop, telling one of the prison guards, "Bring the prisoner out." I looked at Arab Boy, who appeared haggard and sick. I did not say anything.

That night, this prisoner's face came to my mind again and again. I kept asking myself, *Is it right to keep a human being, no matter how guilty he is, in a chicken coop without any holes or windows out there in the yard and under the sun?*

In the morning, I called the prison commandant and told him, "Take Arab Boy out of that chicken coop and transfer him to one of the rooms where other prisoners in his category are held. And destroy the chicken coop. From now on, no one is to be put in a situation like that!"

This example shows how, in certain circumstances, we may get carried away by emotions when hoping to implement justice. These emotions may, in turn, cloud our judgment.

A Lucky Shot

Sometimes during our lives, we make lucky shots, but this always does not happen. The following incident will show you what I mean.

The students at Sultan High School had long wanted a basketball court to practice on and use for playing games played against rival schools. One of the international firms (I do not remember the name) helped build a brand-new basketball court in the Sultan High School in the city of Herat. Since I always promoted sports like soccer, volleyball, basketball, and other athletics for the young, including schoolboys and schoolgirls, the Department of Education asked me to be present for the ribbon cutting of this new facility, say a few words, and give my blessings. I told my secretary to make sure that I appeared at this ceremony.

On the day of the ribbon cutting, I went to the new basketball court. There were many students and teachers present. They cheered when I arrived. The director of education and the school principal both said a few words. One of the students said a few words, including complimenting me for promoting sports and sometimes taking a place on a soccer field and kicking the ball around.

Then, it was my turn to speak. I said a few words and thanked the donor for helping to build the basketball court. When I finished, someone handed me a new basketball and asked if I would throw it as a first shot, as a gesture.

At this time, we were all standing in the middle of the court for the ceremony. After I was handed the ball, I threw it toward one of the new rings. *The ball kept going and going and going, and then it fell through the ring.* The crowd clapped and cheered and thought that I must have been a terrific basketball player, maybe an ex-NBA MVP?! But, as you know and I know, I was neither. All it was, was a lucky shot made at the right moment.

The probability of my making this shot again is less than one in a million.

Liver Cirrhosis

Rooms in Herat hospitals were being filled by sick people from the villages in northeast Herat Province. They all had distended abdomens and were in a lot of pain. Medical doctors could neither treat them nor find the cause of their sickness.

I heard of this problem, so I visited the hospitals and consulted with the doctors, who thought that the problem was a kind of liver cirrhosis that eventually resulted in a patient's painful death. Some patients were sent to the hospitals in Kabul, and even to some outside the country, by the United Nations Health Organization. These patients' livers were becoming hard, which resulted in their deaths after a month or so.

The Department of Public Health sent samples of livers to International Laboratories for analysis and also sought help from experts all over the world. It was determined that the sickness was neither microbial nor caused by a virus.

With a group of medical doctors, agriculturists, and environmentalists, I went to the area where most of the patients had come from so I could seek possible reasons for their illness. This group and I made a survey of the wheat fields, animal shelters, and silos where the villagers stored their foodstuff. We also looked at sources of drinking water and irrigation water.

During the preliminary consultation with this group, I requested that they look for any signs and effects of previous years' drought in the area. Over the past few years, this area had been affected by a series of droughts that, at one time, had caused an influx of tiny mice, which invaded some of the close-by villages. I was contemplating whether the droughts were the cause of this new problem.

I knew that droughts affected the environment and the regimens of plants, insects, and animal life in an area. Could the droughts have had an effect on what these sick people ate, drank, and breathed?

Our group found that wheat plants were much shorter in the field when the wheat was ready for reaping. We learned of another plant in the wheat fields, which, farmers said, sheep, goats, cattle, and other livestock ate without any adverse effect. We took samples of the wheat, the leaves and branches of the other plants, and drinking and irrigation water from the area, sending them to International Laboratories for analysis. When the results came back, they showed no toxicity in any of the samples.

The wheat samples from villagers' silos had some other stuff in it that looked like black pepper. We asked the farmers about this. They said that this was the seed of the plant that they fed their animals without any problem. We asked them, "Do you always get these black seeds in your wheat when you harvest it?" They said that they normally did not get them. The last year, because of drought, their wheat ripened earlier—and the other plants' seeds had fallen at the same time. So, it got mixed with the wheat. I directed the subgovernor in the area to collect some samples of these black seeds from villagers' silos and bring them to me. Then, I had our health and agriculture departments send these samples to International Laboratories for analysis.

Lo and behold, the black seeds were identified to be the culprit. The lab found that they contained a strong toxin that caused severe liver cirrhosis with fatal consequences in animals and humans.

Our office sent a directive to the subgovernors to remove all the wheat that was stored in villagers' silos and replace it with clean wheat. Then, we made proclamations and generated a lot of publicity to educate the people, telling them to replace their wheat with clean wheat and make sure that these seeds would not, in any way, get into people's wheat silos or storage bins for other grains that were being fed to sheep, cattle, and other livestock.

Special advertising and informational pamphlets were prepared to inform the people of Herat and those of other provinces in the region.

The Case of Wakil Junaid

Cross-border smuggling of goods, livestock, and drugs was carried on by bigtime professional smugglers or novices, depending on the type of good and the method and location of the smuggling route. Wakil Junaid, who was a prominent member of a political faction and a bigtime operator, got caught smuggling a large quantity of *chars* (hash).

The gendarmerie was informed and thereafter followed the trail of a large quantity of drugs that had been diverted to Wakil's compound not far from the border with a neighboring country. The courts gave the gendarmerie permission to enter the compound and search for these items. They found a large quantity of hash packed to be carried across the border and a large sum of money. The commission that had been handling the case informed me and told me where they were inventorying these items. I went to the office where they were working and inspected their work.

When I observed the large sum of money with the items, I asked, "Where did this money come from, and why did the gendarmerie bring it as part of the smuggling items?"

One commission member responded, "This money was in the same room with the items that were being smuggled."

I ordered the head of the commission to ask Wakil to be present during the inventory and get a receipt for all the items from the commission. The commission was told to count all the money that they had brought from Wakil Junaid's compound, give it back to him, and get a receipt from him. Actually, it did not make any sense to assume that the sum of money that was in the room was going to be smuggled across the border.

Wakil Junaid was surprised when he got his money back. He had assumed that once the commission got the money, he would never again lay hands on it.

I learned this many years later in Pul-i-Charkhi Prison, of all places. (I was later to be detained there.)

When I was in prison, one of my acquaintances, also an inmate, said, "Wakil Junaid has been brought to the prison and wants to see you!"

I told myself, *Oh my God, he wants to get even with me for catching him in smuggling.* But when I met Wakil Junaid in the prison yard, I was surprised by what he did.

He came to me, stooped, kissed my hands, and said, "Governor, I thank you for your honesty. You caught me in smuggling and submitted my dossier to the courts. I was punished. But you returned my money to me. I never expected that. You are certainly a very honest person, and that is why I thanked you and kissed your hands! Tell me what I can do for you. I have money, if you need it—or anything else."

I said, "No. But thanks for what you said. You are indeed a man of grit. *May God Almighty guide us all to the right path.*"

A Fine of Two Thousand Afghanis

During one of the audience-hall meetings when I was governor, several workers who had gone out of the country to work in the Arabian Gulf area informed me about their troubles when they returned home. They said that they had been stopped and then detained for several weeks by the border patrol for not having a passport. They were told to pay a fine of two thousand afghani for this (then afghani is a unit of money in Afghanistan).

They added that the reason they had gone to work in the Gulf area was to make some money and come back to help their families. "We did not have the fine money on us," one of them said. "All that we had was a check, or a *hawaale,* for the work we had done. They kept us in detention until our families heard about it and sent us the fine money."

I decided to see this for myself. So, the same night and the next day, I inspected the border and central detention facilities that were related to gendarme and police. What I saw shocked me! These places were pitifully overcrowded with detainees, who were held under very unsanitary and unhealthy conditions. I called in the commandant of police and gendarme to my office and made my case. They told me that this problem was the result of a regulation stipulating that all citizens returning from abroad must have a passport. If not, they were required to pay a fine of two thousand afghani to the State. "Since these people could not pay the fine, we are forced to keep them in detention until they pay the fine," the commandant said.

I instructed the commandant to write a report/proposal to me, the governor, about this problem immediately and submit it before the end of the day.

When the report/proposal was submitted to me, I gave a written directive, as follows:

> This regulation is unjust and has caused a lot of undue stress and discomfort to returning citizens to their homeland, who have gone to the Gulf region, working very hard and under very difficult conditions to make some money to help their families.
>
> As the governor of Herat Province, I order the commandant of police and gendarme to welcome returning citizen workers with open arms, help them with transportation to

the city of Herat, and refrain from bothering them with the collection of the fine for not having a passport.

Separately, I shall instruct the secretary of the governor of Herat to write and submit a proposal to the president's office, to absolve workers from paying a fine for not having a passport when they return to their homeland after working in the Gulf region.

Also in the proposal, we shall include specific ideas for helping workers find appropriate work and necessary guidance during their stay, and easy ways to safeguard and transfer to a trusted facility any compensation that they have received for their work.

The commandant (Gul Nabi) was one of the old-timer police commandants. He said, "Sir, your direction is against the regulations."

I said, "Go ahead and write it down under my directive."

He said, "Sir, it is inappropriate for me to write such a thing!"

I said, "No. Go ahead and write what you are saying. It is your duty to do so. Go ahead, sit behind that table, and write what you are saying."

Gul Nabi took the proposal and hesitantly sat on a chair behind a table. He returned after a few minutes and handed the proposal to me.

I wrote an order under his rebuttal: "I understand that the commandant of police should do as I have ordered. The responsibility belongs to me, the governor of Herat Province. Signed, Abdul Tawab Assifi."

My order was immediately carried out, with joyous and welcoming results from the returning workers, the population of the province of Herat, and workers of other provinces who were affected by this regulation.

After sending the proposal for approval to the government, I went to Kabul and met the president. I gave a full account of the condition of the returning workers and the issue of the fine for having no passport, and then I stated my directive for rescinding this requirement. I then told the president that I had prepared my resignation, in case the government did not approve the proposal. In that case, I would be derelict in the application of a regulation that had been approved by the government.

The president smiled and said, "Mr. Assifi, you did the work and then submitted your proposal afterward!"

I said, "Mr. President, that is why I have a resignation in my pocket! Also, sir, because I believe that Afghanistan has a just president, that gave me heart to immediately act on relieving these hardworking citizens returning to their homeland after punishment and detention."

President Daoud smiled again and said, "You did the right thing, Mr. Governor. Good job! Tell my secretary to present your proposal at the next cabinet meeting. I want you to be there to present it to the cabinet, along with the ideas that you have for improvement. Thank you."

I attended the next cabinet meeting and presented my proposal together with my ideas for improving the situation of workers who traveled to the Gulf region to work.

The regulation, fining the returning workers for not having a passport, was rescinded. A commission was appointed to go over the ideas that I had presented for improving the conditions and helping the workers who went to the Gulf area for work.

When, at a later time, I was appointed as the minister of mines and industries, people's representatives told me that the people of Herat wanted to come out to the streets and say good-bye to me when I left the city. I told them that I did not like fanfare of any sort. The representatives then suggested that only a few elders would stand at the road south of the city and the airport to wish me bon voyage, if I would allow this. I agreed to this alternative.

During my departure, a number of elders stood at the side of the road at that location. I got out of the car, said good-bye to them, and thanked them for their kindness. The famous calligrapher of Herat, Mohd Ali Attaar, came forward with a scroll of paper. He opened it and said, "Sir, I have written these prayer verses from the Holy Quran in several styles of script especially for you. Your name is on it. This is to thank you for having my writings published into a book. Please, accept."

I told Attaar that I greatly admired the great artistic works that he had done on all the historic and archeological monuments in Herat. I very gratefully accepted his wonderful artistic document.

Another person by the name of Karim Shams came forward and handed me Shah Maqsud prayer beads, saying, "These beads will help you in your prayers."

I accepted the beads and said, "Thank you, Uncle Shams." I respected him a lot because he was one of the very good businessmen in Herat. I called him uncle because a long time ago, when I was a schoolboy, he had given me a ride in his automobile from Herat and through Badghis to Maimana, where my father was the governor.

Minister of Mines and Industries, 1975 to 1978

After the July 17, 1973, coup and the establishment of the republic, there were major political changes that drastically altered the political and governmental administration of the country. A central committee was formed, and a number of people who had taken part in the coup were promoted and given important jobs in the government.

However, some of these people did not live up to expectations and misused the positions that they were responsible for. Gradually, documents surfaced that negated the trust bestowed upon them.

Consequently, the president dissolved the central committee and decided to bring better-qualified and trustworthy people into a reorganized government and cabinet of ministers.

I was appointed as the cabinet-level minister of mines and industries, responsible for planning, development, and implementation of programs and projects for the following:

1) Exploration and exploitation of mineral resources
2) Supervision, exploration, and exploitation of oil and gas resources
3) Supervision and administration of existing industries
4) Economic studies, plans, and programs for development of new industries
5) Labor relations, including preparation and enactment of a new labor law for Afghanistan

This job was huge. It was further complicated by coordination of work with international professionals and advisors—notably, coordination with Soviet Russian assistants in the field of mineral resources development, such as the exploration of copper and iron reserves. The Soviets played a major role in exploration and the exportation of gas from Afghanistan to the Soviet Union. This necessitated meetings with Soviet experts at the ministry and frequent meetings with Mr. Puzanov, the Soviet ambassador in Kabul.

Some examples of these meetings are given in the following.

During my first introductory meeting with Mr. Puzanov, he complained that there were sixty to seventy contracts between the USSR and Afghanistan related to the ministry that had been delayed at the Ministry of Mines and Industries' offices. He asked the minister's help to get these resolved and executed so that Soviet assistance to the ministry would not be delayed. I promised to look into this and told the responsible staff to give Puzanov an immediate report.

All of the contracts were located within a few days. The minister was given the status of each contract. During my follow-up meeting with Mr. Puzanov, I gave the ambassador a written report saying that six of these contracts were in the ministry offices being processed and that the majority had been delayed either at the Soviet embassy or in Soviet government offices. I then asked the ambassador's help in getting his office to process the contracts ASAP.

Fabricated Accusations

During my second meeting with the president, he asked me, "Do you know that there are several dossiers at the ministry's Inspection and Monitoring [I&M] Department that are related to the ministry staff who have been accused of misappropriating government funds and other wrongdoings? I want you to check into this matter."

When I got back to my office, I immediately called in the president of I&M, Qaari Rahim, and asked him, "How many dossiers do you have in your department?"

His answer astonished me. He said, "Sir, we have maybe three hundred and fifty dossiers, and the people accused have been put on a status of leave without pay."

I said, "Qaari sahib, starting from now, you give me twenty dossiers every day. I will read them at night and give you my instructions the next morning on what you should do!"

Every night after I had gone home, washed up, and eaten supper, I reviewed these dossiers. During my job as governor in Herat, I developed a knack for reading dossiers very fast. After reading each one of these, I wrote my instructions for what should be done. I usually suggested reinvestigating certain points or matters that did not make any sense in light of the conclusion of the first investigation. Then, I appointed new people to reinvestigate the files with advice from the I&M Department. I asked the president of I&M, "Please, give me the names of honest people that you know." I appointed the people he recommended to the reinvestigation committee, instructing them to focus on the points that I believed did not make any sense in the first place.

This process went on for several months. The reinvestigation results were astonishing. Mostly, the facts were opposite the opinion of the first investigative committee.

Within four to six months, most of the dossiers were reinvestigated. The final results were that out of the three hundred and fifty dossiers, fifty were correct. *The other three hundred were false and fabricated accusations.*

For instance, there were six dossiers made for engineer Sharafee, accusing him of wrongdoings while he was the head of the Gas and Oil Exploration and Exploitation Department in north Afghanistan. In one of the dossiers, he was accused of stealing motor oil from the oil barrels imported from the Soviet Union, with the help of an old warehouseman. The two were accused of siphoning oil from the imported barrels into a five-gallon can every night. They allegedly replaced the oil by adding to the barrel an equivalent volume of water from an irrigation ditch in the vicinity. Therefore, Mr. Sharafee was accused of owing the government nine thousand barrels of oil that had been in storage for a long period in the department warehouse. This whole accusation sounded preposterous! The department head, accompanied by an old warehouseman carrying a five-gallon can, went to the storage area every night, siphoned oil from each barrel, and then proceeded to put dirty irrigation ditch water into the barrel!

In the same dossier, it was written that the committee had gone to the border, the Amu Daria (Oxus) River crossing, and checked the oil barrels that were brought from the Soviet Union to Afghanistan. They found dirty water in the bottom of each imported oil barrel.

They had asked the Soviet technicians, "Why is this so?" The technicians told them that this happened when oil barrels were stored upright for a period of several months in outside storage depots. During the day, given the warm temperature and sunlight, the air at the top of the barrels was pushed out. Then at night, when the temperature was lower, the outside humid air was sucked into the barrels, at which point the humidity condensed and stuck to the barrels' sides, which rusted out. If this condition persisted for a longer time, the rusted water, being heavier than oil, collected in the bottom of the barrel.

The technicians then advised the committee, saying that if oil barrels were to be stored for a long time, it was better to store them on their sides, on top of wood supports. That way, the process of condensation would not occur, and rusted water would not collect in the barrels. This information should have convinced the committee that a department head could not have snuck into the warehouse storage yard every night and stolen oil in a five-gallon can!

The other accusatory dossiers that were made for Sharafee were as preposterous as this one! Why was Sharafee singled out? His parents were migrants from one of Russia's southern republics to the north of Afghanistan. When their country was invaded by the Soviet troops, they were forced to flee and take refuge in Afghanistan. As a young boy, Sharafee showed that he had above-average intelligence. He excelled in school and earned a scholarship to study at the Colorado School of Mines in the United States. After graduating and getting a master's degree in the gas and oil field, he came to serve the country that had given his parents refuge. *Was this the reason for fabricating six false accusation dossiers and putting him on leave-without-pay status, introducing the prospect of his being criminalized for life on account of these false accusations and dossiers?*

When the final results of the reinvestigation of these dossiers were submitted to me, I wrote my ministerial directive as follows: "The person who has been falsely accused should be exonerated, reinstated as a legitimate employee, and compensated for lost pay. The members of the committee who have wrongly accused an honest employee and made him (or her) suffer for this period should be punished as falsifiers, according to the law."

Then, I reported my findings and the actions that I had taken to the president. I also reported how I had proceeded to *bring justice back to the people who had been wrongfully accused.*

Pressure within Government

During and after the establishment of the Republic of Afghanistan by President Daoud, certain currents and countercurrents were generated in the country.

The Soviet Union and its allies and loyalists pushed to gain ground for the project of world domination. On the other side were the forces of freedom and justice, sustenance of cultural and religious values, and nationalism, which tried to resist the Soviet superpower and its cohorts.

These currents and countercurrents created great social, political, and cultural pressures on the nation and on those who worked in government offices. The pressure became intolerable. The Soviet propaganda machine labeled the Afghan effort as reactionary.

The fabrication of three hundred false accusation dossiers in an important government ministry was not a simple matter.

Note: Later on, I came to know that all the people who were singled out to be the subject of false accusations were those who were not members of Parcham or Khalq, the two Communist parties assisted and supported by Soviet Union.

The following example elucidates the complicity between Parcham and Khalq and shows how pressure was applied in order to prepare the ground for the Soviet move into the area.

Several days after I had resolved the matter of the dossiers, my secretary, Mr. Asadullah Nouri, told me that Dr. Mir Akbar, the president of the Geologic Surveys Department, wanted to speak to me, the minister of mines and industries, about a private matter once

I finished my routine work in the office. At the end of the day, I asked Nouri, "Is Dr. Akbar still here?"

He said, "Yes. He is waiting."

Dr. Akbar entered the office, came close to my desk, raised both of his hands in a pleading gesture, and said, "Mr. Minister, you have ruined my life. You have destroyed me!"

I said, "Dr. Akbar, I have never hurt anyone in my life! I always go out my way to help people, not hurt them. What you are saying is not correct; it could not be correct! Please, explain what you are saying."

He said, "I am one of the persons who was assigned to work on a dossier. You reinvestigated the dossier and found out that it was false. You directed that the persons who had falsely made the dossier should be legally pursued by the district attorney and sent to court to be dealt with as falsifiers."

"Yes! Which dossier are you talking about?"

He named the dossier and the case.

I asked him, "Did we make a mistake in the reinvestigation and our conclusion?"

He said, "No, you were right, and I am one of the guilty persons in the committee for making the false accusations."

I said, "Dr. Akbar, then why do you make the statement that I ruined your life?"

He said, "But, sir, I did not sign this dossier in the first place. No matter how many times the other members told me to, I would not sign it, because it was wrong."

I asked, "Then what?"

He continued. "I would not sign it for several weeks. Then I was called in to the ministry's head office and was told that we were called in by the Prime Ministry to explain our reluctance in signing these dossiers, for which I was one of the investigators. The whole group was taken by car to the Prime Ministry. There, we were taken to the deputy prime minister's office. He was very upset and said, 'There are some who do not cooperate with us in bringing punishment to the elements who have misused their governmental offices for their personal purposes. The wrongdoers and the elements that are not working according to the government program need to be weeded out of the offices of the government.' Then the deputy added, 'We know how to deal with the people who stop us from cleaning the offices of the government of these unwanted elements. We will punish those who do not cooperate with us.'"

Dr. Akbar then said, "Sir, I was so scared that I pissed in my pants. I am a person of poor background. I have family and kids. I studied very hard for a doctorate degree from Russia, and I tried hard to keep my job and the prospect of future promotions."

I could see Dr. Akbar's problem. Then, there was the other side of the issue: the ones who were falsely accused, put out of a job with a no-pay suspension status, and criminalized for life!

Definitely, there was a dichotomy in the political and social currents and countercurrents. On one hand were the pressures by the Soviet Union and its allies for world domination; on the other were the countercurrents in favor of self-determination and the sovereignty of nations.

Those who assisted the Soviet superpower assumed that the giant would never make a mistake or refrain from achieving its ambitious goals.

The struggle for freedom, liberty, and justice had been started by those who always thought and believed that no other cause was justifiable than serving their own people, no matter how poor and backward-stricken they were.

Sector of Mines

In the sector of mines, two important programs were completed under the Soviet assistance program. These were the exploration of Ainak copper mines and Hajigak iron deposits. During the preparation of Afghanistan's seven-year master plan, the Soviet Union had promised to assist the development and exploitation of Ainak copper and Hajigak iron deposits in Afghanistan.

However, when the Soviet deputy minister of geology visited Kabul to review the projects that were earmarked for USSR assistance, the Afghan delegation that was discussing these projects reported that the Soviets were planning to assist in mining the copper ore and then transport it for refining to the Soviet republics across the border to the north of Afghanistan.

They said that there was not enough electric power available locally for this purpose. Similarly, the Soviet delegation reported that they were planning to transport the iron ore to the north across the border, because there was not enough coal coke available in Afghanistan for smelting iron.

The Afghan government was interested not only in extracting the copper ore from Ainak and the iron ore from Hajigak, but also in creating the industries for refining copper and smelting iron in Afghanistan. This way, the industries and jobs for Afghan workers would help the Afghan economy. In addition, the export of copper bars and iron ingots would have less volume than raw ore, be feasible for international markets, and be more economical and beneficial to Afghanistan's economy.

In preparation for transporting the copper and iron, a railroad from the Iranian border to Kabul and Pakistan had already been designed by the French Sufro Rail Company. A consortium of international donors including Iran had already promised to provide funding for the construction of this important railway. The railroad project would boost the Afghan economy and enhance the marketability of produce and goods, including semifinished products like copper and iron, so they could be taken from Afghanistan and sent to international markets.

The proposal and its reasons were met with the Soviet deputy minister's simple answer of, *"Nyet."*

Khan Nishin Mountain Uranium

During one of my routine meetings with Ambassador Puzanov, he brought up a subject that I was not familiar with. He said that the Germans, when they flew over areas to gather information for making magnetometric and gravimetric maps, did not cover a certain area in Lower Helmand near the river. The Soviet government was prepared to fly over this area and fill in the portions of the maps left vacant by the Germans. There would not be any extra charge to Afghanistan for this mission, Puzanov told me. I responded, "Let me check with our offices about this issue."

When I checked out this matter, I found out that Puzanov was correct: there was a hole in the maps that the Germans had made. After consulting with the president, I met again with the ambassador. I told him that what he wished to do was okay, provided that he immediately shared the information with us.

He said, "Okay."

I received daily reports about the Russian flights in the region. However, after the work was finished, I did not get any report on the result of the survey. One of the technicians informed me that the Russians had had difficulty with their instruments, especially radiometric instruments, which had necessitated frequent repairs.

I consulted with the Department of Geologic Surveys and decided to send a mission on land to collect samples of rocks from that area and analyze them in the laboratory to find out what they were.

Our surveyors went to the site, collected samples, returned, and gave me the analysis report. They had found out that the Khan Nishin Mountain rocks had a rich supply of uranium.

A few days after this, Ambassador Puzanov came for a meeting and offered a proposal for the exploitation of uranium from Khan Nishin Mountain. He said that it may require surface as well as deep-excavation extraction of uranium.

In previous days, I had consulted with the related departments, which told me that our government already had an agreement with the United Nations for the exploration and exploitation of uranium in Afghanistan.

When Ambassador Puzanov asked me about his previous request regarding the Khan Nishin uranium, I told him what I had found out about Afghanistan's previous commitment vis-à-vis uranium.

Industrial Sector

In the industrial sector, there were bids for the construction of several cotton textile factories in Gulbahar, Pulikhumri, Kandahar, Girishk (Helmand Province), Herat, and Murghab. This required product from the cement-making factories in Ghori Pulikhumri (the new cotton factories' needs would double the size of the existing factory there), the six hundred tons of cement per day from Herat, and the fifteen hundred tons of cement per day from the factory in Kandahar (which was going to be funded by Iran). All of these bids were internationally advertised and approved.

The international bids for the cement company of Kandahar, which produced fifteen hundred tons per day, were fifty-five million (by Butler, an American company), sixty-seven million (by a Czech company), and eighty-two million (by a Russian company).

In this period, Afghanistan sought a boost in the rate of development. Weekly reports of an increase in construction and building projects were made. International observers were seeing a healthy phase of rapid growth and modernization in the country, which gave Afghanistan the prospect of being able to catch up with its neighboring countries.

Hydrocarbon Exploitation

As part of my job, in the sector of hydrocarbon exploitation, I took a trip to the north of the country to visit the Soviet-built natural-gas powerhouse and fertilizer factory in Mazar-i-Sharif and to see the sites of exploration and drilling for gas in the Shibirghan area.

During this trip, I also visited the pipeline and metering facilities for exporting gas to the Soviet Union. These facilities were all funded with a low-interest loan and were all built by the Soviets. However, compensation for gas exports was made on the basis of metering facilities on the other side of the border with the Soviet Union. I also visited the two oil exploration sites, Angot and Aq Daria, where oil had been discovered. The oil reserves of these sites were reported to be five million to six million tons.

During one of my routine visits with Ambassador Puzanov, I brought up the subject of Soviet assistance for an oil refinery, which they had promised when the seven-year master plan was being prepared. His response was, "Mr. Minister, your known oil reserves, for a million-ton-per-year refinery, are too small." The Soviet policy at that time was to assist the ministry in drilling for gas reserves only.

During one of my meetings with President Daoud, the president asked me, "Mr. Assifi, in your past work in Helmand and Lower Helmand in Nimroz, you were successful in doing important work with the use of Afghan personnel. Do you think you could find some oil reserves for Afghanistan with the use of Afghan engineers and workers only?"

My response was, "Mr. President, I will make a trip to the north and survey the availability of resources that we could use for this purpose."

The president responded, "Very well. We will discuss this further when you come back."

Accordingly, I made a trip to the north and visited all the sites that were drilling for gas. I also visited the yards and inventoried the equipment, drill rigs, crews, and technical personnel being utilized for gas exploration.

My findings were very promising. For instance, for every drill rig and drill crew that was working for the exploration and exploitation of gas in the field, there were three fully staffed standby units in reserve. I met numerous times with the Afghan staff and personnel and asked, "If we took out one out of three, would it hurt the projects of drilling and exploring for gas?" The answer in all cases was that the then-present program was overequipped and overstaffed, and removing one out of three units would in no way be detrimental to the gas drilling and exploration programs.

I then proceeded and made a budget for five separate fully equipped, fully staffed units that could be used for oil exploration.

Subsequently, I made a detailed report of my findings and submitted it at the cabinet meeting, proposing approval of the budget and asking for expenditure authorization to begin the work of oil exploration.

After this, I appointed qualified Afghan engineers and geologists. Next, I took another trip to the north to determine the location of drilling sites for oil. On the basis of the recommendation of Afghan engineers, a Russian geologist was added to the list of oil exploration geologists. The Afghan engineers identified this geologist on the basis of his expertise in gas and oil exploration. Although he had been sent under a Soviet program to Afghanistan, he had a benevolent character and, they told me, wanted the Afghans to succeed in the quest for oil in the north.

Oil Gushes Out at Qashqari

Within three months after the project was approved, the first drill hit oil in the Qashqari anticline structure. Oil started gushing out of the ground—a fountain of oil reaching high into the sky.

I informed President Daoud of the good news and then flew on a Russian-built military helicopter to the site of the oil fountain at Qashqari. Two cabinet ministers, Mr. Said Wahid Abdullah, deputy foreign minister, and Mr. A. A. Khorram, minister of planning, accompanied me to this site, as they had requested.

The oil specialists reported that oil in the anticline structure existed in three layers, and the top one was estimated to contain forty million to fifty million tons of lightweight oil.

Soviet Ambassador Puzanov, during his regular meetings with me, always complained that the ministry used the equipment and material that was part of the gas exploration program for other purposes. I was prepared for this and had the Gas and Oil Department prepare a graph showing the actual depth of gas drilling. The same graph also showed the planned drilling depth. In this way, I demonstrated that the ministry had actually drilled more for gas than had been planned.

Prior to my next meeting with Puzanov, I had a color-coded progress graph hung on the wall of the room where we would be meeting. I also had my staff make a small pocket booklet of the same graph. At the end of our next meeting, I gave the ambassador a copy of the graph showing the actual progress of the drilling for gas and oil.

Always, the progress of drilling for gas was 70 percent to 80 percent more than had been planned by the Soviet programmers. Simultaneously, the ministry was drilling for oil.

When I next met him, I told the ambassador, "Your Excellency, we are utilizing the equipment that you provided for gas exploration, and we're using the abundantly spare capacity for oil exploration, as well. I understand that you, as friends of Afghanistan, will be happier with our better-than-normal performance and the progress of these programmed projects.

"And by the way, now that we've found more than forty million tons of oil capacity in only at one layer of Qashqari, we have enough capacity to utilize—and so we have a need for the installation of—the planned oil refinery that the USSR promised during the preparation of Afghanistan's seven-year master plan."

Ambassador Puzanov said, "We will send a wire to Moscow and request the beginning of the project for the installation of the oil refinery that you mentioned."

Soon after the oil discovery at Qashqari, oil was found at two more sites, Biland Ghor and Bazar Kami. Then, oil was found all the way out in Ghormaach's Ali Gul anticline structure, which is about twenty-one kilometers long. Actually, we had been drilling for gas in that location when oil started gushing out of the ground. Maybe the saying that "seekers are finders" was showing itself as true in these efforts to find oil in Afghanistan. President Daoud's wish had come to fruition.

Oil Exploration by Other International Firms

Katawaz Area

Total, a French company, had been exploring the Katawaz area in south Afghanistan under a separate contract. Total's representatives requested a meeting with me to report their findings. However, their conclusion and final decision were not very promising. They reported that exploitation of oil and exports from these reserves were not feasible for them. They forwarded the following conclusions:

1) Oil-bearing structures in the Katawaz area were much deeper than the oil and gas in the north of Afghanistan.
2) The oil-bearing structures were fragmented. The reason for this was reported to be the effect of the Quetta Moqur fault and its movements, which caused extreme stresses in the

adjacent layers of Katawaz reserves, resulting in the split and fragmentation of these structures.

3) The factors in items 1 and 2 made exploitation of oil, under these conditions, more expensive and unfeasible for the export of oil to the Indian Ocean and markets of the world, given the oil prices at the time in international markets.

4) The Total Company was prepared to make the $1.2-million penalty payment, as was written in the contract between Total Company and the Afghanistan government.

Note: The Quetta Moqur fault is a main western fault created by the plate-tectonic effects of the Indian continent's moving several thousand kilometers north and ramming into the Asiatic continent, which resulted in an upheaval of land and the formation of the Himalayan and Hindu Kush Mountain Ranges.

As disappointed as I was, I reported the Total Company's decision to the president and to the cabinet of ministers.

I also told the cabinet, "It is my belief that we can pursue this project on our own, if our ministry has the funds to buy the necessary drilling equipment and machinery, and establish a training school for oil drillers, geologists, and engineers, for the exploitation of oil from the Katawaz area for internal use in Afghanistan." I suggested that our ministry should be allowed to conduct further exploration in this area and determine the feasibility of exploitation of oil from these reserves.

The minister of planning said, "You can use funds from the ten million dollars that President of Iraq Hassan al-Bakr had promised Afghanistan."

On the basis of this idea, the Foreign and Planning Ministries made the necessary arrangements for me to go to Iraq, visit Iraqi oil exploration and exploitation works, and see how we could start a training school and drill for oil in the most promising areas of Katawaz, with Iraq's help.

During this trip, I met Hassan al-Bakr and gave him the qarakul cap that President Daoud had sent as a gift. I was accompanied by Ustaad Khalilullah Khalili, the great poet laureate who was my Dari literature professor in the twelfth grade at Habibia High School.

Hassan al-Bakr was very nice in this meeting. He said, "Your ambassador is not only a great poet in Dari [Farsi], but he is also a recognized poet in the Arabic language. I entrust him and you with not only the ten million that we had promised before, but also with more funds, if you need any for your important work."

I spent about a week in Iraq. The Afghan ambassador in Tehran, Iran, was Abdullah Malikyar, my previous boss in the Helmand Valley Project. He kept telling me that the Iranian government had insisted that I visit Iran before going to Kabul. I kept telling him that I was planning to visit Iran for ten days or two weeks, because there was so much to see and do there. Mr. Malikyar then told me to make a stop for two days, maybe, and discuss the projects with which Iran had promised to help Afghanistan. I sent word to Kabul and got permission for this visit.

My visit to Tehran promised to be very interesting. First, I was going to meet my old boss, whom I held in high regard. Second, at that time, the prime minister of Iran was someone who had been my Cornell engineering schoolmate, Mr. Jamshid Amuzgar. We had both stayed at Cosmopolitan House. He was doing his work for a PhD while I was a freshman. I had not told Mr. Malikyar about this.

When Mr. Malikyar and I entered the prime minister's office, Amuzgar got up from his desk and came toward the door, and then he embraced me like an old friend.

The meeting with the prime minister and his team went quite well. I told Amuzgar, "Now I do not have enough time, but I will come to Iran for a more extended visit next time."

After we left the room, Mr. Malikyar said, "I did not know you two were old acquaintances. But I have some bad news for you.

Mr. A. A. Khorram, the minister of planning, was assassinated this morning." This news really hit me like a ton of bricks. I was very much saddened. Khorram had been not only a good colleague but also my schoolmate at Habibia High School.

Margo Desert

The Margo Desert is located in Helmand. From Girishk and Lashkargah, it spreads southwest to Nimroz and Chakansur. With the Helmand River turning north toward the inland *hamuns* (lakes), Margo Desert is quite desolate. I used to travel through it in a four-wheeled pickup with lots of water and gasoline in spare, going back and forth between Lashkargah and the Nimroz-area Lashkari Canal and Kamal Khan projects. In the Baluchi language, *margo* means "death."

During my work at the Ministry of Mines and Industries, I frequently met with Mr. Puzanov the Russian ambassador. However, meeting with ambassadors from other countries was infrequent. I was pleasantly surprised when the American ambassador, H. E. Theodor Eliot, made an appointment for a meeting with me.

Ambassador Eliot was a tall and very pleasant person. I enjoyed talking freely with him during the meetings or when I was invited to the American embassy for the Fourth of July celebration.

I told my secretary, Mr. Asadullah Nouri, a very competent secretary and a fine person, to go and welcome the ambassador at the entrance to the ministry and then escort him to my office. I also said, "Inform the deputy minister of mines and industries, Mr. Samad Salah, to come to my office for the meeting." Mr. Salah had advanced degrees in engineering and geology from German universities, and he was a very intelligent, scholarly, and competent person. I learned from him many things in the field of his profession, and I considered myself fortunate to have him as my deputy.

Ambassador Eliot had some very interesting news for me. He said that an American firm by the name of City Service had shown interest in the survey and exploration of oil in the Margo Desert. I asked, "What ever made them get interested in this idea?"

The ambassador said, "They have been studying satellite data and think that there are possibilities." He then added, "Let me know if the Afghan government is interested in this."

I said, "Okay!"

I brought this matter up during the next cabinet meeting of ministers. The attending ministers were all in favor of it. President Daoud said, "We welcome this idea. Please, ask Ambassador H. E. Eliot to tell the American company that they can start the work anytime soon. Also ask him to tell us what we can do to help."

(There are many other stories of accomplishments during the period of Daoud's presidency. However, for the purposes of brevity, I will not write about these in detail.)

President Daoud's objectives, and his desire for teaching the Afghan nation to learn to stand on its own feet, did not fit in well with the expansionist plans of the Soviet superpower at that time. I believe that *having superpower does not make a country super.*

What big countries need to learn is to have the *heart and vision* to allow the small nations of the world to learn to stand on their own feet, to progress in achieving self-sufficiency, and to lessen the burden on bigger countries that plan and make programs for assisting these less-developed countries on the path of progress.

In the following pages, I provide an eyewitness account and the story of the slaughter of President Daoud and his family. I also depict the Communists' tyranny, terror, and murder of innocent people that followed.

After the Soviet-assisted Communist coup d'état, I was a political prisoner held by the Communists for twenty-two months (from 1978 to 1980) in the infamous Pul-i-Charkhi Prison in Kabul. In the following pages, which you may be interested in reading, I document the daily reign of terror and murder by a bunch of small-brained, Soviet-trained people in the human slaughterhouse of Pul-i-Charkhi Prison.

PART 2

THE ORIGINS OF THE TRAGEDY OF AFGHANISTAN

Preface

This portion of the document is an eyewitness account of the April 27, 1978 (Saur 7, 1357), Communist coup in Afghanistan,[2] and it describes aspects of the chaotic two years that followed, leading to the Soviet army invasion of December 1979.

As a member of the pre-Communist cabinet who was with the president when he was overthrown and murdered, this is my experience of the events as they occurred. I also relate my experiences as a political prisoner during the following two years in the notorious Pul-i-Charkhi Prison, expecting to be executed at any moment.

Secret Notes

Against all odds and against the strict orders of the prison authorities, I secretly kept notes on tiny pieces of paper and paper tissues, hiding them in cracks and under slabs and stones. I had promised myself that if I came out alive from the Pul-i-Charkhi slaughterhouse, I would

---

[2]   The Communist coup had apparently been planned for late summer, but the arrest of the Communist leaders triggered it in April.

write about these atrocities, the torture and killing of innocent people by the Afghan Communists and their Soviet trainers and supporters. This part of the book is, hopefully, an exposé for the free people of the world, asking them to take heed and not allow the recurrence of similar tragedies anywhere in the world.

The first sections are an account of the 1978 coup itself and the massacre of President Daoud and his family, which I describe hour by hour and even minute by minute, as I, at risk myself, witnessed it in the presidential palace with other cabinet ministers. After that slaughter, those of us cabinet ministers who were still alive were eventually moved to Pul-i-Charkhi Prison.

The largest section of this part of the book is made up of specific and documented daily accounts of atrocities committed during the twenty-two months that I was held at Pul-i-Charkhi—from early May 1978 to mid-1980, during the first two Communist regimes and the early months of the third, which was installed by the invading Russians on or about January 1, 1980.

During that time, I observed (and experienced myself) the imprisonment and torture of Afghans; the execution of many hundreds of Afghans who stood up to the Communist regimes and the Soviets; and the elimination of an entire generation of trained, experienced Afghan leaders.

As noted above, I secretly managed to record my observations on a daily basis. Dated items about events that took place in the prison are transcribed from these secret daily notes, as is much else. (For the convenience of some readers, when I specify dates, I also include in parentheses the dates on the traditional Afghan calendar.) In many cases, I have included the reasons for the policies and actions of the Communist regimes, their factional infighting, and their eventual failure in Afghanistan *as I understood it at that time, with only the information available to me in the prison.* (Any additional information is given in occasional footnotes.)

I provide stark examples of the atrocities that were daily and almost routine. I also tell of our ingenuity while prisoners, in an environment of terror and slaughter, in establishing a secret communication system.

The final sections, dealing with my release from prison, give a glimpse of conditions in Kabul under the Communist regime directly installed and controlled by the Soviets and enforced by the presence of the dreaded Soviet army. Life in what I called "Prison Kabul," and the pressures placed on me to cooperate with the Communist puppet regime, made it intolerable for me to remain there. With the help of valiant friends, I was able to get my wife and children out of the country and then managed to walk out of my ancestral homeland myself, evading the Afghan Communist and Soviet forces and the "butterfly mines" scattered by Soviet air forces.

Some Background

From 1933 to 1973, Afghanistan lived peacefully under the reign of a king, Zahir Shah. For most of that time, the government was led by members of the royal family who served as prime ministers, including the king's cousin Sardar (Prince) Mohammad Daoud.

During those years, the Afghan government emphasized education, and a number of students were sent abroad to France, England, Germany, and the United States for advanced education and training. A small but growing class of highly educated modernizers was developing and moving into the government.

As prime minister (1953–63), Daoud, an army general, established increasingly friendly ties with the Soviet Union, sending a number of military officers to the USSR for training. He was apparently unaware that Soviet intelligence agencies co-opted a number of these trainees, who became secret long-term Soviet agents. (At that time, the United States was not interested in Afghanistan; however, the USSR and, before it, Imperial Russia had sought influence or control in Afghanistan—its pathway to the Indian subcontinent and the Indian Ocean.)

In 1963, following a policy disagreement with the king, Daoud resigned. For the first time, the position of prime minister was given to someone outside the royal family, one of the Western-educated modernizers, Dr. Mohammad Yussof, who filled his cabinet with European- and American-educated modernizers. A new, more liberal constitution established a constitutional monarchy with potentially democratic institutions. In 1965 and 1969, under five liberal prime ministers, national parliamentary elections, determined by universal suffrage and secret ballot, were successfully held. A third election was scheduled for the autumn of 1973.

During this period, a Communist Party was secretly formed in Afghanistan with guidance from the Soviet embassy in Kabul. It split into two competing factions, Khalq (meaning, "the people") and Parcham (meaning, "banner").

In mid-1973, while the king was vacationing in Italy, Daoud, in an almost bloodless coup, overthrew the 1964 constitution and the monarchy, declared a republic, and took office as president. The king abdicated. To the nation, there appeared to be largely a dynastic shift within the royal family.

Daoud was apparently unaware that some of the men he trusted and who had carried out his coup had secret Soviet ties. This group, largely Parchami, was initially influential in establishing Daoud's government based on a Soviet-style model with a central committee. But after Daoud found concrete evidence that some high-ranking members of that agency were abusing their newfound power for their own financial benefit, he abolished the central committee, rejected Soviet advice, cleansed his government of those he knew to be Parchami, and replaced them with a new group of educated, experienced modernizers.

Daoud was unaware that among those he still considered trustworthy—and whom he retained in his government and in the armed forces—were several individuals who had secret ties to Parcham and Khalq or who were directly linked to the Soviet Union through its embassy.

Most of the reorganized cabinet, including the author of this memoir, were loyal Afghan patriots who were dedicated to building a modern nation.

With degrees in engineering from two major American universities—Cornell University and Colorado State University—and decades of administrative experience in the Helmand Valley Development Project, establishing a new Cadastral Survey Department and organizing a Rural Development Department, and as the former governor of a major province, I was serving as minister of mines and industries in April 1978, when a bloody coup, led by the same officers who had helped Daoud overthrow the monarchy five years earlier, overthrew and murdered President Daoud and his family.

With the help and direction of the Soviet Union, these officers installed an Afghan Communist regime, which led to widespread popular resistance, the Soviet invasion in December 1979, and all of the tragedies that followed.

It all began during a cabinet meeting on a seemingly ordinary Thursday morning. Explosions interrupted my presentation of a proposed new labor regulation.

The Coup

On Thursday, April 27, 1978 (Saur 7, 1357), I had an early breakfast, said good-bye to my wife and kids, and left our apartment for a 7:00 a.m. meeting with a delegation from the International Labor Organization (ILO). As minister of mines and industries, I was also responsible for Afghanistan's labor affairs. The ILO had helped us revise an old labor law.

The meeting was scheduled to be held at the office of the Labor Relations Department on the first floor of the Ministry of Mines and Industries. Afterward, I would go to a special cabinet meeting at 9:00 a.m. to present the new labor law and request that the cabinet approve it.

I had submitted the new law for government approval at the regular cabinet meeting on the preceding Tuesday. However, at that time, the minister of finance, who also served as deputy prime minister, raised some questions that led to a long discussion. The new labor law gave laborers the right to hold peaceful demonstrations if the government and judiciary offices did not respond to their grievances and demands. The finance minister was arguing that workers did not need to demonstrate, because Daoud's new constitution guaranteed them a large number of representatives in the Parliament.

I pointed out that the labor law had been prepared by my ministry with the help of the ILO and that it adhered to the standards, norms, and rights customary in the free world. I argued that we could not limit the rights of Afghan citizens. If peaceful demonstrations were stifled, what would be the alternative? Riots? Rebellion?

At this point, President Daoud intervened and suggested that we continue our discussion elsewhere and come with our conclusions to a special cabinet meeting—which we were now holding this Thursday morning.

But before the Tuesday meeting had adjourned, the president asked the minister of justice, Mr. Wafi-ullah Samiee, a question related to a totally different subject, namely, the detention of a number of Parchami and Khalqi figures, leaders of the two factions of the Soviet-guided Communist "group," because they had held a mass demonstration several days earlier to protest the assassination of one of their Communist ideologues, Mir Akbar Khaibar.

President Daoud and a few members of his inner circle had made the decision to arrest them. Daoud had not consulted with cabinet ministers. I hadn't known about the arrests until I heard of them on the news. This did not seem to be of major importance at the time. It would prove to be of catastrophic importance, however.

On Tuesday, the president had asked the justice minister, "According to the law, how long can the leaders of Parcham and Khalq be kept in detention?"

Mr. Samiee replied, "The existing law stipulates a minimum of two weeks and a maximum of three months."

President Daoud repeated his question and added, "Have you looked carefully at the related articles of the existing law that are applicable in this instance?"

The minister of justice responded, "Yes, sir. According to the existing law, the punishment for breaking the law in this instance is detention from two weeks minimum to three months maximum."

Once the Tuesday meeting had ended, we all went back to our jobs at the respective ministries. As President Daoud had directed, I met with the finance minister and several others on Wednesday to discuss the labor law. After a brief discussion, the finance minister agreed to have the new law approved at the special cabinet meeting on Thursday morning. It was all rather routine.

Special Cabinet Meeting

April 27, 1978 (Saur 7, 1357)

On Thursday morning, I first met with the ILO team at the Ministry of Mines, thanked them for their work on the new law, and began to leave for the nearby presidential palace. In the corridor of the ministry, I noticed several young men who were unfamiliar to me walking around. They seemed surprised to see me there so early.

About 8:00 a.m., I arrived at the presidential palace, where cabinet meetings were usually held at about 9:00 a.m. in the cabinet meeting room, a large room on the ground floor. The building had been constructed by the former king, Zahir Shah.[3] He had used it as his office and for holding meetings with visiting heads of state, ambassadors, high-ranking government officials, and representatives from various Afghan provinces.

---

[3] *Shah* means "king" and follows the name of the ruler. Thus "Zahir Shah" indicates "King Zahir."

After overthrowing the monarchy in 1973 and declaring the establishment of a republic with himself as president, Daoud had set up the offices of the presidency in the same building, so it was now officially called the presidential palace. But (ironically, in view of events) this palace, which included some greenhouses for winter flowers, has always been popularly known as the Gulkhana—"Palace of Flowers." Gradually, other ministers arrived for the special meeting that Thursday morning, exchanged greetings, and took their regular seats around the long, rectangular table. I gave the proposal package and signature sheet to Dr. Naween, the minister of information and culture, who was acting as the secretary of the cabinet that day; he usually filled in, in the absence of the regular secretary of the cabinet, Mr. Said Waheed Abdullah (who was also the acting foreign minister). Although some ministers had not yet arrived, President Daoud came in and took his place at the head of the table. He asked me to report on our discussions concerning the questions that had been raised about the labor law. I said that I had met with the appropriate people on Wednesday, that we had discussed the questions that were raised at Tuesday's cabinet meeting and reached agreement, and that I was submitting the final version of the agreed-upon labor law for Daoud's and the cabinet's approval. Mr. Said Abdul-Illah, the deputy prime minister, confirmed my statement. The president said, "Then let us finish the signatures and approval." The proposal package and the signature sheet were circulated. After the sheet was signed by all those present, the documents were placed in front of the president for his approval. Whether or not he signed, I do not know, for, just then, one of the office staff came into the cabinet room and gave a small piece of paper to Minister of Interior Qadir Nuristani. Nuristani got up and left the room. He came back after a few minutes, went to the head of the table, bent down, and said something privately to the president. President Daoud got up from his chair and slowly walked out of the room, with Mr. Nuristani following. After a few moments, Deputy Prime Minister Said Abdul-Illah left the room, as did Dr. Naween. Some ministers—the minister of defense, General Rasuli, and the minister of public works, engineer Ghausuddin Fayeq—were not present at that morning's meeting. The rest of us sat and waited for almost half an hour in the cabinet room, not knowing what was happening or whether the meeting would continue or not.

A Loud Noise

Dr. Naween came back into the room. "Why are you guys still sitting here?" he asked. "There's no meeting anymore." But before he could finish that sentence, a loud noise, which sounded like an explosion or cannon fire, startled everyone. The ministers started collecting their papers and, one by one, left the room.

Since this special cabinet meeting had been scheduled specifically for the approval of the new labor law that I had submitted, I was hesitant to leave. However, I realized that the meeting was over, so I proceeded to collect my papers, put them into my briefcase, and walk out into the corridor, very anxious to learn what was happening. I saw the minister of finance, Said Abdul Illah, coming down the stairs from the president's office on the second floor. I met him at the bottom of the stairs and asked, "What's going on?"

He said, "The president is trying to get the facts, but there is a rumor that about two hundred tanks from the Fourth Armored Division have started moving toward Kabul." The barracks for that armored division were close to the military school, north across the Kabul River at Pul-i-Charkhi. Most of the ministers who had been in the cabinet meeting room either stayed in the first-floor corridor or went into the office of Mr. Akbar, the president's secretary and chief of staff, or the rooms of the president's other secretaries on either side of the corridor. What was happening was still unclear. Was this a coup against the government, or was it, as some rumors had it, a movement of an armored division to protect the presidential palace against an uprising by some Communists who wanted to release the leaders of Parcham and Khalq from detention?

As time went on, we learned that the president was in communication with his generals who were in charge of military divisions located around Kabul City. Power and telephone services to the presidential palace were still operational. I went upstairs to the second floor, entered the president's secretary's room, and then opened the door to go into the president's office. President Daoud was sitting at his desk, talking on the phone to Sahibjan, the commander of the Presidential Guard unit that was responsible for the security of the president, the presidential offices, and the palace grounds. Another officer was also present in the room; he wore a military field uniform and had a radio communication unit on his back with an antenna sticking up from it. Apparently, the president was also using the military radio communication system.

I went back downstairs and returned to the first-floor corridor, where I stayed most of the rest of that day. There, I was able to speak with those who passed through or came down from the president's office. Gradually, the suspicion of a coup d'état was becoming stronger. The cannon fire that we had heard had been directed at the Ministry of Defense, which was about three hundred meters to the east of the presidential palace.

Tanks Surround the Palace

After a while, Sahibjan,[4] the Presidential Guard commander, came down the stairs. I asked him what was happening. He said, "A number of tanks have surrounded the outside walls of the palace. They say, 'We have come to defend the palace against a possible coup.' I will communicate with them and tell them, 'If you have come to defend the palace, then why are your guns pointing toward us? You should turn your guns to point away from the palace.'" Saying that, he left the corridor. I went to other rooms on the first floor to see if others had any information about what was happening. Some ministers were in the office of the president's chief of staff, Mr. Akbar. Some were in other rooms or hanging around in the corridor. The phones were still working, so most had called their own offices, trying to find out how things were in the city. No one had any definite information. There was confusion and many rumors.

Akbar-jan's phone was still working, and he let me use it to call my home. I talked to my wife and told her that there was a coup going on. My wife, Fariha, is a person of strong character. She keeps her cool even in times of crisis and adversity. She said that the kids were in

---

[4]   *Jan* is an affectionate suffix often attached to names of friends, relatives, and admired individuals; it may also be part of a formal name, as it is in this case and some others that appear herein.

school but that she would find a way to get them home. I told her, "I love you and pray to God Almighty to protect you all!" I went back to the corridor and waited for Sahibjan to return and tell me what had happened as a result of his communication with the tank units positioned outside the palace. But when he came in, he went quickly up the stairs toward the president's office, motioning to me that he would talk to me when he came back. Eventually, he did so. He told me that he had communicated with the soldiers in the tanks and told them to turn their guns away from the palace. Some moved partway and stopped turning; others did not turn at all.

"I told them again," Sahibjan said, "'If you have come to defend the palace, the sign will be to turn your guns so they are pointing away from us. If you don't, then it will mean that you are attacking the palace, and we will be forced to blow your tanks away.'"

Antitank Units Fire at Tanks

Sahibjan continued speaking. "After some time passed and the tanks didn't turn their guns away from the palace, I ordered our antitank units to hit first one tank and then another tank of those that were closest. The first tank blew up—pieces of it scattered into the street and nearby trees—and then the second tank was hit and blew up like the first one. After the second tank blew up," he went on, "the occupants started coming out of their tanks and running away. Some climbed up the walls of the Cartographic Department building, and others went over the walls of the Ministry of Mines. About sixty of them surrendered to the palace guards, and we took them to the basement of the palace, where we will hold them for the time being. Now that the tank units have been defeated," he went on, "the areas around the palace up to the Wazir Akbar Khan district are under the control of the palace guards." But at this time, some of the coup leaders were calling from the Bagram airbase, where they had apparently taken control; not having other options, they were threatening to use airpower to subdue the palace guards and the president. They were telling the palace guards to give up; otherwise, they warned, they would use aerial bombardment and level the president's palace to the ground.

A Jet Plane Overhead

I could hear the sound of a jet plane overhead and heavy antiaircraft machine guns firing from the palace. I wanted to see what was going on, so I exited the palace through the front door and started walking on the lawn between the palace and the small mosque that stood some 150 meters to the west. A light rain had fallen earlier, but it was not raining now. I looked up when I heard a jet plane overhead the second time. The plane circled and dove toward the palace. Since I was just outside of the palace, it seemed as if the plane was coming toward me. A vapor trail came out from under the wing, and then I heard another blast. I saw that the building was still intact, but there was debris scattered around the lawn, and some pieces were burning. I bent down and began stepping on the burning pieces one by one to stamp out the flames. As I was doing this, I heard a clicking noise in front of me. An officer had clicked his heels and was standing at attention in front of me, his head slightly bent in salute. I recognized him. He was Abdul Haq, one of the Ulumi brothers whom President Daoud liked very much. Throughout the Ulumis' careers, he had helped them receive higher education and be promoted in the armed forces. Officer Ulumi said, "Sir, you should not walk out here like this. It is dangerous, and you might get hurt."

I said, "Officer, it doesn't make much difference whether I'm out here or inside the palace—the chance of getting hurt is about the same. And by the way, where did all this debris come from?"

He said, "I think the planes were aiming to hit the palace, but instead they hit the gate behind it, between the palace and the Salam Khana."[5] He went on to say, "I assure you, sir, that they will not be able to cause you any harm unless they first go over our chests."

I said, "That remains to be seen."

---

[5] Literally, "greeting room": the reception hall where the king or president formally receives and greets large groups of representatives or other guests.

142

He clicked his heels, saluted, turned around, and walked back toward the building. I no longer heard planes overhead, but I could hear the crackling of machine-gun fire in the distance.

After some time, I, too, went back into the palace, where I stayed until early the next morning. I think it was about three or four o'clock in the afternoon when I returned to the palace, but, to tell the truth, I was not aware of the time. It seems that in times of severe crisis, we do not keep track of time; instead, happenings and events are etched in our minds and time seems to stretch.

I began talking to some who were present in the entrance corridor and first-floor offices, trying to learn what was going on in Kabul City and surrounding areas. I wanted to know whether there were any countercoup movements made by the military units stationed around the capital. President Daoud was still in his office, trying to contact various military command centers. From the information I got, I knew that one unit had started moving toward the center of Kabul in an attempt to join the palace guards.

One thing was obvious, and that was the increasing crescendo of the palace guards' gunfire, including machine-gun fire. At this time, I could not get any further information as to whether the president was in contact with military division commanders or whether the commanders in charge of the military divisions were, in fact, in command of their troops.

The next time the commander of the palace guards, Sahibjan, walked by, I asked him about this. He said that the president was still trying; other than that, he was noncommittal. After saying this, he walked out of the room. The day wore on; gradually, it became dark outside. The lights were turned on, as electricity had not been cut off on the palace grounds.

The President and His Family Come Down

Someone told me that most of President Daoud's family had come from their homes in the city and made it to the palace during the day. They were now upstairs with the president. I could sense that an atmosphere of bewilderment and doom was setting in among those who were present. I noticed that people were looking toward the stairs. I saw President Daoud slowly coming down. He nodded to us in recognition and then went on down the corridor and sat on a bench at the left, farther from the stairs. Coming down the stairs close behind him were the deputy prime minister, Said Abdul-Illah, and Qadir Nuristani, the minister of the interior. Then, some members of President Daoud's family came down, led by his brother Sardar Naim Khan,[6] who was Afghanistan's foreign minister and had once been the Afghan ambassador to Washington during Zahir Shah's time. Behind him was Omar-jan, the president's older son, who had not seen his father in a year because they had had some disagreements. Then came other close family members—women and children, including Princess Zainab, President Daoud's wife, and Princess Bibi Zohra, Sardar Naim's wife. As this large group came into the corridor, the people who were already there, in an effort to make room for them, gradually drifted into the side rooms or into the rooms used by the president's secretarial staff. All of us who had come that morning for the cabinet meeting were now trapped in the building. I could hear increasing noise of gunfire from the palace grounds and from farther away.

When Sahibjan passed by again, he said, "They are threatening aerial bombardment and saying that they will level the palace to the ground with half-ton bombs." Night fell.

---

[6] *Sardar* means "prince" or "nobleman." *Khan* is an honorific suffix indicating a man of substance, of property, or of distinction; it is somewhat similar to "esquire" or "sir."

The Reception Room

I decided to go to the reception room where guests customarily waited to meet the president. I went in and sat down on a bench in front of the window facing the front lawn of the palace. My head and shoulders were above the windowsill. Although I tried, I could not see anything outside; it was pitch-dark. Close to about eight o'clock, President Daoud walked into the room. Seeing me sitting in front of the window, he came over and sat on another bench at a right angle to the one I was sitting on. Gradually, other ministers came in and sat down on the chairs around the room. The last one to come in was the president's brother, Sardar Naim Khan, who sat down in the corner opposite Daoud. There was a coffee table in front of the president. An attendant came in and placed a cup of green tea on the table. After a few minutes, another attendant came in and put another cup of tea in front of the president. Without looking up, Daoud pushed the second cup in front of me. He did not drink the tea, and neither did I. President Daoud was somewhat stooped, looking at the table in front of him, deep in thought. No one spoke. The sounds of gunfire and machine-gun fire could be heard outside.

After some time, Deputy Prime Minister Said Abdul-Illah came into the room carrying a small transistor radio, which he placed on the table in front of President Daoud. The radio was on and we could hear a military band, apparently on the Kabul station that used to be run by the government (there were not many other radio stations broadcasting in Kabul). Apparently, they announced earlier that there would be an important forthcoming announcement on Kabul Radio.

The Radio Announcement: A Lie

We listened to the bang-bang of the military band. Then an announcement began, made by someone who was not identified but whose voice was recognized as belonging to Tank Commander Mohammad Aslam Watanjar, an officer whom Daoud had favored, helped to train, given exceptional opportunities, and promoted to high rank. In the announcement, which was being said anonymously and on behalf of what was termed as the "People's Democratic Party," the speaker stated, "Daoud, a member of the Yahyaa Dynasty, and all his family and co-workers have been killed by…" and so forth and so on. (I do not remember the exact wording of the entire announcement; one's memory tends to freeze at such moments.)

The announcement was repeated several times, in both Pashto and Dari, the official languages of Afghanistan. Said Abdul-Illah, standing by the table, reached down to the transistor radio and turned it off. A few minutes passed in silence.

President Daoud's Last Words

President Daoud spoke at this time. In a very calm and steady voice, he said, *"It is my mistake!"*

These were the last words that I ever heard from President Daoud.

Obviously, the announcement was a lie; President Daoud was still alive, and so were we. What was its purpose? First of all, it was an announcement before the deed: it meant that the aggressors were planning to kill the president and his family—and all who worked with him. Second, the attackers were attempting to scare or caution the other military units not to move or try to help the palace guards who stood firm against the coup. Third, they were frightening the people of Kabul and of Afghanistan, warning them not to attempt any countercoups.

At this time, two thoughts passed through my mind.

First, I thought that I was sitting in precarious position, there by the window. The room was lighted and bright, and outside was pitch-dark. If someone had made it onto the palace grounds to kill the president, he could clearly see into the room—and I was in the direct line of fire. But I decided to stay where I was. I thought that if I was destined to be the first one to be killed, then so be it. I thought that it was better to be firm than to move away from the danger of the moment. This may seem like an unduly fatalistic decision, but, at such a moment, one may not be logical or even intelligent. Sometimes in life, we are put into a situation where, on the spur of the moment, we have to make life-or-death decisions. This is the situation of soldiers in war. In the months that followed, I came very close to death several times. And in most of these instances, I did not even have a chance to make a decision.

My second thought was, *Ask the president to explain his mistake. What did he mean?* But I didn't ask; it was not an appropriate occasion for a question or a discussion. We all sat where we were. No one said a word. The sound of gunfire could be heard from outside. After some time, President Daoud stood up and slowly walked toward the door, his brother Sardar Naim Khan following behind. They went out of the room and into the corridor where their families were. After that, Said Abdul-Illah and most of the ministers in the room gradually went back into the corridor. Some others who had not been in the cabinet meeting that morning, including the acting foreign minister, Said Wahid Abdullah, had come to the palace. The corridor was becoming crowded. Some went into Akbar-jan's office. I stood near the stairs.

What I knew up to that point was the following:

- The palace guards, under the command of Sahibjan, had stood firm and defended the palace and its premises, including the Wazir Akbar Khan district. They had blown up two tanks, causing the soldiers to abandon their tanks and flee. About sixty surrendered to the guards.
- President Daoud had tried to contact his generals at different military divisions to join the palace guards, but with no success. So far, no one had joined forces with the guards to defend the president or his government.
- The coup conspirators were threatening to bomb and level the president's office to the ground, killing everyone in it.
- The Kabul radio and television stations had been taken over and were now occupied by the conspirators. They had made an announcement from there that "Daoud, a member of the Yahyaa Dynasty, and all his family and co-workers have been killed."

- The conspirators were members of Parcham and Khalq, two factions of a Communist group (not yet formally called a party) that had been trained and indoctrinated by the agents of the Soviet Union to take over Afghanistan's government with backing and support by the USSR. Their leaders had recently been arrested; just two days before, Daoud had asked about the possible length of their detention.

The Decision to Leave the Palace

It was decided that the president should leave his office at the palace with an escort unit and move to one of the military divisions near Kabul. He could then take command and conduct the countercoup fight from there. The president ordered Said Wahid Abdullah, the deputy foreign minister, who had come back to the palace, to go to the Foreign Ministry and take care of his papers. He told Sardar Timur Shah-jan, Zahir Shah's brother-in-law, to accompany Said Wahid Abdullah, and they both left the premises. The president then ordered Sahibjan to organize a palace guard escort. Sahibjan reported that he would shortly have two fully functioning T-62 tanks and several weapons-carrier units ready with several antitank rocket launcher units, and that he would also get the president's gray bulletproof Mercedes car ready.

At this time, someone brought in two Kalashnikov guns, giving one to Said Abdul-Illah and the other to Qadir Nuristani.

I approached Said Abdul-Illah and asked him to tell the president that I had a proposal. He said, "What is your proposal?"

I told him, "I want the guards' commander to give me a machine gun, several fully armed soldiers, and one soldier with an antitank rocket launcher, and let us form an attack unit. I understand that the palace guards are in command of the whole area around the palace, all the way into Wazir Akbar Khan Carte [district]. I volunteer, and maybe some others in this room may also volunteer, to go with this unit, approach the Kabul radio and TV station from the back, and surprise the conspirators who are guarding the station by first blowing one or maybe two of their tanks, and then attacking the station guards and going into the broadcasting studios." I told him that I was sure that the regular station personnel would cooperate with us and broadcast several radio announcements saying that:

- The previous announcements made by the traitor Watanjar were not true;
- President Daoud was alive and in command at the presidential palace;
- Palace guards had defeated the tank units that had come on the false pretext of guarding the palace against disturbance;
- Sixty tank soldiers had surrendered and were in the custody of the palace;
- President Daoud asked the military divisions to move their armed units and join forces with the palace guards against the traitors;
- President Daoud was asking the citizens of Kabul and Afghanistan to stay calm, not to believe the false announcements made by the traitors, and to join forces and disarm any coup elements who wanted to disturb the peace and freedom of our country.

I knew that our chance of success was very small. I also knew that I would not survive this attempt. However, if we had even a 5 percent chance of success, it would be worth the sacrifice. Otherwise, I would be just sitting there and not doing anything useful.

The president was now sitting on a bench on the other side of the corridor. He looked toward Said Abdul-Illah with a questioning expression on his face. Said Abdul-Illah moved closer to him, bent down, briefly told him what I had said, and then stood up again. After about ten minutes, he edged toward the wall and closer to me. I asked him, "What did the president say? Did he approve?"

He replied, "The president said, 'They will all be killed. It's no use.'" Eventually, the palace guard commander, Sahibjan, came in reported to the president that the escort was ready. Omar-jan, President Daoud's son, approached his father and said that he would go out and inspect the escort. Then he and Minister of the Interior Qadir walked out through the front door to see if everything was okay. Soon after they went out, I heard a buzzing sound near my ears and machine-gun fire from outside. At the same time, the plaster on the wall behind me was shattered. The sound of the machine gun was loud; apparently, it was being fired at close range.

A machine gun on the lawn was being fired at people who were coming out of the front door—and fired into the corridor, too. Someone shouted, "Turn off the lights! Turn off the lights! They can see inside!" The lights in the corridor and offices were turned off.

Someone else shouted, "Omar-jan has been hit!" and "Qadir is wounded!" The two guards who were standing at either side of the front door were hit. Now the corridor was dark. I could hear the sound of the footsteps of the men who were bringing Omar-jan's body into the building. Qadir had gone into Akbar-jan's office to find somebody to bandage the wound on his arm.

I could hear women's voices crying and mourning; I assumed that they belonged to Omar-jan's mother and his wife.

One of the ministers—I think it was Minister of Agriculture Wasefi— said, "Brothers, it is appropriate for us to leave this room for the president's immediate family members."

I moved out of the corridor and into the side room where I had been earlier, going toward the window near the place where I had been sitting some time ago. The room was dark now, and I could hear the sound of gunfire from the surrounding palace grounds. Stooping low, I came close to the window where I had sat next to the president and tried to peer outside, but this time without raising my head above the windowsill. I was trying to figure out the location of the machine gun that had killed and wounded Omar, Qadir, and others. While I was doing that, I heard footsteps outside. They were approaching the window.

Whoever passed the window was shuffling past and was probably stooped down so as not to be seen from inside the room. I walked slowly to the next window facing the lawn and repeated my visual survey of the outside. Again, I could hear steps outside approaching and shuffling past the window. I kept repeating my moves from room to room until I came to a side door in the corner of the last room. Several guards were standing there. Heavy machine-gun fire could be heard coming from outside.

While I was talking to the guards, an officer came in from behind the wall. Upon seeing me, he said, "Sir, you should not be standing here. You could get hurt." I noticed that he was the same officer I had seen earlier while I was walking on the lawn and stepping on the burning debris, but now he was wearing an officer's field uniform.

The Telephone Room

I asked the guards, "Where are the other ministers? Where did they go?"

One of the guards replied, "Sir, they went to the telephone office room."

I asked, "Where is that?"

One of them said, "Let me show you, sir. It is beyond this passage." Saying that, he led me into the telephone office room, where I found the other ministers sitting together in a circle. From time to time, Sahibjan came through the door, looked around, and said a few words. I and the others sat in this room until the next morning.

The Second Day of Being Attacked

Friday, April 28, 1978 (Saur 8, 1357)

Before dawn, Sahibjan came into the telephone office room and said that his guards had been defending the palace very well but that, so far, no other military unit had come to join them. The traitors

151

were threatening to begin aerial bombardment with half-ton bombs, hoping to level the whole place and kill everyone in it.

The White Flag

The next time he came in, Sahibjan said, "The president has ordered me to negotiate with the other side for a peaceful solution. President Daoud says, 'Young ones will be killed.'" Sahibjan went on to say, "We will raise a white flag, a symbol of peace, open the front gate, and allow a delegation to come in and talk with the president."

Gradually, the night was receding. In the early light, we could see outside when a white flag was raised on the main tower of the presidential palace.

After some time, we saw first one weapons carrier, and then a second one, come into the compound. Some men, maybe about ten of them, were walking in front of and alongside the first carrier.

They came in slowly. The weapons carriers stopped in front of the palace mosque. Then, five or six of the men walked toward the president's office and entered through the front door, which led to the first-floor corridor.

The Mass Murder of President Daoud and His Family

President Daoud, most of his family members, and two ministers, Said Abdul-Illah and Qadir Nuristani—altogether, about forty unarmed people, old and young, women and children, too—were in the corridor.

Five or ten minutes passed. Then, we heard the sound of machine-gun fire from the corridor. It went on for some time before it stopped. *Intuitively, we knew that the conspirators had fulfilled the claims they had made in their announcement on Kabul Radio the night before.*

It was one of the most inhuman and barbaric acts perpetrated in the last part of the twentieth century, in a country that was at peace—a slaughter of innocent men, women, and children. The rest of us were waiting in the telephone room for our turn to be murdered. I thought that we were like sheep in a slaughterhouse. It reminded me of an incident that occurred when I was the governor of Herat Province. A slaughterhouse funded by the World Bank had been built. As governor of the province, I was being shown the place. As we came to the section where sheep were lined up to be slaughtered, I wondered, *What would be the feeling of sheep? Are they able to sense that they are going to be killed? Even if they do, they cannot do anything to avoid it.*

Now, while we sat in the telephone room, my thoughts went to the predicament of the sheep in the slaughterhouse. We in the palace certainly knew what was going to happen to us; yet, we all waited like sheep. It was a strange situation. No one cried out, got up to run, tried to escape, or concocted a plan of action. Had we given up hope? Or did the process of reasoning and thinking prevent us from taking any physical action? Obviously, humans are different from sheep, but still we waited there, like sheep. Given the impossible alternatives, we were all in a stupefied state of mind. We just waited there to face whatever was going to happen to us. So be it.

After some time, the door opened. Two soldiers, apparently from the subverted units, brought Qayeum Wardak, the minister of education, into the room. They said that he had been hiding in one of the rooms in the *haram saray,* the king's private quarters. Apparently, he was familiar with the layout of the buildings in the palace compound.

The soldiers opened the door again and ushered in two ministers who had not spent the night in the telephone room. First, Dr. Naween, minister of press and culture, came in, and then Mohammad Khan Jalalar, the minister of commerce, was brought in.

When the conspirators searched the rooms in the palace, they found these two men in the cabinet room and brought them from there. Passing through the corridor, Naween and Jalalar had witnessed the carnage, the blood and bodies of men, women, and children strewn all over the place.

153

Naween's face was so flushed that it had a bluish tinge. As a gynecologist, he had seen a lot of blood in his professional life, but nothing like what he saw now: the blood and dead bodies of people he had respected during his life.

Jalalar's face showed that he was in a state of shock. It was pale and colorless, and his eyes were bulging from their sockets. He had probably read many accounts of revolutions and the rivers flowing full with blood, but now he witnessed with his own eyes the reality of slaughter and the carnage of innocent women and children.

After some time, the crew of attendants and staff who worked in the palace were allowed to leave.

The conspirators came to us with President Daoud's grandson, saying that they had found the boy still alive and badly wounded. Blood was oozing from his groin, and he could hardly walk. The attendant staff asked if we would help take him out to safety. Since we thought that we were not going to survive, we thought it would be better if they took him out of the palace themselves. So we told them, "Please take him out with your group, as he will have a better chance of survival. Afterward, you can contact someone on the outside to provide a safe place for him to stay."

Killers Come into the Room

Several hours had passed, but we were aware neither of time nor of how soon the end would come. We were waiting, with our minds in a state of shock and numbness. Then, the door opened. Two guys came in.

One seemed to be the commander. The other, a smaller man wearing a blue-gray air force field uniform, held a machine gun. He was pointing and waving the gun, ready to fire. We all stood up and raised our hands. I noticed that the guy with the machine gun was pale and that his eyes were bulging.

These two were probably the same ones who had killed the president and his family in the corridor. The commander had a pistol but did not carry a machine gun. He appeared to be in control and did not seem flustered by the horrible deed that he and his men had committed earlier in the corridor. He was probably one of the coup leaders.

This man knew everybody in the room and was showing off to his subordinate how knowledgeable he was. He started from the right, introducing the ministers one by one to his gun-toting comrade and joking about them.

Pointing at Jalalar, he said, "This is the Jewish boy."[7] Next, he indicated Dr. Naween and said, "He is the spy from the Iranian SAVAK." He then spoke to Qayeum Wardak, saying, "I haven't seen you for some time. Where have you been?" Then, he shook hands with Mr. Muhibbi, the minister of higher education; apparently they knew each other from the past.

The commander chatted in Pashto with Azizullah Wasefi, the minister of agriculture, who was standing in the corner. He said, "You didn't come to our meeting in Jalalabad!" Wasefi said something unintelligible under his breath.

The commander then looked at Dr. Abdul Majid, the minister of state. Dr. Majid was a man of small stature but significant achievement. He had degrees in science, microbiology, and public health from American universities. Highly respected by all who knew him, he had been a lecturer at Kabul University and had served in several diplomatic and ministerial posts—as minister of education and minister of health during Zahir Shah's reign, as well as minister of state in President Daoud's cabinet. Our tormenter said, mockingly, "You know, they call him the minister of state now, but he is actually the minister of court." (There was no minister of court in President Daoud's time because there was no longer a royal court; that position had existed only during the period of the monarchy.)

---

[7] *Jalalar* is, in fact, of Turkish origin. It indicates a first-generation Afghan.

The next group of ministers to whom the commander turned were engineers. The commander spoke in Pashto to Juma Mohammadi, minister of water and power, who had studied at the College of Engineering of Kabul University and at the University of Colorado. And then he introduced his sidekick to engineer Kareem Ataii, who had degrees in electronics and communications from German universities.

He next came to me, introducing me as "a great engineer." He asked me, "Do you remember that I was your helicopter pilot during a trip that you took to Nimroz and Lower Helmand River?" At this point, it clicked in my mind. I remembered him: Asadullah Sarwari. Several years earlier, I had known him slightly. At that time, a delegation had been appointed to negotiate with Iran for the relocation of several border pillars that had been destroyed when the Helmand River changed its course at a certain location and meandered more than a kilometer onto the Afghan side. Representing Afghanistan were Habib Karzai, a director at the Ministry of Foreign Affairs, and Brigadier General Rahim Nawabi from the Ministry of the Interior. As an engineer, I was appointed by the Prime Minister's Office to accompany and assist the Afghan delegation.

The meetings between the delegations were held alternately, one day in Afghanistan and the next in Iran. We went back and forth by helicopter, and our pilot was Asadullah Sarwari. He had become part of our delegation; wherever we went, he was there. He was strongly built and had helped unload helicopter fuel barrels from the back of his copter to refuel in the middle of the desert, halfway to Lower Helmand.

The border pillars had been set up almost a century before by a British engineer-surveyor named McMahon who worked with the All India Survey system and documented his survey with descriptive and technical notes tying the location of pillars to known landmarks on both sides of the river.

The Iranian delegation insisted that we relocate the pillars on the basis of those descriptive notes. However, since the river had changed its course and destroyed the pillars as well as the landmarks, the new location of the pillars would be shifted a kilometer into Afghan territory. I could see the wisdom of the Prime Ministry in assigning an engineer to help the delegation.

At my request, the delegation took a few days' recess to allow me to study the technical data that McMahon had provided in the form of triangulation points and coordinates. Fortunately, a cartographer, Abdul Ghafoor Khan, was also with us. We didn't have the GPS and computers that many enjoy today, but between the two of us, by using methods I had learned in the surveying classes I took at Cornell University's School of Civil Engineering in the pre-computer 1950s, shooting the North Star with a theodolite and using the logarithmic tables for calculations, Ghafoor and I were able to find the exact location of two landmarks. We then proceeded to relocate the destroyed pillars by way of triangulation. At dawn, we snuck onto the other side of the river by helicopter and found the remains of the destroyed pillars.

Sarwari had been impressed by what we engineers had done, which is why he now used the word *great* when introducing me. Perhaps he thought I'd be flattered,[8] but what was really going on in my mind at the time was this: when a killer praises his victim, it may connote a priority in the process that he is planning to carry out, like, "That sheep is fat, so it will be given priority in the slaughter." However, the two executioners left the room without shooting us. After a while, some armed soldiers came into the room and ushered out two of the ministers who were near the door. I thought that the soldiers were taking us two by two to be killed somewhere else.

I listened for the sound of machine-gun fire, but I did not hear any. I thought, *Probably they are taking us farther away to another place for the killing.*

---

[8]   Sarwari subsequently became head of the secret police and was known for his personal participation in torture. His cold brutality won him the nickname "King Kong."

After about fifteen minutes, the same soldiers came back and motioned for two more of the ministers to come out.

This process went on, two of us at a time—until my turn came. The two soliders took me and another minister—I don't remember who—outside. They led us to an old Chevy that was parked at a distance and made us sit in the backseat with one soldier on either side and two soldiers in front with the driver. All of them except the driver had guns.

Nobody told us ministers where we were going. The car exited through the palace gate. Outside the gate, I saw body parts and clothes on nearby tree branches. Those were probably from the explosion of the two tanks that the palace guards had hit the day before.

Ministry of Defense

The Chevy took us to the Ministry of Defense, which was not very far from the outer walls of the palace compound. It was several stories high, and its façade was made of gray-white marble. This was the building that the first cannon shot had been fired at the morning before.

Our captors drove us to the rear of the building and ordered us to get out of the car. Then, they led us down into the basement, where there were several large rooms that were probably used by the ministry's clerical staff. We were taken down the stairs to one of the rooms, where we found the other ministers, the ones who had been taken out of the telephone room before we were, sitting on benches and chairs.

The room had only high, barred window slits. One could not see outside without standing on a table. The soldiers kept on bringing the remaining ministers from the telephone room into the basement. We realized that they had only that one old Chevy available to transport the ministers from the palace to the Ministry of Defense. That's why they brought us two by two. None of us knew what was going to happen to us. Time passed minute by minute. No one even thought, *What is going to happen next?* Our minds were numb. The only thing that passed through my mind was to pray for the safety of my wife, my children, and the rest of my family.

We were held in the Ministry of Defense basement for more than a week. Our captors herded us into a large conference hall on the top floor of the building for meals; at night, they moved the tables to make space for mattresses to sleep on. After breakfast in the morning, we were herded down to the basement again to spend the rest of the day. The up-and-down trips became a routine during the time that we were held there.

The upstairs hall had large windows. We could peer out and see what was going on in the vicinity, but we could not see any city traffic. Some military trucks, weapons carriers, and Russian-made jeeps were moving, and some were parked around the building. We did not have any contact or communication with our families or anyone else in the outside world.

We did get some news from others who were brought into the room. The leaders of the coup and the new Communist regime announced several times on Kabul Radio that all ministers and high-ranking military generals should immediately report to the Ministry of Defense. Some of these people reported and were subsequently seized and brought down into our room or other rooms in the basement. Among those who reported to the Ministry of Defense and were brought down to our basement room were Dr. Ibrahim Majid Seraj, the former minister of education who had, some time ago, resigned from his post; Dr. Omar Muhabbat, deputy minister of education; Mr. Samad Ghaus, deputy minister of foreign affairs; Mr. Said Waheed Abdullah, acting minister of foreign affairs; and Mr. Ghausuddin Fayeq, minister of public works. Fayeq had not attended the cabinet meeting on Thursday, so he was not in the palace when the coup erupted. After he heard the announcements, he reported to the command at the Defense Ministry, was brought down to our room in the basement, and sat down next to me.

Some people were released from detention without any explanation.

April 30, 1978 (Saur 10, 1357)

Muhammad Khan Jalalar,[9] minister of commerce, was released from detention on the morning of April 30, 1978.

May 1, 1978 (Saur 11, 1357)

Dr. Ibrahim Majid Seraj, the former minister of education; Dr. Abdullah Omar, minister of health; and Dr. Omar Muhabbat, deputy minister of education, were released in the morning. Mr. Muhibbi, minister of higher education, was released in the afternoon. Dr. Majid, minister of state, and Abdul Qayeum Wardak, minister of education, were also released this day. Other people were taken out of the Ministry of Defense but were not released.

Taking People Out to Kill Them

May 3, 1978 (Saur 13, 1357)

Sometime after 9:30 in the evening, a military officer named Rafee came into the room, looked around, and asked Mr. Wafi-ullah Samiee, the minister of justice, to leave the room with him. As they were about to leave, Said Waheed Abdullah, the acting minister of foreign affairs, called out, "Say, Rafee, shall I come, too?"

---

[9] Although never a member of the Afghan Communist Party, Jalalar went on to serve in the cabinets of all the Communist regimes of both factions, Khalq and Parcham. Such a thing is generally considered to be indicative of a person with Soviet connections. Jalalar is widely believed to have been a secret Soviet agent in the pre-Communist cabinets as well as those of the People's Democratic Party of Afghanistan. Jalalar is an ethnic Turkoman, a first-generation citizen of Afghanistan. His great-uncle was a Soviet general. Following the collapse of the Communist regimes in Afghanistan, Jalalar illegally entered the United States, where his sons were established, via Canada. He did ultimately manage to obtain a residence permit.

Rafee looked back into the room and said, "Oh yes. Why don't you come out, too?" Apparently, Waheed knew Rafee from the past; Rafee had been a member of the group that had overthrown the monarchy in Daoud's 1973 coup.

A while after these men were taken out, Fayeq, who was sitting next to me, got up, knocked on the door, and told the guard standing outside, "I need to go to the restroom." The guard opened the door, and then they were both gone.

The restrooms were on the first floor, near the stairs leading up from the basement. After some time, Fayeq came back. He had a troubled look on his face. He bent close to me and slowly said, "Things do not look good. The two ministers who were taken out of our room, and some more people from other rooms, were all standing in the basement hallway close to the stairs, and there were a lot of uniformed soldiers with machine guns everywhere in the basement, on the stairs, and in the upstairs hallway."

I decided to see for myself. I went to the door, knocked, and told the guard that I needed to go to the restroom. He opened the door, said, "Come with me," and led me up the stairs. I deliberately moved rather slowly, both going up to the bathroom and coming back, so as to get a better look at who was there. I noticed that Samiee and Waheed Abdullah, who had been taken from our room, were standing near the wall in the basement hallway. Others whom I also knew were standing a little farther down the hall, and several generals and high-ranking officials were standing around. There was a somber mood and troubled faces all around. I understood what Fayeq had meant. That night, in addition to the two ministers from our room, about eleven more men from other basement rooms were taken out from the Defense Ministry, including General Abdullah Rokayai; General Abdul Qadir Khaliq; Mohammad Rahim, who had been the royal court advisor; and Mohammad Musa Shafiq, the last constitutional prime minister during Zahir Shah's reign.

Later, I found out by way of the underground grapevine that all these men were killed the same night, at a site called the Polygon, the firing range at the military base near Pul-i-Charkhi, outside the city.

I also learned that Said Waheed Abdullah was tortured, until he died, in an effort to make him talk and give his coup interrogators the details of recent trips that President Daoud had taken to Middle Eastern countries to discuss better relations with the West and peace and nonalignment in the region. We were told that at the end, the torturers were hitting Waheed in the chest with bayonets while he said to them, "Communist traitors, you are selling our country to the Soviets."

While we were kept in the basement of the Ministry of Defense, we were not allowed to have any outside contact whatsoever—not with our families or anyone else. So no one knew whether we were alive. In fact, during in the radio announcement that Watanjar had made on the night of the coup, the conspirators stated that the president *and all who were working with him* had been destroyed—which suggested that we were dead.

Communication with people in Kabul and Afghanistan was totally cut off. We were kept in the dark, and the people of Afghanistan were kept in the dark. No one knew what was really happening.

The only sources of information for the public were the official Communist-regime radio broadcasts and propaganda, some international radio news broadcasts like the BBC's, and rumors.

The conspiracy leaders were vanquishing hope and instilling fear in the hearts of the people of Afghanistan. They were trying to establish a system of government that was based on terror and fear. Apparently, some of the coup leaders who had been trained in the USSR were schooled in these methods. Also, the Soviets were providing advisors and expertise to mastermind the decisions and actions of the coup leaders and operatives.[10]

The Transfer

May 8, 1978 (Saur 18, 1357)

About ten o'clock that night, we captives felt that something was going to happen. We could hear the noise of heavy machinery and people talking outside. Heavily armed guards with machine guns came into the room and ordered us all to file out, one by one. We were taken to the rear of the ministry, which was completely dark except for the lights of what looked like weapons carriers and tanks parked at a distance. The smoke of diesel exhaust was billowing in the searchlights and headlights. There were also military buses surrounded by soldiers with machine guns.

We were ordered to proceed in single file toward the buses. When I came to a bus, the soldiers motioned for me to get in. The bus had only one door, which was on the front right side. There were several armed guards in the front and the back. I got in and sat down in a seat located near the middle of the left side.

Mr. Fayeq, who had been following me, got in and sat next to me. I peered out the window but could see nothing except the machine-gun-toting guards standing close by. It took about an hour to load the buses. Then, the bus drivers were ordered to move the buses.

---

[10] The Soviet embassy had pressured the two antagonistic Communist factions, Parcham and Khalq, into unifying in preparation for the coup and had apparently been actively involved in planning the coup, although not in its timing (it was scheduled for some months later but was triggered by the leaders' arrests). A number of the key tank commanders and air force officers involved received military training in the Soviet Union and are believed to have had ongoing ties with the KGB or the GRU, the latter of which is the Soviet (now Russian) military intelligence service.

I could not see the heavy military vehicles that were in front and back of us. I could not even count the number of buses. The soldiers had apparently loaded all the remaining detainees from the basement of the Defense Ministry into the buses. This operation was being carried out in the middle of a pitch-dark night. The whole caravan of equipment, buses, and vehicles moved slowly.

After some time, I realized that we were on the road that led to Jalalabad. Mr. Fayeq whispered in my ear, "When we reach the Pul-i-Charkhi bridge on the Kabul River, if our bus turns to the left, they will be taking us to the compound of the military base. In that case, we should say our prayers, because that will mean our end. If the bus turns to the right and crosses the bridge, they will be taking us to the Pul-i-Charkhi Prison, which means that we may have a chance to live a bit longer."

I started saying my prayers.

Since it was completely dark outside, I could neither discern nor get a fix on our whereabouts. It seemed that a long time had passed and we were still moving. Then our bus stopped. I looked out the window, trying to guess where we were.

I could hear men talking outside the bus, but I could not understand what they were saying. When our bus started to move again, I saw that the vehicles in front of it were turning to the right. After a while, I noticed that we were crossing what seemed to be a bridge. I turned to Fayeq, who was sitting beside me, and asked him, "Are we going toward the prison?"

He said, "Yes, I think so." Our bus was moving slowly. Eventually, we came close to a structure with high walls.

Our caravan of machinery, vehicles, and buses stopped. I could hear a lot of shouting. Apparently, we had reached the Pul-i-Charkhi Prison, and the prison guards were asking our command vehicle for that night's password.

Then, our bus started to move. It passed through a big gate and then through another gate, coming into a lighted courtyard. I could see that we were inside the Pul-i-Charkhi Prison, surrounded by its high walls.

Pul-i-Charkhi Prison

May 8, 1978 (Saur 18, 1357)

The transfer of us captives to Pul-i-Charkhi Prison had taken more than two hours, and it was midnight now. The caravan of tanks, weapons carriers, buses, and other vehicles had slowly brought us from the Ministry of Defense to the prison's inner yard. It was very dark. The only lighting was from vehicle headlights and searchlights on top of the military machines, which were shining toward our buses and blinding us, so we could not see the prison buildings.

I could hear people talking outside the buses, probably the contingent that had brought us from the Defense Ministry talking with the guards and officers in charge of the prison. It was a dreadful situation.

I didn't know where they were taking us or what they would do to us.

After some time, soldiers pointed their guns at us, commanded us to get out of the buses, and then herded us, single file, into the building.

I was led through a corridor, up concrete stairs to the second floor, and into a small room—a cell that had a solid steel door with a porthole for the guards to look in.

The prison construction had not been completed, and the unfinished concrete floor was rough and strewn with rubble and debris—bricks, gravel, sand, lime, and dirt. There was no chair, bench, or stool—no furniture of any kind.

One by one, three other ministers were brought into the room: Ghausuddin Fayeq, the minister of public works; Kareem Ataii, the minister of communications; and Juma Mohammad, the minister of water and power.

The steel door was shut with a clang and was locked after each man entered. With nothing to sit on, we all stood around, not knowing what to do next. I realized that our captors had put four engineers in one tiny cell; it was probably made for single occupancy, but now there were four of us standing there.

We were still wearing the suits that we had worn to the cabinet meeting ten days before. They were now wrinkled and grubby. We stood there, thinking that perhaps we were in a staging area to be taken to some other location. But that did not happen.

Mr. Fayeq soon revealed a nervous problem: he was apparently claustrophobic. He went to the door, banged on it, and called for the guard.

When the guard eventually peeped in through the small porthole, Fayeq begged him to keep the door open. The guard refused, but Fayeq kept banging on the door and begging the guard not to lock it.

The rest of us in the cell asked Fayeq to stop, telling him that it was no use to bang on the door because the guard would obviously not leave it open. After an hour or so, we managed to persuade Fayeq not to bang on the steel door. After that, he just stood at the door and looked into the corridor through the small porthole.

After a long time standing around, I told my friends, "I don't know what you fellows are going to do, but I'm going to stretch out on the floor and get some sleep." I had a feeling that we were going to spend more time in that cell, and I was right. In my past fieldwork as an engineer, I had trained myself to be able to sleep in the desert, on dirt and rough surfaces. I had disciplined myself and learned how to cope with very rough conditions.

But the situation that I was in now—herded in the middle of the night into a partially constructed, unfurnished little prison cell with three other men—was one that none of us could have prepared for. Still, I stretched out on the floor, put a piece of brick under my head, closed my eyes, and tried to sleep. After the long night passed, my cell mates and I could see glimmers of daylight.

One thing that immediately affected us was the nonexistence of restrooms, which we found out about when we needed to relieve ourselves, banged on the door, and asked the guards to take us to a restroom. They told us that there were none, that they would have to take us outside the building for this.

When we asked them to take us outside, they told us that it was not possible because the outside latrines were being used by female prisoners.

We did not know it then, but we later learned that the female prisoners were women, children, and babies of the large extended royal family who had been brought from their homes in the city. Among them were several members of President Daoud's family who had not been at the presidential palace and thus had escaped the slaughter there. Among them was Princess Bibi Zohra, the king's sister, who was the wife of Sardar Naim.

As mentioned previously, construction of the prison barracks had not been completed. The cell that I was in had one small, steel-barred window placed high and facing north. In order to look out, one had to climb on something, but there was no stool or table in the cell.

Life is full of ironies. As minister of mines and industries, I had known before that a new prison was under construction to the east of Kabul City.

One day after a cabinet meeting, the minister of the interior, Qadir Nuristani, asked me, "Minister Assifi, have you seen the new prison that we are constructing?"

I said, "No, I haven't."

He said, "Would you like to see it?"

I said, "That's a good idea."

He said, "Do you have time to see it now? I'm going there to see how the work is progressing."

I said, "Okay. I'll call my office and tell them that I'll be late coming back so they can cancel my meetings scheduled for this afternoon."

Qadir took me to the prison construction site in his German-made jeep. Though ministers were entitled to drivers, he drove himself. When he started the jeep, I commented jokingly, "Mr. Minister, you were once a traffic officer, so I assume that you know the traffic rules quite well. But are you a good driver?"

He said, "Trust me, Mr. Assifi. I'll get you back to your office safely."

When we got to the Pul-i-Charkhi bridge and crossed the river, I could see the high walls of the new prison. Qadir drove me around the construction site, showing me the different blocks, the barracks, and the general layout. Some buildings were under construction, and others looked, at least from the outside, as though they were partially completed.

Qadir said, "This prison is where prisoners will be trained in different trades.

There are going to be literacy and vocational training and school facilities. There will also be gymnasiums, sports grounds, a health clinic, and a hospital as part of the prison complex. The concept is that the prisoners will be given a chance to learn trades, and hopefully they will become better and useful citizens by the time they are released."

I said, "Mr. Minister, this is a very well-designed facility. Who was your architect?"

He said, "Well, we did not design it. We got the plans and specifications from the United States of America."

I asked, "How did you do that?"

"When President Daoud was prime minister," he said, "the US government invited him to visit America. In planning his itinerary, he asked to see a modern prison during his trip in the United States. This request was granted. After visiting the site of one of the modern prisons, he then asked his hosts, the US government, for a copy of the architectural and construction plans for that prison. After coming back to Afghanistan, he gave this set of plans to the Ministry of the Interior. Many years later, when he became the president of Afghanistan, he remembered this. And when I became the minister of the interior, he ordered me to try to find these plans and bring them to him. I found them in the ministry archives.

"Daoud told me, 'Mr. Minister of the Interior, include the construction of a prison in your plans. I will instruct the other related ministers to cooperate with you in finding a suitable location for the construction of a modern prison on the basis of these plans. Good luck!'"

After we visited the construction site, Qadir took me back to the high walls and main gate of the prison and then guided me to a nearby building, a four-story masonry and concrete structure with small, steel-barred windows. He said, "This building, block no. 1, has better accommodations: one cell for one prisoner, with an attached bathroom. There are also some larger cells suitable for about ten prisoners."

He showed me several rooms at the entrance and said that they were for the prison command offices. We walked through the building and saw other sections and the small, single-occupancy cells that were still under construction. The steel doors had not been installed at that time, but when I looked into several of these rooms, I had a strange premonition.

I told Qadir, "Mr. Minister, I have a feeling that someday I may be in one of these cells!"

He laughed and said, "Mr. Assifi, you have a very rich imagination. Don't worry. That won't happen!"

But now it was happening—and Qadir Nuristani was not with us. He had been in the corridor of the presidential offices with President Daoud and his family on the day after the coup, when the conspirators' thugs entered the corridor and opened machine-gun fire. Their intent was to kill everyone who was there. However, it was later discovered that three people in the corridor were still alive, although they were badly wounded and bleeding heavily: the president's daughter-in-law, Gulalai Malikyar; one of Daoud's grandsons; and Qadir Nuristani.

Qadir, bleeding badly, was denied treatment in a hospital and shortly thereafter died. And now, contrary to his assurance, I was inside his still-unfinished Pul-i-Charkhi Prison. I felt that my strange premonition was becoming a reality. And in fact, on the first night in Pul-i-Charkhi Prison, when I was taken to cell no. 14 on the second floor of political block no. 1, I had a feeling that I had seen the room before.

The next morning, several hours passed before we were allowed to go down to the latrines in the backyard of the prison to relieve ourselves. Our captors didn't allow the men to go out until after the female prisoners were taken back to their rooms in the western section of the building.

On the eastern side of the prison yard, the soldiers had dug a number of crude latrines—just holes in the ground. They had curtained these holes with broken wood planks left over from concrete forms. The prisoners had to line up to take their turns using these holes. In a corner of the yard, there were two old barrels filled with well water for washing up, but there were no buckets, nothing with which to scoop up water from the barrels. I saw several cans laying on the ground. We used these to get water from the barrels to wash our hands. While we waited in line, we saw other prisoners who were allowed to come out to the prison yard, but we could not speak to them.

No Communication Whatsoever

All around us, there were guards armed with machine guns. They told us that prisoners were not allowed to speak to one another.

We were told that absolutely no communication whatsoever, or by any means, was permitted among the prisoners or between the prisoners and people outside of the prison. No paper, no pen or pencil, and no books were allowed inside the prison. We soon learned that this rule was enforced by way of severe punishment for those who tried to communicate with anyone either inside or outside the prison. One who disobeyed this rule was punished with solitary confinement—or, in some cases, by the imprisonment of a member of the violator's family. Later on, we heard that some prisoners had even been executed for disobeying these rules.

Since we were cut off from the outside world, I did not know the situation of my wife, our children, my father and mother, and the rest of my family—or how they were. And my family did not know if I was alive or had been killed. If I had not been killed, they had no information about where I was being kept. The only thing they knew was that we cabinet officials had been kept for a period of time in the basement of the Ministry of Defense.

On the other hand, we who had been present in the basement of the Ministry of Defense knew a little about all the others, those who had been slaughtered in the corridor and the distinguished figures who had been taken out of the basement on the night of May 3, 1978.

We never saw those men again. They were taken out of the basement to be tortured and killed somewhere else.

In response to questions from foreign journalists who had arrived in Kabul to cover the story, the leaders of the new Communist regime mentioned the names of some of these men and claimed that they were killed because they resisted government forces. But we knew that they were lying.

At first, our families did not know who was dead and who was still alive, but through underground information channels, they found out that some had been killed and others had been transferred to Pul-i-Charkhi Prison.

After I was transferred to Pul-i-Charkhi Prison, families and relatives of missing people started gathering outside the prison gate, asking about their family members in the hope that they might be still alive.

Very soon, the number of inquirers grew so large that alarmed coup leaders decided to bring in soldiers, heavy military equipment, and helicopter gunships to disperse them by force. Eventually, they made a list of those being asked about, checked inside Pul-i-Charkhi Prison, and then informed the relatives who came every day to wait for information outside the prison gate.

The families of prisoners were told that once every two weeks, on alternate Tuesdays, they would be allowed to bring something that their imprisoned relative might need. A family member was allowed to ask a guard to find out what his or her imprisoned relative needed. Thus, only orally, and through a guard, was communication to or from the prisoner and his family allowed.

No written communication was permitted. Every item brought for a prisoner was opened and inspected by the prison command; only then was it permitted to be given to the prisoner.

Eventually, this became a routine. When my wife learned that I was in prison, she sent me some clothing—loose Afghan shirts and pants, and a warm *chapan* (a loose, quilted overcoat). With these, she included a shaving kit, which, surprisingly, I was allowed to receive. It contained a small pair of scissors, which would prove to be extremely useful. The rule of "no direct contact or communication" also applied within the prison, but prisoners found ways to pass information to each other without the guards' knowledge.

An Unbearable Circumstance

Everything was becoming unbearable because of the reign of terror inside the prison and in the outside world.

The guards kept on bringing in more prisoners and taking others out. At night, we could hear the cries of prisoners who were being tortured. Most ominously, at night the corridor lights were turned off, and then we heard the sound of gradually increasing footsteps in the corridor—footsteps not of just one person, but of several.

We all knew that they were coming to take some prisoners out of their cells. Then, we would hear the clanging of steel doors being opened and shut, but we could not determine which cell the guards had entered.

And then there was absolute silence.

The next morning, a rumor went around that some prisoners had been released. But why would the guards have to come at night and turn the lights out to release them?

We later learned the names of those who had been taken out, and we gradually came to realize that those who were taken out this way never made it to their homes. They were taken out of their cells either to be tortured—in the prison or somewhere else—or to be transported to the nearby execution grounds. Who would be next? The anticipation of painful torture and the expectation of death at any moment was pervasive and unbearable.

Terror has strange and devastating effects on people. Being constantly terrorized erodes one's strength and courage.

To my dismay, I saw some men whom I had thought of as pillars of strength and courage gradually dissolve into pitiable, whimpering objects.

I was in a deadly environment in the prison. The smell of death was all around me. Although this was an unbearable situation, I still had the ability to stretch out on the floor, say my prayers, and fall asleep. And a strange phenomenon was happening in my dreams: they were in Technicolor, and they were beautiful. I would see myself floating out of the prison, flying around, going to many places, and seeing many things.

I also dreamed of possible events in the prison. The strangest part was that a week or two afterward, some of the events that I had seen in my dreams really happened.

Sleeping on a Concrete Floor

We prisoners were each given two very thin gray blankets and a bag with clumps of cotton inside to make a mattress for sleeping on the concrete floor. Each prisoner was issued a metal plate to use as a dish. No forks, spoons, or knives were allowed, because they could be made into a weapon.

Every morning, each prisoner was issued a loaf of dark bread that was baked at the Kabul silo built years earlier by the Russians. At noon and evening, pots of food were brought to the corridor outside our cells.

One person from each cell would take the "dishes" to the corridor, to bring his cell mates soup that looked like dishwater. Rice was issued twice weekly.

The soup sometimes would have long strands of what looked like camel or oxen meat in it. Occasionally, a potato would be found floating in a lucky one's dish.

This food was always cold. Given its qualities, it was very hard to swallow. A fellow prisoner told me that I could heat up my food on a candle stove. He told me how to make one: you put holes in the side of an empty can to let air come in, and then you put a candle inside and light it. I went to work immediately and made a candle stove out of an empty powdered-milk can. We in my cell could then put our plates on top of the can and heat our food. It worked very well.

The only problem with the candle heater was that the plates or pots on top would get awfully black from the candle soot, but that was not a big problem compared to the problem of eating cold, inedible soup.

I believe that what kept us alive in the prison was the loaf of dark whole-wheat bread that we got every morning. The crust was edible, and the inside, which was not quite baked, could be molded into statuettes or chess pieces, depending on one's artistic prowess.

More Prisoners Are Brought In

Every night, two to three hundred new prisoners were brought into Pul-i-Charkhi.

At night, prisoners on the top floor could see the lights of a caravan of vehicles moving east on the Kabul–Jalalabad road.

The caravan would split in two, some vehicles going north toward the military grounds, and the others coming toward Pul-i-Charkhi Prison.

We learned later that those in the other vehicles that turned off and went to the military base were taken there for execution.

All through the night, we could hear the cries of the new prisoners who were being tortured. I called this "the human grinding machine." These men were tortured to extract admissions of treason. As time went on, we learned that the prison authorities did not have sufficient staff and equipment to torture the large number of people who were sent to the prison, so they made it easier for themselves by taking half of the prisoners who were brought in straightaway to the Polygon execution grounds at the military base.

May 15, 1978 (Saur 25, 1357)

On this morning, I saw Roshandil, the former governor of Ghazni Province, sitting under the high wall in the backyard of our block no. 1, which was also called "the political block."

Governor Roshandil was the son of Professor Roshandil, a well-known and enlightened Islamic scholar who had been my theology teacher at Habibia High School, Afghanistan's oldest high school, which had an American principal and American teachers.

I slowly walked close to Roshandil and said, "Salaam." He looked very tired and haggard, with bloodshot eyes. He looked up at me and tried to rise. I said, "Governor, please don't get up. But when did they bring you here?"

He said, "They brought me several days ago, but they only allowed me to get out with the other prisoners today."

Mr. Roshandil was about ten years my senior. He had a good reputation as a governor and for his other work as a teacher and a civil servant.

June 5, 1978 (Jauza 15, 1357)

A joint delegation from the government and the prison command visited the Pul-i-Charkhi Prison cells and prisoners. They issued an order that all radios, cassette recorders, books, holy books, prayer rugs, prayer beads, and other items that prisoners might have brought with them into the prison be confiscated. They also ordered the prison commander to collect all the cotton bag "mattresses" that had been issued. It was also stipulated that prisoners be given only two very thin blankets—one to sleep on, and the other to sleep under. The joint delegation had commented, "This is not Hotel Intercontinental."

June 16, 1978 (Jauza 26, 1357)

Lights Off, Taking Prisoners Out to Kill Them

About ten o'clock the previous night, the lights were turned off. We could hear the heavy footsteps of several people in the corridor. The sound grew louder and then stopped. It sounded as if the people had stopped in front of our cell. The horror of turning the lights off and then coming into the cells to take one or more prisoners out to the slaughter grounds had been going on for some time.

We would not know until the next day who had been taken. Earlier, I had thought to establish a signal between those in my cell and the men in the adjacent cell, whom I knew.

We agreed on a signal: one thump on the wall if the guards did not take anyone out of the cell; two thumps if they took someone out.

On this night, we heard the door of the next cell being opened and then, after a brief moment, being closed.

Then came the signal: two thumps. Someone had been taken out.

Our cell door did not open, but we could hear footsteps and other doors being opened and shut.

We realized that the guards had taken several people out of their cells. It was a night of horror and dread. The omen of death hung in the air, stifling all of us.

After what seemed to us like years, the process appeared to end for now. The lights were back on in the corridor. But the question remained in my minds: Who had they taken, and how many of them did I know?

Eventually, I mustered some courage and knocked on my cell door. The guard appeared at the porthole, asking why I was knocking. I said that I felt sick and needed to go to the outhouse. Actually, my aim was to find a chance to pass the neighboring cell. The guard said, "Wait a minute," and disappeared.

After a while, he came back and opened the door for me. I went down the corridor and walked down the stairs to the first floor, with the guard behind me. He stood at the entrance as I went down the steps to the backyard and walked toward the latrines.

The backyard was lit by a few bulbs hanging from wires. I took my time, trying to observe my surroundings and hear the sounds outside the walls.

I came back toward the entrance, walked up the steps, went inside, and climbed up the stairs to the second floor. The guard was not following behind me.

I entered the corridor where our cell was located and went to the door of the cell next to ours. The door was unlocked, and I entered. Inside, Wasefi, the minister of agriculture, was sitting on his blanket.

He looked up at me. I said, "Whom did they take out?"

He pointed at the empty blanket on the floor and said, "Akbar-jan. His glasses are still here. May God Almighty have mercy on him!"

I had known Akbar-jan from long ago. A northerner, he was a career diplomat who had worked as a civil employee at the Ministry of Foreign Affairs all his life. He was highly educated, had a law degree from Kabul University, and had done postgraduate work in international affairs, law, literature, and social sciences during his tenure as a diplomat. A man of great integrity and high moral character, Akbar-jan was respected by all who knew him. President Daoud knew of his work and background and had appointed him as the president's chief of staff.

We never saw Akbar-jan again.

The next morning, we learned that Lala Baz Mohammad, a longtime friend who was the manager of President Daoud's household, and three of his sons—Adjutant Majid, the governor of Chardi, and a younger son—had also been taken out of their cells that night.

We never saw them again, either, later learning that they had been taken to the Polygon—the firing range at the military grounds—and shot.

One day after Akbar-jan had been taken out of the prison and killed, I heard the prison guards calling his name loudly in the corridor, asking for him to take what his family had brought for him. This was the day when prisoners' families were allowed to bring clean clothes and other things in a bag for their imprisoned family members. But these items were brought for Akbar-jan after he had been executed—and it happened several more times.

I realized that Akbar-jan's family did not know that he was dead.

Someone else may have been taking Akbar-jan's items and sending dirty clothes back to his family to have them washed. I could not determine who it was, whether one of the prisoners or a prison guard.

As time went on, the repetition of this incident further horrified me. I imagined a scenario in which I, too, was killed and my wife did not know it.

I thought, *If I am not alive, my wife should know it. Otherwise, she will be sending me clean clothes and other things and getting back dirty clothes, thinking that I am still alive.* I didn't want her to suffer that way. It was necessary for me to establish communication with my wife so that when my messages stopped, she would know that I was no longer in prison and alive.

The question was, how could I send and receive messages?

We prisoners were not allowed to get notes or write to our families, not even to tell them that we had received what they brought for us or to mention what we needed. Letters, notes, and any other kind of communication with family members or anyone else on the outside were prohibited. The cost for breaking this rule was the pain of the most extreme punishment.

The prison commander and guards thoroughly searched all the items that were brought to us and those we sent back. Even the seams of clothing were torn open and searched for hidden notes.

I thought about this problem very carefully, trying to find a way to communicate. How could I outsmart the prison command and the guards without endangering my family members or myself?

A desperate, critical, but well-thought-out resolve had to be made. Since the guards always searched our rooms, our meager belongings, the items that were brought to us every fifteen days, and those items we sent back, I decided not to take the suicidal chance of writing notes.

I needed to devise a way to communicate, one that presented the minimum danger of being caught. But how could I communicate without any means of communication? Moreover, there were many obstacles, seeing as we were not allowed to possess, and therefore did not have access to, any electronic devices or gadgets.

As mentioned before, our cells, our clothing, and any items that were brought in or that we sent back were constantly searched and carefully inspected. In addition, we were not allowed to have any paper, pens, or pencils.

Our only permitted contact was at the fifteen-day intervals when our families were allowed to bring us items besides clean clothes, such as medicine, and when we sent back dirty clothes and empty containers or bottles to be refilled.

We were only permitted to send brief oral messages to our families, and we had to do this via the guards—messages like, "Tell my family that I need some cold medicine." The guards were not supposed to deliver long messages or any other information that was related to us.

I could devise a method, but how could I let my wife know about it? To begin with, I thought it safer to use a method that would not be hidden. I chose to communicate openly and, so to speak, right under the guards' noses. I did have one favorable thing going for me: my wife was a very clever and intelligent person. She used to joke that (using an Afghan saying) she could "read notes that are written on the back of a paper." I thought, *Maybe. If not the back of a paper, then how about notes on the front of a paper?*

My first step was to secretly inform her that I was thinking about how to communicate with her. No method without any risk whatsoever was possible, but maybe I could devise a way that would involve minimum risk.

Secret Communication

My wife had learned that I was not getting much food in the prison, so in the bag that she had previously brought, she included some vitamin pills and a bottle of cherry syrup that she had made herself. This was the key to my method.

In the bag that I sent back, I included the empty cherry-syrup bottle. I showed the guard the empty bottle and asked him to tell my wife to send me some more cherry syrup next time. I told him to tell my wife that the top of the bottle was very dirty and that she should make sure it was clean and secured tightly.

In fact, there was nothing wrong with the top of the cherry-syrup bottle. As my wife would know, it was clean and tight when I got it the last time. This was my first signal to her.

The prison guards who were assigned to our block had been trained as security guards, and most of them were not Communists. They were fully aware that the political prisoners under their charge were highly educated and respectable people. As a result, during the two or three months that we had been in the prison, our relationship with the guards was very good. They treated us in a respectful manner.

But they were afraid of the prison commander, and they continuously heard the Communist propaganda from government radio and television stations. They also knew, having witnessed it themselves, that many prisoners were tortured and executed on a daily and nightly basis.

So, the prison guards were very careful about how they treated us. They treated us respectfully but were very careful that the prison commander did not know of this. It was a situation of touch-and-go or maybe life-or-death for them.

The guard assigned to our cell was called Sawtinman Baseer. (*Sawtinman* indicates a low police rank, rather like *corporal*.) Very often, he would come and stand in the doorway of our cell, constantly looking behind him toward the corridor.

When he was sure that no one else was watching, he would pass on a bit of information. Sometimes, he was helpful in certain ways if, under the circumstances, he could be. For example, I had earlier asked him if he could bring me some pieces of torn paper cement bags. I told him that I would put them under the blanket on which I slept on the bare concrete floor to reduce the moisture. The dampness of the concrete had caused most of us to suffer from arthritic pain in the back and joints.

Baseer complied with my request. He also brought me a pencil. I cut the pencil into six pieces, keeping one piece for myself and distributing the rest to other prisoners.

Then I proceeded with my plan. First, with the scissors from my shaving kit, I cut about a two-inch-square piece of cement-bag paper, and then I wrote on it with my one-inch-long pencil: "I will begin sending you messages on top of the paper bags that you send my clean clothes and other items in. The message will be in the form of numbers based on the English alphabet. A = 1, B = 2, C = 3, and so on. The numbers will be written next to each other to form a word. The next word will be below the first one, and so on. At the end of the sentence I will put a line and then add the numbers for a total amount. Anyone looking at these numbers will think that it is a purchase list. You can use the same method in answering my previous message. I will periodically change the method of communication and will inform you ahead of time." I folded the two-inch-square message tightly until it was about a quarter inch in size. I put this small package into a thin plastic sheet I had saved from the bags of vitamins my wife had sent me, and I sealed the sides with a candle flame so the tiny packet would not get stained. Then, I took off the top cap of the cherry-syrup bottle and pried out the paperboard liner. I put my tiny package underneath it, with a lot of cherry syrup under, on top of, and around it, before replacing the inner liner to cover the note.

I put some more syrup around the cap and tightened it on the top of the bottle. After smearing on some more syrup, and I cleaned the bottle.

When I gave Baseer the bag with my dirty clothes and the empty cherry-syrup bottle, I told the guard to tell my wife that I would like some more of the cherry syrup. I also asked him to tell her that she should make sure that the top is clean and secured tightly.

I had to wait another fifteen days to find out whether a secret communication channel between me and my wife could be established. Would my wife catch the implications of the dirty cherry-bottle cap?

Meanwhile, the atmosphere in the prison was growing more ominous. The torture and killing of prisoners had become routine. Everyone was expecting to be taken out at any time to be slaughtered.

I felt a sense of hopelessness growing in the minds and bodies of prisoners who had been there longer. They were haggard and losing weight. Their faces pale, the prisoners were like walking dead—I not excluded.

The Enemies of Revolution?

The number of prisoners in the blocks was increasing night by night.

I saw some new prisoners during the daily fifteen-to-twenty-minute period when we were allowed out of our block to relieve ourselves and then clean up with water from the barrels. The new prisoners showed signs of having been tortured. They sat meekly by a wall in the sunshine, not knowing how long it would be before they were taken back to the torture chamber or the execution ground.

I was hesitant to contact the other prisoners, especially the new ones; it was dangerous.

I had to be very cautious. I would speak with these new prisoners only when guards were not around or when I could act in a way that was not obvious or noticeable. When I found an opportunity, I sat next to one of the newcomers and asked questions such as the following:

- How are things outside the prison?
- Why were you brought to the prison?
- How many of your group were killed right away? How many are imprisoned?
- What did they do to you? Did they torture you? What kind of torture?
- Do you need anything? Are you in pain? ("I can give you some pain medicine, if you want," I said at these times.)

Most of the new prisoners did not speak. They were frightened and did not trust anyone they did not know. They had been told by the prison guards or those who had tortured them not to talk to anyone.

After a few days, some of the new prisoners got to know me and trusted me enough to confide in me and tell me some of their stories. They told me how things were at their places of work and what was going on in the city and the country at large.

Invariably, they offered some words of advice for me based on their own experiences.

As I got to know more of them, I was surprised when hearing of the backgrounds of the newer prisoners who were brought in. Unlike those of us who were the first prisoners, few of the newcomers were officials or held significant positions. Most were from the middle class or working class and of the younger generation. They came from all sectors of the Afghan population, from the countryside as well as the city. Many of them were from the urban working class or the rural peasantry. Actually, I could not identify a large number from any specific segment of society.

I was trying to find a certain identifiable category that could match the rhetoric of the Communists' ideology. Which people in Afghan society did the Parchamis and Khalqis imprison, torture, and kill? *If they imprisoned only one or two elements of Afghan society, then the rest would not have been terrorized into submission.*

The only group of people that I could see in the prison who might have fit the category that Communist propaganda and rhetoric had in the past identified as the "enemies of revolution" were some generals, ministers from past governments, and members of Zahir Shah's extended family. Many of these were very hardworking and honest people serving their country.

But how about the students, teachers, clerks, janitors, ordinary workers, farmers, small shopkeepers, and other ordinary people who constituted the majority of the prisoners in Pul-i-Charkhi?

The Communists had said, "We shall make a revolution that will shed the blood of capitalists, rich merchants, big landowners and landlords, and the like. We shall make rivers flow full of the blood of these parasites who have been sucking the blood of our society. These are the people who have enslaved Afghans and ruled for centuries over the hardworking nation of workers and farmers of Afghanistan."

But I could not see many capitalists, rich merchants, big landowners, or landlords among the prisoners. Instead, in the mass of prisoners that I saw in Pul-i-Charkhi, I saw the very people for whom the Communists claimed that their promised revolution, or now their coup d'état, was being perpetrated. They were imprisoning, torturing, and executing the very same people whom they had identified as the beneficiaries of revolution.

So, what was going on? I had little information about events outside of the prison. I asked myself, *What could be the reasons for what they are doing?*

As time went on, I came to some conclusions:

1. The Parchamis and Khalqis, contrary to their own propaganda, had soon been forced to realize that the Afghans did not accept their ideology or their rule. They also realized that now they had to govern millions of people and a country.

2. They benefited enormously from Soviet experience and direction: the establishment of the Soviet Union by brutal methods in Russia, i.e., the killing of a large number of Russians by Lenin and Stalin and their associates. (I knew that it was estimated that the Russians lost more people at Stalin's hands than they lost in World War II.)

3. They were supported fully by Soviet expertise and advice on how to subjugate a nation that would not accept materialistic and Communist ideologies, based on the following things:

   a) They used tested methods from before the establishment of the USSR, such as "carrot and stick," and experimental scientific methods such as Pavlov's experiments.

   b) They drew upon the Soviet Union's experience in subjugating neighboring countries, including the countries of Eastern Europe after World War II.

   c) They were not imprisoning "capitalists, rich merchants, big landowners, and landlords" as they had threatened to do, because somebody had to make money. They had to have financial resources to run a government. They needed taxes and customs duties from trade. In other words, they needed some financial milking cows in the country.

I concluded that the Communist invaders were meeting resistance from all sectors of Afghan society, so they felt that they had to imprison and crush people from a complete cross-section of Afghan society.

Their proclaimed objectives before the coup were little more than propaganda, which was needed to persuade dissatisfied young people to believe those claims and cooperate with the Soviets for a successful coup. Once the coup had been carried out and the Communists had control of the government, their main objective was to stay in control and subjugate the Afghan people by all means possible, which meant imprisoning, torturing, and killing anyone who questioned or opposed them, as the Soviets had successfully done.

Judging from the information that I gathered from these prisoners, and knowing the fact that an increasingly large number of soldiers as well as ordinary folks were being imprisoned and killed, I realized that there was a general uprising in the country in towns and rural areas alike. Opposition to the new regime was occurring in military units, too.

One day, the commanding warden of Pul-i-Charkhi, Said Abdullah (known to the prisoners as the Bloodsucker), called all the prisoners from their cells to come downstairs and enter the backyard of our block. Once we arrived, I saw guards armed with machine guns all around us, as well as some stationed on rooftops and other high perches. At that point, Said Abdullah gave a speech.

Fourteen Lakhs

He told us, "The people's democratic government is fully aware of everything that is going on in the country and is in full control. There are some elements who are employed by the West and the dirty imperialist American CIA. The government is fully aware and in control, and will destroy all these enemies of Afghanistan.

"Our great brothers of the Soviet Union are in full support of the People's Democratic Republic of Afghanistan." He repeated several times during his speech the number of fourteen lakhs.[11] Why was he using a specific number? Was this a number from his own dumb brain, or had he heard it from higher-ups in the party?

I finally realized that this number more or less represented 10 percent of the estimated population of Afghanistan at that time. One lakh is equal to a hundred thousand, so fourteen lakhs would be $14 \times 100,000 = 1,400,000$, or 1.4 million, which would be 10 percent of 14 million, which was the estimated population of Afghanistan at that time.

Said Abdullah was telling us that the Communists would be willing to get rid of 90 percent of the population in order to establish their control and rule in Afghanistan. The warden did not have brains enough to have figured this out by himself. He had to have learned it from others in the People's Democratic Party of Afghanistan (PDPA).

Wherever this figure had come from, it was horrifying. It demonstrated how murderous the Communists actually were; they were telling us that they would not stop at anything to control and rule the country. To accomplish that, they would go to the length of wiping out 90 percent of the population!

So, where were those idealistic objectives of the revolution? Did revolution mean killing 90 percent of the people?

Ideological Propaganda

The prison command brought TV sets and put them at the end of the corridors in each block during the evening news hours. They wanted

---

[11] In a numbering system widely used in South Asia, from Afghanistan and Pakistan to Indonesia, one lakh is equal to a hundred thousand.

the prisoners to listen to government propaganda and indoctrination, with which they were trying to persuade the Afghans that they had carried out the coup only to get rid of Daoud's government. They put up a propaganda façade to persuade the people that they were not Communists. They were trying very hard to get the Afghans to accept their rule and not see their true colors. These were all tactics to buy time for them to become entrenched and gain full control of the government and the country.

However, it had not taken very long for the people of Afghanistan to see them for what they were and recognize that the purpose of the coup had been to establish a Communist government based on the Soviet.

The following were some telltale facts:

The two factions, which had buried their antagonisms long enough to join together for the coup, called themselves the People's Democratic Party of Afghanistan; "People's Democratic Parties" in other countries were Communists.

The PDPA government was immediately recognized by the USSR and the Soviet bloc countries in Europe and elsewhere.

The government was organized along the same lines as the Soviet Union and other Communist countries, with a politburo, a central committee, and so forth.

The PDPA leadership was made up of recognized Communists. Popular resistance to the Communist regime was increasing day by day. Even in prison, through underground channels, we heard rumors of general uprisings in different parts of the country on a daily basis. No matter how much the PDPA tortured, imprisoned, and killed, it did not help them; the people of Afghanistan did not accept their rule.

The increasing number of prisoners who were brought into Pul-i-Charkhi Prison from different military units indicated that soldiers in those units were trying to organize countercoups to overthrow the Communist regime. Many of these men were executed right away; others were tortured to extract statements admitting their participation in these countercoups and then were killed.

Only a few lucky ones remained to live a little longer.

Meanwhile, I gathered information about our block no. 1 for my notes through my own observations and contact with other prisoners and some of the prison staff. All of my information regarding the other blocks in the prison was obtained through personal contact and observation, or via the information channels that we prisoners gradually developed with the prison staff. All of our information came from these sources, as we had no other.

The government radio and television stations were spreading the regime's propaganda. We knew that that the propaganda was not true, but we could not be sure about the information we got from prisoners and other underground sources. It had to be validated. This was unnerving.

We needed to find some other, reliable sources of information that would give us a better picture of what was really happening. And we needed a whiff of good news to help us keep alive a glimmer of hope in the face of an unfathomable future; it was like being trapped in a dark tunnel and searching for a point of light, from some opening that might promise escape.

July 21, 1978 (Saratan 30, 1357)

A day with some good news: I learned that between 9:30 and 10:00 the previous night, eighteen army personnel and air force pilots had been released from Pul-i-Charkhi. Later, I found out that my brother-in-law, Major General Karim Ali, a man of high moral character and integrity who was a highly trained and well-qualified staff officer and an army engineer, was one of them, and he had gotten home safely.

In view of all the horrors that were going on in Pul-i-Charkhi Prison, it was a temporary relief to hear that a few prisoners had been released. However, the respite did not last very long.

July 22, 1978 (Saratan 31, 1357)

The following day, at about ten o'clock at night, two prisoners were taken out of their cells. We could hear that something was going on; doors were being opened and closed. For some reason, the corridor was not darkened this time.

I looked into the corridor through the porthole in our door and saw the face of Mir Abdul Rashid, the chief of police of Kandahar. He saw me and raised his hands in a gesture, asking me to pray for him. I responded by raising my hands and saying a few words of prayer for him. I thought to myself that, since the lights in the corridor were on, hopefully whoever was being taken out would be released and sent home like the soldiers released the night before had been.

Mir Abdul Rashid was an excellent, well-educated police officer. He held degrees from the Afghan Police Academy as well as police training centers in several other countries. He was honest and hardworking. Everyone who knew him had words of praise for his moral character and integrity.

After Rashid was taken out, I tried to find out whether he had gone home, but all my efforts were futile. Sadly, I came to the conclusion that he had been killed.

Why Kill Salah Ghazi?

The next morning, I learned that Salah Ghazi, a cousin of the king whose father, Sardar Shah Mahmud Khan,[12] had once been prime minister, had also been taken out the night before. Further inquiry showed that he, too, never arrived home.

---

[12] Shah Mahmud, one of the king's uncles, served as prime minister from 1946 to 1953.

Salah Ghazi was one of several members of the royal family who were with us in what was called "political block no. 1"—the east wing of block no. 1. We constituted a group made up of high-ranking government officials, cabinet ministers like me who had been brought from the Ministry of Defense, military generals, members of the royal family, and others who were brought from different locales in Kabul.

Women and children of the extended royal family were also imprisoned in political block no. 1, but in the west wing. Children of all ages, including some babies, were held there with the women. Since the times for the use of latrines and outside facilities were staggered, we men in political block no. 1 never saw the women.

Salah Ghazi's wife and their three-year-old son were held in the west wing. One day, I came back to my cell earlier than usual and, as I passed Salah Ghazi's cell, I, saw, through a half-open door Salah lying on his blanket. His son was there playing on his chest. To this day, I have never forgotten that scene. Salah Ghazi was killed several days after that.

But why did the regime leaders choose to kill Salah Ghazi just then? Why did they single him out from the other members of the royal family?

Earlier, we had heard that a delegation from Amnesty International was going to visit the prison. The warden of Pul-i-Charkhi decided to isolate the members of the royal family, take them from the various cells where they were held, and put them all together in one or two cells for the occasion.

We also heard that these people were told not to complain about the actual conditions in the prison and to say only nice things about the treatment that they received.

The Amnesty delegation was accompanied by people from the newly organized secret police intelligence agency. Obviously, these agents were there to make sure that the prisoners behaved as they had been instructed. Later, when we found out that Salah Ghazi never made it home, we wondered whether he had perhaps said something during the Amnesty visit. Understandably, when the other members of the royal family were asked about it, they were reluctant to say anything.

We were all being terrorized into absolute submission.

Although I was not sure whether I could mentally and physically survive the circumstances of the prison, I nevertheless decided to keep notes on a daily basis about what was happening there. I knew that it was extremely risky. Of course, prison rules forbade any communication—or any writing at all. Our rooms were constantly searched for the forbidden paper, pen, or pencil, or any indication of contact.

On the other hand, as the saying goes, "Where there is a will, there is a way!"

I had the will, and I started to study the possibilities and try to find ways.

What I am writing now is the result of that resolve, and of my making it alive out of Pul-i-Charkhi and Afghanistan.

Sometimes, we prisoners knew about what was happening via the clandestine information channels before events became publicly known or announcements were made. For instance, when a number of prisoners from military units in Kabul and around the country were brought into the prison, and later on, after the Khalqi and Parchami factions began fighting each other and some well-known Communists and even Communist government ministers were brought in, we found out about the internal coup attempts within the party before anyone else in the outside world knew of them.

A Summary of Events to Date

It may be useful here to briefly review the general situation in Kabul and Pul-i-Charkhi Prison, and the reasons for so much killing.

More than three months had passed since the beginning of our imprisonment. In the beginning, we had been kept for about ten days in the basement of the Ministry of Defense, and after that, we were kept in Pul-i-Charkhi Prison, located on the outskirts of Kabul City.

A bloody coup d'état, planned and supported by the Soviet Union and its embassy in Kabul and undertaken by the competing Parcham and Khalq factions of the Communist Party (called the People's Democratic Party), which were temporarily glued together by the embassy, had toppled the government of the Republic of Afghanistan in a very short period of time.

The coup, planned with Soviet advice, was very well executed by a small number of Soviet-trained military officers, secret Communist Party members[13] who were established in critical command centers of the army and air force military units in and around Kabul and in military command centers of adjacent provinces. Their job was to attack and put a choke hold on the command. Simultaneously, Communist officers had taken command of the Fourth Military Unit and the Fourteenth Tank Forces at the base in the Pul-i-Charkhi area east of Kabul City.

As we in the cabinet met on the morning of April 27, 1978, a large number of Soviet-made T-54 and T-62 tanks from these units— reportedly about two hundred of them—were mobilized and were moving toward the president's offices at the presidential palace.

Apparently, the objective was to set up a siege around the central command of the presidency. Although the Presidential Guard later succeeded in breaking the siege, no other military units came to join forces with the guards' unit.

---

[13] Notably, Tank Commander Watanjar, who announced the coup on Kabul Radio, and General Abdul Qader, the commanding general of the air force, both of whom had been trusted and promoted by Daoud, were told to neutralize control centers and loyal non-Communist commanders, and immobilize all army and air force units—which they did.

A day later, President Daoud, his family, and several other important men were killed, and from that day on, the Communists began killing or imprisoning a large number of community elders (respected for their age and wisdom), cabinet ministers, other officials, non-Communist army and air force generals, and other prominent figures.

Although the total number of devout Communists was not very large (three to four thousand altogether in Parcham and Khalq combined), they were nevertheless able to gradually take control and command of the whole country by taking the command centers of the military and the police forces; the radio, TV, and printing facilities; and all the communication systems in the capital city and the provinces.

Everyone was waiting to see what was happening and to learn who was in command.

The coup conspirators immediately released the leaders who had been arrested. These leaders set up a governing body and established a central committee and a politburo. The new government was headed by Taraki, Karmal, and Amin, and the regime combined their mutually antagonistic factions. Decisions and commands issued by the central committee of the politburo of this new government were implemented by a small number of devoted Communist army and air force officers and a larger number of sympathizers and opportunists.

At first, the Afghan people went into a state of shock, disbelief, and numbness.

On one hand, the Communist government issued decrees and made propagandistic announcements to portray itself as legitimate. On the other hand, having murdered Daoud and his family, the Communists kept on imprisoning and executing large numbers of people who might oppose their rule.

They apparently believed that by keeping the public uninformed, issuing false statements and propaganda, and terrorizing people, they could succeed in subduing the Afghan people into accepting their rule.

They also believed that by employing a number of semieducated operatives who had been indoctrinated and expeditiously promoted to carry out the orders handed to them, they could enlarge the circle of their command and rule.

Obviously, the coup had been well planned.

Although the coup (as we later learned) had been scheduled for a few months later, it was carried out quite successfully by the commanders involved, with advice and coordination of their efforts provided by their Soviet KGB counterparts. Also, the Soviet advisors who were helping the newly formed government had plenty of experience in subjugating their own people and the citizens of other countries that they had invaded and occupied in the past.

At first, confusion and uncertainty would not allow any countercoup action; Afghanistan hadn't experienced a government upheaval for fifty years. Most Afghans waited to see what the outcome would be.

Then, gradually, the people realized that the Communists and their Soviet patrons had taken over the government by force and did not care whether the people accepted them or not. They would force the Afghans to submit to their rule by means of fear, through inhuman punishment, torture, and murder.

As time went on, the Communists faced increasing resistance from the strong-willed Afghan people, who are endowed with strong human spirit, deep religious belief, and pride. It appeared that a rebellious resistance to a Communist regime that was being forced upon them was beginning to spread throughout the country.

The Polygon

My observations during the more than three months since I was first imprisoned in the basement of the Ministry of Defense and then brought to Pul-i-Charkhi Prison were of an increasing number of executions, torture sessions, and imprisonments.

The number of prisoners who were brought from Kabul and taken directly to the Polygon firing range for summary execution, or brought into the prison for torture and imprisonment, increased day by day. By now, it was about three to four hundred more people per day. In Pul-i-Charkhi, political block no. 1 had filled up with prisoners. So had block no. 2. The other blocks were also being filled up.

Of course, Pul-i-Charkhi was not the only prison in Kabul. The Communists were also using empty warehouses and buildings for imprisonment, torture, and killing purposes. Prisons in the provinces and larger towns were also being used.

The Communists were using debilitating methods of torture and execution to erode and weaken the capacity of the Afghan people to endure and resist. They seemed to have learned well from their Soviet advisors, or perhaps they invented new methods of their own. They were becoming experts at torture and execution, and they gained more experience in terrorizing the population.

Prisoners who were brought into Pul-i-Charkhi were tortured so that they would sign forced confessions. They were then taken out at night to the slaughter ground of the Polygon at the military base across the Kabul River.

When there was a southwesterly breeze, I could hear the sound of machine-gun fire from the Polygon, followed by single shots—the coup de grâce—to make sure that every victim was dead.

I would count the number of single shots to estimate the number of people who had been killed at any one time.

Gradually, we prisoners got information about the details and the method of these killings. The PDPA regime was continuously using heavy machinery to dig trenches at the Polygon. The trenches were used to bury the bodies of prisoners who had been brought there to be gunned down. Prisoners were taken from Pul-i-Charkhi Prison or brought from other places in the city, at which point they were taken directly to the slaughter grounds at about midnight to be killed.

With their hands tied behind their backs and their eyes covered, they were made to stand close to the edge of a trench; then, they were machine-gunned. Next came the single shots to the head to make sure they were all dead. The bodies were heaved into the trench and buried by bulldozers' pushing dirt into the trench.

Later on, we heard that one prisoner whom the executioners thought dead was actually wounded and buried alive. He managed to get out of the trench and escape to a nearby village. The villagers tended to his wounds. Eventually, he was able to make it to the outside world and tell his story. Since I was in prison, it was impossible for me to verify the report, but we prisoners all hoped it was true.

My observations showed that of those who were taken out of Pul-i-Charkhi Prison, only a very small number were actually released to go home. Most were brought in, tortured, and then taken out to the Polygon for execution.

Cherry-Syrup Communication

I had to wait two weeks to find out if my wife had gotten my message in the cherry-syrup bottle.

Sure enough, she sent my clean clothes in paper bags after the fifteen-day interval had passed. With them there was another bottle of cherry syrup. Also, there was a column of numbers on the paper bag, and these were added up to a total.

I deciphered the message and was happy to learn that Fariha, our kids, and my parents were okay.

So, my wife and I had succeeded in establishing a system of communication for receiving and sending messages every fifteen days. From then on, we communicated. I continuously changed the method and means of communication.

When using numbers on paper bags, messages had to be very brief. I began sending my messages in tiny, sealed plastic pouches, concealing them in used toothpaste tubes, ChapStick cartridges, or any spent or used item in which I could hide them. I used not only an empty space but also spaces that were filled with a cream, Vaseline, or a powder or liquid in which my wife sent her messages to me.

We prisoners were very eager to have more information about what was happening in Kabul and other cities and rural areas around the country. So, my next effort was to find a way to smuggle a tiny radio into the prison in order to listen to the BBC medium-wave news broadcasts. This would give us information about what was really happening in Afghanistan and the outside world.

All foreign-based radio stations except the BBC broadcasted their news on shortwave frequencies, but, in those days, shortwave radios were larger than medium-wave radios. A very small medium-wave radio could easily fit into one's palm, and it usually included headphones for listening.

A very small radio like that could easily be hidden in a can of powdered milk without raising any suspicion. It was very unlikely that the guards would empty a can of powdered milk and look inside it for hidden objects. If they did, I was quite sure that they would just confiscate the radio. The chance of punishment, therefore, was not all that high.

I calculated that it was worth the risk.

In a secret message to my wife, I asked her to buy the smallest battery-operated medium-wave radio with headphones that she could find. I also asked her to send me a can of powdered milk. I told her to put the radio in a plastic pouch, seal it, hide it in the can under the powdered milk, and send me the can with my clean clothes.

By this time, I was getting to know the mind-set of our guards better than I had a month or two before. Although the people in command of the prison were Communist Party members belonging to either the Parcham or the Khalq faction, our guards were not Communists. They had been members of the security forces before the coup and, as such, had been kept on as staff and assigned to guard duty in the prison.

As I mentioned before, they treated us quite respectfully, knowing that we were highly educated, honest, and respected people who had been serving the country before our imprisonment. After a while, I realized that the guards were rather sympathetic toward us.

Although it was dangerous for them to do so, the guards, if they found out that there was something going on that could harm us, warned us ahead of time. This slightly eased our tension.

In making the decision to get a radio into my cell, I had evaluated all these factors before proceeding with my plan.

When I gave the bag of my soiled clothes to the guard, I told him that I was suffering from malnutrition and asked him to tell my family members, who were waiting outside, to send some powdered milk with my clean clothes next time.

Meanwhile, I continued to make my secret notes.

August 3, 1978 (Asad 12, 1357)

Two more prisoners, General Qasim and Officer Daoud, were brought into our block.

August 7, 1978 (Asad 16, 1357)

Six more prisoners were brought into our block no. 1. Among them were two of my old associates: Police Chief Sultan Aziz Qaderi (my cousin's husband) from Samangan Province, who was deputy police chief of Herat Province when I was the governor there, and Ghafoor Waseel, who had been my deputy governor and chief financial officer (*mustoofi*) of Herat Province.

Another new arrival was Dr. Ghazanfar, the chief of the Central Microbiological Laboratories at the Ministry of Public Health. Dr.

Ghazanfar was very well-known for his impeccable integrity and impressive professional qualifications.

Tuesday, August 8, 1978 (Asad 17, 1357)

Two buses full of Afghan army officers were brought into our block at night.

Also on this night, about 145 prisoners were transferred from other prisons in Kabul to Pul-i-Charkhi Prison. These prisoners belonged to the Ikhwan, or Muslim Brotherhood, a group of religious devotees.

Faizani

Most were taken to block no. 2 and the south block, but about thirty prisoners, together with a Mr. Faizani and General Mir Ahmadshah, were brought to political block no. 1 at night.

After cleaning up the next morning, I met Mr. Faizani in the prison yard. Engineer Ghausuddin Fayeq, one of my cell mates, introduced me to him. I had not met him before, but I knew that he was a recognized religious scholar.

He started our conversation with the following words: "I am sorry that unfortunate circumstances in the country have resulted in putting you here in Pul-i-Charkhi as a political prisoner.

"Mr. Assifi, your place is not here in the prison. You will be released very soon. The people of Afghanistan, all over the country, have seen through the façade of lies and the deceit of this group that has taken over the government. All over the land, there is a general uprising by the people against these Communists and Soviet agents.

"I promise you," he went on, "that no matter how much this terrorist and tyrannical group is supported by Soviet Russia and its East European allies, it will not be able to last very long. Soon, their establishment will topple and the perpetrators will be brought to justice. I pray for your good health and safety."

This statement surprised me, since we were all waiting to be executed at any minute. To make such an open statement in front of several other prisoners showed that this man was obviously a person of ideals.

Mr. Faizani's Ikhwani group was not kept very long in political block no. 1. We did not see them anymore. The very next day, I heard that they had been transferred to block no. 2. Later events determined the fate of this group.

August 12, 1978 (Asad 21, 1357)

Sixty army officers from the Qargha Division were brought in late at night.

Exercise

Lack of exercise was another problem in the prison. There was no space in the cell where four of us were held. We could not even walk around the room without stepping on someone else who was lying down or sleeping on his blanket on the floor.

The only exercise that we had during the day was when we went outside to the latrines, washed up afterward, and walked around in the yard for maybe ten or fifteen minutes.

Prison command allowed us out five times each day for this.

The morning session would take place before sunrise. We were allowed at least half an hour after cleanup for our morning prayers.

I decided to do the first part of the morning routine more quickly so I could use the rest of the time for getting some exercise. After I washed, I went upstairs to my cell, said my prayers, came back down to the yard, stood in a corner, and did some calisthenics. After that, I ran in a circle until the time was up.

I did this every morning. After a couple of days, another prisoner, Mr. Wakil Khosti, who had been a member of Parliament during Zahir Shah's reign, saw me exercising and asked if he could join me in my routine. I told him that it was up to him. From then on, he stood behind me and followed everything that I did.

After a few days, I noticed that the number of prisoners doing the exercise routine had increased; now, we had maybe ten or fifteen people doing the exercises.

This went on for some time.

Then one day, the prison commander called the prisoners down to the yard and gave one of his speeches. Whenever he gave a speech, a number of guards with machine guns positioned themselves all around us for the sake of his security.

After saying the routine words and sentences that we had been hearing all the time on official radio and TV stations, the commander said that "they" (meaning he) was aware that the minister of mines (that's me) had the nefarious purpose of disrupting the peace of the prison and was organizing the prisoners for this purpose, under the guise of exercise.

Then he added, "We will empty one charge of the machine gun into the belly of each one of you before you can succeed in your destructive purposes!" Well, that was the end of my exercise. Some time later, I heard that Wakil Khosti, the fellow who had first joined me in my exercises, was executed.

Monday, August 14, 1978 (Asad 23, 1357)

A total of 123 new prisoners were brought into our block today.

Tuesday, August 15, 1978 (Asad 24, 1357)

General Farouq, the chief of military operations, and eighteen officers from the Fifteenth Heavy Armored Division of Kabul were brought into our block at night.

Wednesday, August 16, 1978 (Asad 25, 1357)

Thirty prisoners from block no. 2, including Faizani and General Mir Ahmadshah, together with some other prisoners from the Ikhwan (Brotherhood) group of religious devotees, were taken out at night and killed at the Polygon execution grounds across the river.

Rumors of a PDPA Split

For some time now, we had been hearing through the underground rumor channels that the previous rivalries between the Parcham and Khalq factions of the Communist Party had heated up. Consequently, after a showdown between them, the leadership posts in the party command structure were taken over by the Khalqis, led by Hafizullah Amin.[14] The Parchamis were pushed aside to secondary jobs, such as ambassadorships, which got them out of Kabul.[15]

The Parchami leader, Babrak Karmal, and several of his key associates were sent off as ambassadors.

---

[14] In September 1978, with Soviet approval, Taraki tried to assassinate Amin but failed. Amin assumed the presidency and, in October of that year, had Taraki killed.

[15] There was constant tension, conflict, and infighting between the two Communist factions. The first PDPA president, Nur Mohammad Taraki, was the nominal head of Khalq but was willing to follow Soviet instructions and cooperate with Parcham. The strongman of Khalq, Hafizullah Amin, was less pliable.

Thursday, August 17, 1978 (Asad 26, 1357)

Kabul radio and television stations reported an attempted coup, led by a number of high-ranking persons, against the newly formed Khalqi government.

Judging from this announcement, it did not appear to me that the persons named as being involved in the coup attempt were solely from the Parcham faction. However, on the same day, August 17, government radio and television announced that the following were implicated in the attempted coup: General Abdul Qader, defense minister in the PDPA cabinet and a Parchami; Major General Shahpur Khan Ahmadzai, the army's chief of staff operations; and Dr. Mir Ali Akbar, president of Jamhoori Hospital.

Dr. Mir Ali Akbar

General Shahpur Ahmadzai and Dr. Mir Ali Akbar were brought into Pul-i-Charkhi Prison and were kept on the first floor of the east wing of block no. 1. They were held in solitary confinement for about a week before they were allowed to mix with the other prisoners.

General Shahpur Ahmadzai and Dr. Mir Ali Akbar had been brutally tortured.

The torturers had extracted from both of them confessions regarding their involvement in the coup. Shahpur Ahmadzai's eerie groans and screams from the pain of the wounds that he sustained from torture were very unnerving. We could hear these groans, which echoed in the prison halls in the middle of the night, and we could feel his pain. It reminded us of our own impending fate and our predicament of being in the hands of these butchers who would stop at nothing to achieve their goal of ruling the country.

Dr. Mir Ali Akbar was a very nice person and a good doctor. I had known him several years prior. At one time, I was hospitalized in Jamhoori Hospital because I had severe amoebic dysentery, which I had contracted after being forced to drink from an irrigation ditch's tepid water in the Dasht-i-Margo Desert when I was chief engineer of the Helmand and Arghandab Valley Project. Years later, I was hospitalized again in Jamhoori Hospital for an appendectomy and to treat an infection that arose from it. Both of these times, Dr. Mir Ali Akbar went out of his way and was very kind to me.

I found out that Dr. Mir Ali Akbar was in one of the cells on the first floor that had a high, barred window facing the backyard where we went to wash. During one of our washup breaks, I went and sat below his window, pretending to warm myself in the sunshine. Once, I heard his voice reading the Holy Book, the Quran, out loud. I called to him and said his name. He was quiet for a while, listening to find out who was calling him from the outside. I called his name again and told him who I was, and then I asked if he needed any medicine or money.

He called back to me, saying, "Mr. Assifi, do not stay where you are, and don't talk to me. It is dangerous for you. I don't need anything. And, please, do not stay there!" Nevertheless, from then on, when no one was around, I talked to him, but every time he asked me not to endanger myself by associating with him.

After some time, we heard on the government television news that a special government court had ruled that General Shahpur Ahmadzai and Dr. Mir Ali Akbar were ordered to be executed for treason for having taken part in an attempted coup against the government. This was the first time that the Communist regime had publicly announced the execution of any individuals. They had been, and still were, killing hundreds of people day and night without making any announcements or providing a list of their names.

This was like a tragic show or playacting. Human life did not mean anything to them. All they wanted was to grab command and stay in power.

After this announcement, both of these men were taken out of solitary confinement. I saw them outside during the cleanup period, but they sat away from the other prisoners and did not mingle.

Once, I saw Dr. Mir Ali Akbar washing his hands and feet in a corner. I went and sat next to him, started washing my hands, and again asked him if he needed anything. By now, we had all had heard of and knew about the ruling of the special government court for his execution.

Dr. Mir Ali Akbar again cautioned me not to come too close to him. Then he said, "Mr. Assifi, I know that I am going to be killed at any time now, but I assure you that the people of Afghanistan have recognized who these people are and will never accept the rule of the servants of the Soviets at any time. I pray for your long life, good health, and prosperity. And once again, for your safety, I beg of you not to come too close to me or talk to me. I do not want any harm to come to you."

I was amazed and looked at him with awe. I told myself, *This is an amazing man. He knows that he is going to be killed at any minute now, yet he does not think of himself. He is thinking about my safety and well-being!*

At that moment, I felt that I was close to a man with the highest degree of courage. I considered myself privileged to speak to a person like this. From then on, I did what he had asked me to do. Whenever I saw him from that point forward, I nodded my head in respect from a distance and could see the greatness of his spirit in his eyes.

Eventually, the doctor was taken away for execution. But all the while, I was sure of one thing: *they could execute him, but they could not terrify him or break his spirit.*

August 19, 1978 (Asad 28, 1357)

Twelve new prisoners were brought into Pul-i-Charkhi on this date.

August 20, 1978 (Asad 29, 1357)

Twenty-four air force officers in one group and twelve in a second group were brought into Pul-i-Charkhi Prison.

August 22, 1978 (Asad 31, 1357)

Four new prisoners were brought into our block, and fifty more prisoners were brought from the northern province of Kishm Badakhshan and taken to the block that was designated for "critical [dangerous] prisoners."

August 26, 1978 (Sunbula 4, 1357)

Shah-jan Ahmadzai (Ashraf Ghani's father), who was once the president of the government's Logistics and Transportation Department; Kochi Ahmadzai, Ahmadzai's brother; and a number of prisoners from the army artillery unit at Ghazni were brought into our block.

Gravel Craft, a Stone Age Industry

When we prisoners went outside to wash, we usually had a few minutes before guards told us to go back to our cells. One day, I was sitting outside under the wall of the block and looking at pieces of gravel under my feet. I noticed a flat oval stone that had a reddish color. I picked it up, looked at it, and liked it.

I had dreamed some time earlier that I was outside looking at the ground in the yard and saw a piece of stone that looked like a jewel among the other rocks.

Before going back to the cell, I picked up that pebble again and put it in my pocket.

When I was in my cell, I took the pebble out of my pocket and kept looking at it. I thought, *If I rub this piece of stone against some other pieces of stone, then I can craft it into a better-looking object.*

This is when my "gravel craft" project started. It kept me doing something creative instead of just lying on my blanket or jumping up and down on it like a crazy chicken for the sake of getting some movement into my frozen limbs and joints, with my cell mates complaining, "Hey, what are you doing, shaking up the dust?"

Anyhow, I thought this would be a temporary diversion from the horrible environment of the slaughterhouse that I was in. So, I kept on working on the pebble. I found some other, rougher pieces of stone in the yard. I could recognize various bits of stone and guess at their geologic origin and natural hardness. I rubbed my pebble against the harder stones that I picked up from the yard.

Gradually, my stone acquired a flat surface with an elongated oval shape. It smoothed out with a natural polish.

The second phase of my work involved writing my oldest daughter's name on this surface and, on the back of the stone, her birth date. I wrote with my small, cutoff piece of pencil. But this writing would rub off and not last for a long time. I needed to etch the writing, but I had no tools for etching or engraving. Since the prison commander did not allow us to have any metal utensils like forks, knives, and spoons for fear that we might make weapons from them, we had no tools of any kind.

But I simply had to make a tool for etching on the stone. I thought about this for some time and finally found a solution.

My engineering knowledge, which included the composition of metals and other materials, gave me an idea. I asked one of the guards if he could get me a sewing needle. He said, "Okay, I'll find you one." The next day, it was very nice when he brought me two needles.

A sewing needle is made of materials that do not become dull very quickly. It can be used for sewing for a long time without losing its property. And needles are made of a combination of materials that are hard and brittle; you cannot bend a sewing needle without breaking it. So I broke one of the needles into two pieces. The broken edges were quite rough and sharp, which was ideal for etching my piece of stone.

But how could I hold the needle without hurting my fingers? The solution to this problem was not very difficult. All I needed was a handle to hold the needle.

For a handle, I used an old toothbrush that I had with me. I heated the needle on a candle flame and then pushed it into the end of my plastic toothbrush. It went in like a hot knife cutting butter. When the needle cooled, it was tight in the grip of the plastic handle. I started the etching process. The tool that I had improvised was perfect for the job.

The last part of this project was the most difficult. The problem was that I needed to put a hole at one end of the oval ornament so that my daughter could put a chain through it. How could I drill a hole in this piece of stone? I needed a small drill.

The solution to this problem came to me from a childhood memory. I remembered that when an item of china broke, my mother always kept the pieces. Then, one day, a man would come and knock at the door, asking if we needed any broken china repaired. My mother would tell him to come in, and then she'd give him the broken pieces.

Such people were experts at repairing broken china. First, this man drilled holes on the two sides that were going to be glued together. Then, he made a glue from egg whites and some white powder, which, I think, was lime. He glued together the pieces that fit, put metal clips through the holes, and tightened them for the final job. So, the pieces were glued and stapled. In this way, a teapot, a cup, or a plate was repaired for home use.

I remembered the tool that this repairman used to make holes in the broken pieces of china: a bow with a thread tied to each end. He then twisted the thread around the handle of the drill and used it, like a violin player, to make the holes.

I used the other piece of the broken needle for the drill bit. I made a bow and tied thread to each end. I then made a handle for my needle drill bit. Now I had the tool for drilling holes into the stone piece. I drilled the hole, and the pebble looked beautifully done.

I sent this as a birthday present for my daughter on the day that my wife and son brought my clean clothes. I gave it to the guard and told him, "Please, give this to my family and tell them to give it to my daughter as a present." This was done, and it generated requests for more of the same kind from other members of my family. I was very glad to comply.

When the other prisoners saw what I was doing, many of them asked me to show them how to do it. Some would ask me to artistically write names, dates, or other inscriptions on the pieces of polished stone that they had made, and they always asked me to put a hole in the piece that they had created.

Unfortunately, the bloodthirsty commandant learned about this industry. He assumed that the minister of mines and industries was hatching another plan against the workers' government, using this stone craft to unite the prisoners. As a result, one night, without any warning, the guards and soldiers raided our cells, searched for the pieces and tools that we had created, and took them away. Well, *that put an end to my gravel craft industry.*

August 27, 1978 (Sunbula 5, 1357)

A number of prisoners from the army's Eighth Division were brought into our block.

Interrogation of prisoners took place at several locations in Kabul and in other provinces. A final and brief interrogation, a precursor to execution, was conducted in the chambers of block no. 1 of Pul-i-Charkhi. These interrogations were headed by the commandant of military factories, with advice from Soviet specialists.

Tuesday, August 29, 1978 (Sunbula 7, 1357)

Seventeen new prisoners were brought into our block. Among these were Malik from the military factory, and a number of prisoners from the Upper Qargha Seventh and Lower Qargha Eighth Divisions.

Also, three Parchami cabinet ministers who had organized the coup that was reported a couple of weeks prior were brought into the west wing of our block no. 1: General Abdul Qader, defense minister; Sultan Ali Keshtmand, minister of planning—and one of the top Parchamis;[16] and General Rafiee, head of military operations and minister of public works.

These men were all part of the Parcham faction of the government. They were kept separate from the other prisoners in political block no. 1. Actually, we knew that they were there, but we never saw them in person.

Since the power shake-up within the two rival groups, the leadership of the People's Democratic Party of Afghanistan had been taken over by the Khalq faction, with Hafizullah Amin as its leader. Apparently, the reported coup against the government had been organized by the Parcham faction. Hafizullah Amin's government sent many Parchamis and a number of non-Parchamis to Pul-i-Charkhi Prison. Walking around in the backyard of the prison, I could see some members of Parcham walking among the prisoners.

---

[16] Kishtmand, the only Hazara and only Shia in the Parchami leadership, was a founding member of Parcham, was close to Babrak Karmal, and, on-and-off, was a member of the central committee and politburo, depending on power shifts among the various leaders. Kishtmand was sentenced to death in August 1978, but Amin commuted his sentence to a prison term. After the Soviets installed Karmal as president, Kishtmand was made deputy prime minister and (again) minister of planning, and was restored to the central committee, the politburo, and the Revolutionary Council.

The Soviet advisors deemed it necessary that a government acceptable to the Soviet Union be formed under the leadership of the Parchamis, whose leader, Babrak Karmal, was a longtime Soviet agent. Such a government would include a conglomerate of various political entities: Parchamis, Parcham sympathizers, Khalqis, and a visible hodgepodge of non-Communists from various sectors of Afghan society. In today's terminology, this was a so-called broad-based government.

This was the basic formula devised by the Soviet leadership for a stable government that was acceptable to them in Afghanistan and that would be accepted by the Afghan people, too.

The Soviets repeatedly tried to implement this formula or some variation of it. All these Soviet efforts failed because they had based them on "unverified assumptions" about the characteristics of the Afghan people. The Soviets based their plans and methods on their experiences with Russians, Eastern Europeans, Uzbeks, Turkmens, Tajiks, and other peoples whom they had conquered and subjugated. An important component of their failure in Afghanistan was their assumption that Afghans were similar to those peoples and that they could apply their plans and programs on the basis of assumptions derived from their experiences with those peoples. It seemed that both the initial and later Soviet plans all had the following ingrained flaws: they were based on unverifiable assumptions; they were purely materialistic, with intrinsic antireligious elements; and they were all "top-down." The Soviets did not recognize the indomitable spiritual strength of the Afghan people, and they did not consider the Afghan people's love of freedom and dignity.

I believe there is a saying, "To everyone their own means"—or did I make that up?

My Conversation with a Parchami

Friday, September 1, 1978 (Sunbula 10, 1957)

Several more Parchami prisoners were brought into our block, one of whom was Mohammad Hakim, deputy commandant of the military academy.

Some time later, during a cleanup session, Commandant Hakim introduced himself to me as the nephew of Yahyah-jan Sarwari, who happened to be a second or third cousin of my father. In the traditions of Afghan culture, tribal and family relationships are considered very important. (These relationships are given especially great importance among the Pashtuns, who make up more than half of the population in Afghanistan. I am Pashtun.) He also told me that he had studied military sciences at one of the military colleges in the United States.

Because of Hakim's active participation in the command structure of the PDPA, my association with him was limited, but because of our family ties, we exchanged a nod whenever our paths crossed.

Another one of the Parchami prisoners who introduced himself to me was a Dr. Faqir, who also said that he was related to me by tribal connections. He was helpful in giving me some information about the list of Parchamis, about which I had questions.

Once, I asked him, "Is Jalalar a member of Parcham?"[17]

He said, "No."

I said, "How come he was never imprisoned with other ministers of the former government? And as I have heard, he is working as a minister with the PDPA."

Faqir said, "I don't know."

---

[17] See note 8 in this chapter. Jalalar is believed to have had direct connections to Soviet agencies.

I asked him another question: "Is Farouq Yaqubi a member of Parcham?"

He said, "No."

I asked, "How come, then, he is working at an important job with the PDPA?"

He said, "I don't know."

I told him, "Well, Dr. Faqir, you don't know much about your own party, do you?" Then I asked him some other questions: "The party of the joint Parcham and Khalq government is called the People's Democratic Party of Afghanistan. My questions are these: Did the people of Afghanistan vote to put your party in power? Are you going to ask the people of Afghanistan to vote to keep you as the legal government of Afghanistan?"

He said, "Well, Mr. Assifi, the word *democratic* means that it is democratic among the party members."

I said, "Don't the people of Afghanistan have any right to say what they want?"

He replied, "What would an illiterate people know about what is good for them? We, not a lot of illiterate and ignorant people in the country, know what is good for them and what they should want!"

I had to write about this conversation with a Parchami. It showed so clearly the Parcham mentality and how members of that faction had been brainwashed by the Soviet indoctrination and propaganda machine into accepting certain beliefs.

So the PDPA had decided to imprison, torture, and execute some people to make others submit to their rule and a government of tyranny. They had set the rules and justified to themselves the killing of up to 90 percent of the population of Afghanistan. They claimed to know what was good for the people of Afghanistan.

Or maybe what they did was meant to establish the rule of the Soviet Union.

Tahir Badakhshi, a well-known leader of the Afghan Maoist Communist (Shola) Party, had been brought to Pul-i-Charkhi. He was imprisoned in the west wing of block no. 1 and was kept away from the other prisoners.

Sunday, September 3, 1978 (Sunbula 12, 1357)

Ten busloads of new prisoners, which I estimated to be about three hundred people, were brought into Pul-i-Charkhi Prison.

The Beating of Ludin

I do not remember the exact date of the following incident, but it is important that I mention what happened on this day in the prison's backyard. We had washed up for the afternoon session and were walking around in the yard before going back to our cells.

Suddenly, I noticed that the atmosphere was getting tense.

Before I could gather my thoughts, I saw that the commandant, Said Abdullah, was there, with a pistol in his holster and what looked like a submachine gun in his hand, the kind of square black submachine gun that the Germans had given to the Interior Ministry's police force some time ago. The commandant was walking briskly toward us prisoners, accompanied by a bunch of soldiers carrying machine guns.

I also noticed that other armed soldiers and guards were getting into position at key points around the prisoners in the yard. The prisoners opened a space among themselves for the commandant's group. He was shaking the submachine gun, with the barrel pointing toward us, as if he was going to open fire at any moment.

Said Abdullah shouted, "Aziz Ludin!" He kept repeating Ludin's name and shouting, "Where is Ludin?" We could not see Ludin among the prisoners. We were scared stiff, and all of us knew that something drastic was going to happen at any moment.

I was hoping that Ludin was not in the yard—but, if he wasn't there, then where was he? There was no place where anyone could hide.

Then, Ludin, who had been washing up, came running, his hands and face still wet. He started toward the commandant. Said Abdullah and his soldiers jumped at him, beating him down to the ground with fists, gun butts, heavy boots, and everything else they had while shouting curses and bad names. The commandant was yelling at Ludin. "You had the audacity to mention our Great Leader's name with your dirty mouth? You had the temerity to mention our Great Leader, Taraki, the Genius of the East, with your dirty mouth?" Ludin was smashed to the ground. His small white cap and glasses fell off, were trampled upon, and vanished in the dust.

We prisoners were all frozen and could do nothing. All we could do was back away, so as not to get trampled on by the commandant and his soldiers. We were thinking that they might even kill Ludin right there.

I was watching from the corner of my eye. I saw one of the prisoners who had been squatting by the wall next to block no. 2 get up and walk toward the men who were beating Ludin. He stepped in among them, grabbed the commandant's upraised hand, and said, "That's enough! He got his punishment—don't beat him anymore. *Stop!*"

This man spoke in Pashto. The commandant recognized him and stopped the beating. I recognized him, too. He was General Shahpur Ahmadzai, who had been sentenced by the revolutionary special court to die. His tortured groans had echoed through the nights.

General Shahpur Ahmadzai was someone to whom the other prisoners would hardly speak. They had heard that he had given a scathing speech at the military academy, during which he had made derogatory remarks about his mentor, President Daoud.

Daoud had helped Ahmadzai receive advanced military training and education and had promoted him to high rank in Afghanistan's army, raising him to the position of chief of staff of all the Afghan armed forces.

In Afghanistan's culture of honor, there is nothing worse than showing disloyalty to one's own father or one's mentor, or to a person who had helped one achieve a higher station in life. Yet this man, for the sake of pleasing the people who had seized the reins of government, had betrayed his chief mentor. He was considered a traitor. Still, this same man, knowing that he was to be executed at any moment, put himself at risk of being killed right then and there in order to protect a weaker man. His word was still a command.

We prisoners had seen dramas revealing the intricacies of life that could have been written by Shakespeare. The two men—General Shahpur Ahmadzai and Dr. Mir Ali Akbar—whose executions had been announced by a "special court," were so different in personality, and their deeds in the past and in the last hours before their deaths were so extraordinary, that it was mind-boggling to the utmost degree. Yet, what do we know about their real motives and purposes? Do we really know all the facts? I myself would hesitate to pass judgment, lest I make a mistake on the basis of unverified—or, in this case, probably unverifiable—assumptions.

Monday, September 4, 1978 (Sunbula 13, 1357)

Sher Pacha of the Hazrat-i-Shor bazaar, an elder and the head of the Mojadidi family and a very influential religious figure in Afghanistan for many years, was brought in to the adjacent block no. 2 along with nine other men.

Members of the Mojadidi family had been prominent religious leaders in Afghanistan and other countries in the region for many years. They were associated with the Naqshbandi order of Sufism. I had known many very fine Mojadidis who were assisting those who were making positive developments in Afghanistan. They played a moderating role in religious matters, helped the process of peace, and espoused the proper understanding of Islamic doctrine and beliefs. They were very influential. That is why the Communists had chosen to kill them. We prisoners heard a rumor that between thirty and forty members of the Mojadidi family had been imprisoned and then forced into large wooden crates, the type that were used for hauling heavy equipment. The crates were then closed up. Later on, Afghan soldiers were ordered to use them for target practice, to shoot at the crates without knowing that there were people inside. I was not able to verify the truth of this rumor, but later I found out that many members of the Mojadidi family whom I personally knew had indeed been executed by the Communist regime.

Tuesday, September 5, 1978 (Sunbula 14, 1357)

Suleiman Layeq was brought into the west wing of block no. 1, where the other Communist government ministers were imprisoned. Suleiman Layeq, a Parchami, was a well-known writer and poet. His poems were written in both Pashto and Dari, in a so-called revolutionary style.[18]

On the same day, three hundred new prisoners from Badakhshan Province were brought into block no. 2.

The Radio

My wife had been able to fulfill my request for a small battery-operated medium-wave radio with earphones. She had successfully gotten it to me in a can of powdered milk. So now I was in possession of a radio.

My cell mates and I immediately began operating it, disconnecting its loudspeaker and listening with the earphones to the BBC's international broadcasts to Afghanistan. We took turns. One of us would listen and then tell the others what he had heard on the news.

---

[18] Layeq was a member of the Mojadidi family who became radicalized and broke with his family to become an early and active member of Parcham and the PDPA.

Now we had access to information about what was happening in Afghanistan and the world.

It was great!

We had to take extreme care and exercise caution in implementing this operation. It was really a dangerous mission. One of us would stand guard near the door and watch out for possible intrusions by guards or even the bloodthirsty commandant, Said Abdullah.

The radio operation went well, except for some flaws that exposed us to grave danger later on. As time went on, we became more relaxed in discussing the news with other prisoners whom we knew. This gradually turned us into the sole source of new information about events.

When we passed the information on to other prisoners, they would always ask, "How do you know?" or "Where did you hear this from?" Eventually, human frailties opened us to attention, and gradually the attention of prison command.

Once, the commandant himself came bursting into our cell and searched all the nooks and crannies, but he did not find anything. As a cautionary practice, we always hid the radio under powdered milk and its earphone in a totally different location.

Another time, the commandant burst in and vigorously searched again at a time when I was stretched out on the floor listening to the news. I had the earphone in my ear with its wire extended through my undergarment sleeve and going to the radio that was in my pocket. Fortunately, I was wearing a thick, loose chapan—a quilted robe often worn as a winter coat. I closed my eyes, pretending to be asleep, and kept on listening to the news. I was in a very precarious situation indeed. Seeing me on the floor, the commandant demanded an answer to his question, "What's wrong with him?"

My cell mates told him, "He's sick."

Fortunately, he left me alone and did not kick me or make me stand up; otherwise, I would not be alive to write these notes.

Thursday, August 24, 1978 (Sunbula 2, 1357)

On this dreadful night, a large number of the Ikhwan al-Muslimin were blindfolded. Their hands tied, they were loaded onto waiting buses. Elsewhere, I mentioned that we prisoners witnessed a horrifying scene when soldiers opened fire with machine guns and killed all who were in the buses, and another three or four in a cell by throwing hand grenades in through broken windows. Due to circumstances, the prison command could not kill the rest of these prisoners on that dreadful night.

However, they made special arrangements to kill the remainder of those prisoners they had decided to execute.

Wednesday, September 20, 1978 (Sunbula 29, 1357)

The remaining ninety prisoners from the adjacent block no. 2, together with fourteen more from political block no. 1, were taken out at daylight and killed at the Polygon execution grounds across the river. Thus, the guards killed all the prisoners from the Ikhwan al-Muslimin group (Muslim Brotherhood) who had been brought to Pul-i-Charkhi Prison.

Thursday, September 21, 1978 (Sunbula 30, 1357)

Eleven new prisoners were brought in today. Among them were Hakim, the brother of Azizullah Wasefi (the former minister of agriculture), and the brother of the Ariana Airlines president.

Tuesday, September 26, 1978 (Mizan 4, 1357)

At about nine o'clock at night, fifty-four prisoners, nine of them from political block no. 1 and the rest from other blocks, together with forty-five more prisoners, were taken out of Pul-i-Charkhi in two buses to be killed. Like the others, their hands were tied behind their backs and their eyes were covered.

Then, from mid-October to mid-November, there appeared to be a temporary lull in executions. At that time, I could guess at only two reasons for this lull:

1) The coup attempt made "by a number of high-ranking persons" and announced on August 17 had resulted in a power shake-up within the two rival Communist factions. The leadership of the government had been taken over by the Khalqis, with Hafizullah Amin in charge.
2) The Communist government, in showing the changes brought by the new leadership and in response to Amnesty International's visit to the prison, was putting on a show for the press of the Western world.

There was a relaxation of the previously tight rules in the prison. For instance, prisoners could talk to each other during the cleanup sessions. We were also allowed to go into each other's cells during cleanup sessions.

A PX was opened to provide some basic needs and wants of the prisoners, like powdered milk, cigarettes, matches, dried fruits, toilet paper, and soap.

Israrullah

As I said before, the crust of each prisoner's daily loaf of bread was edible, but the center was not, so some prisoners molded the doughy part into chess pieces. These hardened in a few days. One of the prisoners, Corporal Israrullah from Badakhshan Province, was quite a character. He had sewn a chessboard inside his old and tattered chapan overcoat. He would open his chapan and spread it on the ground, take dried-dough chess pieces out of his pocket, and invite anyone who passed to play chess with him. During this period of relaxed rules, one could see a bunch of prisoners sitting on the ground around Israrullah, two guys playing chess and all the others kibitzing. Of course, we did not have much time to play real chess. But the few minutes that we did have to play or watch somebody else play were a relief from all the torturing and killing that was going on in the prison.

Israrullah had no relatives or friends in Kabul. Nobody brought him clean clothes or anything that he might have needed. Once, during the cold season, I asked my wife to send two or three wool sweaters. She did not know why I wanted them, but she sent them. When I got them, I gave them to Israrullah and told him to keep warm.

I thought to myself that the relaxation of rules was for show. Hafizullah Amin and his guys wanted the people to think that his regime was freer than the previous PDPA government. But everyone knew that he had been a powerful member of the previous one, also.

The following are some examples of the "lull phase" in Pul-i-Charkhi.

Saturday, October 7, 1978 (Mizan 15, 1357)

Abdul Karim Hakimi, the president of the government's General Statistics Department, was released from Pul-i-Charkhi. A number of other prisoners were released from Pul-i-Charkhi on the following dates.

Sunday, October 8, 1978 (Mizan 16, 1357)

Four from political block no. 1 and twenty from other blocks were released.

Monday, October 9, 1978 (Mizan 17, 1357)

Three from political block no. 1, and a hundred and twenty from other blocks, were released.

Wednesday, October 11, 1978 (Mizan 19, 1357)

Three from political block no. 1 and twenty from other blocks were released. Also on this date, the bed sacks that had once been taken away were reissued to prisoners.

Saturday, October 14, 1978 (Mizan 22, 1357)

It was announced that the women and children of the royal family would be released from the prison, and they would be permitted to go wherever they chose.

Sunday, October 15, 1978 (Mizan 23, 1357)

Two members of Daoud's cabinet—Dr. Majid, the minister of state, and Qayeum Wardak, the minister of education—were both released today. I had earlier dreamed that they would both be released.

Wednesday, October 18, 1978 (Mizan 26, 1357)

On this day, sixty-two women and children of the extended royal family were allowed to meet and say good-bye to their relatives in the male prisoner section of political block no. 1.

Monday, October 23, 1978 (Aqrab 1, 1357)

About 11:00 in the morning, the sixty-two women and children of the royal family boarded minibuses and left the prison. Also, on the same day, twenty-one prisoners from other blocks, together with Lala Baz Mohammad's two younger sons who were still in the prison, plus twenty-one prisoners from the "dangerous block" and twenty-six prisoners from the southern blocks, were all released from Pul-i-Charkhi.

Monday, October 30, 1978 (Aqrab 8, 1357)

Brigadier Rahmatullah, air force pilot Ashraf, and Lieutenant Sultan from cell no. 13 were released.

Wednesday, November 1, 1978 (Aqrab 10, 1357)

Army officers Gulraheem Jawhari and Haji Hussain (who was fat) were released.

Wednesday, November 8, 1978 (Aqrab 17, 1357)

Sixteen prisoners from the south blocks were released.

Friday, November 10, 1978 (Aqrab 19, 1357)

Juma Mohammadi Released

At about 9:30 that night, our colleague and cell mate in cell no. 14, Juma Mohammadi, the minister of water and power, and Ghulam Ali Ayeen, a former governor of Herat, were both released. Juma Mohammadi had earlier told us that he had sent Mr. Hakim Malyar, a well-known member of the Khalq faction, on a scholarship to Australia, and that he was certain that as soon as Hakim Malyar returned, he would make sure that Juma was released from the prison.

Tuesday, November 14, 1978 (Aqrab 23, 1357)

Said Kamal Shinwari, the president of the Religious Properties Department, was released per the recommendation of one of the prison guard officers (nicknamed Zaabit-i-Chaar-meela[19]) who wanted to marry his daughter.

Friday, November 17, 1978 (Aqrab 26, 1357)

Nur Ahmad Etemadi, the former prime minister,[20] was brought from another cell into ours, to take the place of Juma Mohammadi. Mr. Etemadi was frail and not very well, so we decided not to let him do

---

[19] A chaar-meela is a four-barrel heavy anti-aircraft machine gun.

[20] He was prime minister from 1967 to 1971. He also served as ambassador to Italy, Pakistan, and the USSR.

any of the daily chores, like cleaning the room, bringing food from the corridor, and cleaning the food pans.

On this Friday, family members and other relatives were not allowed to come near the Pul-i-Charkhi prison gate. No clean clothes or anything else was allowed to be brought in for the prisoners. The brief respite from killing was over. Interrogations, the operation of the human grinding machine (i.e., torture), and executions restarted in full force.

Killing as Usual

Thursday, November 23, 1978 (Qaus 2, 1357)

At about ten o'clock at night, the prison was darkened. Thirty to fifty prisoners were brought from the other blocks. They were taken via a back entrance into the commandant's office to be blindfolded and have their hands tied behind their backs. Buses specially made for transporting the prisoners were brought into the inner yard. They were made of stainless steel plates with small portholes for windows and a loading ramp in the back. The blindfolded prisoners were loaded onto the buses and taken out to the Polygon for killing.

Sunday, November 26, 1978 (Qaus 5, 1357)

Fourteen prisoners who had been imprisoned earlier because of their connections to former Prime Minister Mohammad Hashim Maiwandwal[21] were brought from the maximum security section to our political block no. 1. Among them were General Abdul Razaq, the former head of the air force; General Nayek Mohammad Sahaak; Haji Faqir, a respected elder from Jalalabad; Baz Mohammad, Zurmat's representative in Parliament; and Saif-ur-Rahmaan's father, a white-bearded religious scholar. Also, Mr. Abdul Ghafoor Parwani, a well-known mathematician and teacher at the military academy who had

---

[21] Maiwandwal, a former ambassador to Washington, was prime minister from 1965 to 1967. He was jailed by Daoud and murdered while in jail, reportedly by Parchamis, without Daoud's knowledge.

written a textbook on trigonometry that was used in several high schools in Kabul, was brought to Pul-i-Charkhi from ano*ther prison in Kabul.*

Tuesday, November 28, 1978 (Qaus 7, 1357)

The lights were turned off, so the prison was dark. About 150 prisoners were brought from the other blocks to the commandant's office to be blindfolded and have their hands tied. They were then loaded onto three buses and taken out to the Polygon killing grounds across the river.

Saturday, December 2, 1978 (Qaus 11, 1357)

About ninety prisoners were taken out of Pul-i-Charkhi Prison.

Thirteen prisoners from our block (political block no. 1) were taken out to be released. They included General Forouq, a former chief of general staff; engineer Rasul from Khost; pilot Said Mohammad; Said Waheed-ullah, a pilot; and the brother of Amin who was the president of the Gul Bahar textile factories. These prisoners were from the group brought in on Asad 10 (August 1, 1978).

Friday, December 22, 1978 (Jadi 1, 1357)

A Kandahari from the Ministry of Culture's advertising department was released on this day.

Sunday, December 24, 1978 (Jadi 3, 1357)

Dignitaries during Zahir Shah's Time

Five new prisoners were brought into our political block no. 1. They were Noorgul Zaazi, the owner of Aryub Cinema, his brothers, and two others. On this date, three high-ranking ministers from King Zahir's time were also brought in to Pul-i-Charkhi Prison. They were Dr. Omar Wardak, former president of Parliament; Dr. Samad Hamed, former deputy prime minister; and Dr. Walid Hoquqi, former attorney general and minister of justice.

Omar Wardak and Dr. Hoquqi had been tortured somewhere else. Dr. Wardak's face was scarred and swollen. All of the men mentioned above were put in solitary confinement cells and were taken out to the backyard latrines at different times from the other prisoners. Other prisoners had been brought earlier, such as Dr. Ravan Farhadi,[22] who had been deputy minister of foreign affairs during the king's time, and Dr. Aziz Ludin, a professor of economics at Kabul University.

De Facto Center of Learning

At the beginning of my imprisonment in Pul-i-Charkhi, any communication between prisoners, with the outside world, or inside the prison was absolutely forbidden.

This no-exception rule regarding communication was enforceable when there was a smaller number of prisoners, but as the number of prisoners increased, the ratio of guards to prisoners was lower and enforcement weakened, to the benefit of the prisoners who were still alive—although the prison command could still implement the "no communication, without exception" rule wantonly and at their own pleasure.

I had been among the first batches of prisoners brought to the prison. This group was composed of highly educated cadres of the previous governments. As time went on, the number of prisoners, the torture, and the executions increased while the ratio of highly educated people to midlevel-educated people kept on decreasing. However, the failed August 17, 1978, anti-Amin coup led by the Parchamis involved a large number of highly educated professionals, Kabul University professors, and doctors who were not necessarily Communists. Some of the names that I remember are as follows: Dr. Nadir Omar, professor of physiology, School of Medicine, Kabul University; Dr. Hashemi, professor of physiology, School of Medicine, Kabul University; and Dr. Abdullah Kazim, professor of economics, Kabul University. I have already mentioned Dr. Ravan Farhadi and Dr. Aziz Ludin.

---

[22] A French-educated diplomat and subsequent postwar, post-Communist Afghan ambassador to the United Nations.

These men and others were non-Communists who had been drawn into the coup attempt against Hafizullah Amin's Khalqi government.

Consequently, a large number of these men were brought into the human grinding machine of Pul-i-Charkhi Prison in several waves. The somewhat relaxed enforcement of the rule forbidding communication and contact between the prisoners created a de facto community of learning and an exchange of knowledge between prisoners of varied expertise and professions. This somewhat relieved the mental stress inflicted in the disastrous prison environment.

I saw an opportunity for adding to my knowledge. I started learning specifically in two fields:

1) Linguistics, which I learned from Dr. Farhadi, who had a PhD in philology from a French university
2) Human physiology, which I learned from Dr. Hashemi

As it happened, I did not know much about Communist theory at that time. I asked other prisoners if they knew anyone who might help me. Someone told me that a prisoner named Maalim Nabi Siah from Farah Province, who used to teach chemistry at the military school, was a theoretician of Shola-i-Jawid, the Maoist Communist Party.

I searched out and found Maalim Nabi Siah, and he agreed to help me learn about Marxist theory. After I learned more about these principles, I realized that, contrary to the assertions made by Communists, some of the basic principles of communism could not be verified by research and modern scientific knowledge.

Meanwhile, I was helping three prisoners in my own areas of expertise.

Having spent years at American universities and working with Americans in Helmand, I helped Dr. Farhadi to extend his English vocabulary. Dr. Farhadi knew English quite well, but his vocabulary was rather formal and literary; he wanted to learn more idioms and popular expressions used in America and England. I also taught physics to one prisoner and tutored another in mathematics. I cannot recall exactly how many of these individual one-on-one learning and knowledge exchange courses started among the prisoners, but I can say that there were many.

It was amazing.

The prison command had put a bunch of professionals and scholars inside the stifling atmosphere of the prison with the aroma of death all around. But instead of cowering in fright in the face of the danger of being tortured or killed at any moment, they spent what time they could by learning from each other. These courses went on for quite some time, I believe even to the end of our stay in deadly Pul-i-Charkhi Prison. From this experience, I concluded that *human beings with knowledge and strong beliefs can turn around the most difficult situations in life, if given a chance to survive.*

In other words, it is what we do in life that matters.

Wednesday, January 3, 1979 (Jadi 13, 1357)

Fifty prisoners from the south block were taken out to the execution grounds. And twenty-eight more prisoners—twenty-seven of them from the south block, and Shah-Dawlah from political block no. 1—were taken out to the execution grounds. Shah-Dawlah and twenty soldiers from the tanks had attempted to make a coup against the Communist Parcham–Khalq government.

Thursday, January 18, 1979 (Jadi 28, 1357)

Thirty-one women and babies belonging to Hazrat Mojadidi's family were brought to the west side of political block no. 1.

Saturday, January 27, 1979 (Dalua 7, 1357)

Three prisoners were released on this date: Abdul Mohammad and Zahir, both students at Kandahar Polytechnical College who were imprisoned for refusing to attend Russian-language classes, and Captain Fazil-haq from Herat Province.

Radio Problem

Monday, February 12, 1979 (Dalua 23, 1357)

On this date, I did not think that I would survive the nightmarish night. At about midday, Sawtinman Baseer came to my cell on his usual patrol. He opened the door and stood in the doorway, periodically looking behind himself, toward the corridor. My cell mates were still outside for their cleaning period, and I was alone in the room.

After asking how I was, Baseer quietly added, "If you have anything in the room that you do not want anyone to know about, then get rid of it."

After saying that, he closed the door and left. This fellow had always been courteous toward me and my cell mates. I realized that he was giving me an important warning. The only thing that we had in the room that we did not anyone else to know about was our radio. Baseer must have known about it or, at least, guessed. As I was thinking about this, my cell mate Fayeq returned. I said, "Fayeq, take our radio and the earphone outside. Pretend that you are washing up. When you're sure no one is looking, bury the radio under gravel and sand at one place and then the earphone in another. Both the radio and the earphone are in plastic bags, so they won't get ruined. Make sure that you mark the location in your mind. We'll retrieve them later. Go quickly, and don't waste any time, my friend."

Fayeq immediately collected the radio and earphone from where we had hidden them, and then he left. He was a man of action who did things very fast. He could do this job much better than I could ever have done it.

Fayeq came back after about fifteen minutes. Looking at me, he said, "It is done. Nobody can find it." He then smiled.

By this time, our other cell mates were back, so we informed them of what we had done. The prison cleanup periods were timed to precede the five prayer times during the day; we had to wash before praying.

231

The guards led the prisoners down to the courtyard and allowed them about twenty to thirty minutes. Then, they herded everyone back to their cells in the block. The times for prayer were an hour before sunrise; at noon; in the afternoon; half an hour after sunset; and about eight at night, before going to sleep. That evening, I did a quick washup during the fourth period and returned to my cell before the others. I had finished saying my prayers when I heard a lot of noise—the clump-clump of footsteps and then the bang-bang and people running, as if there were a buffalo stampede. There was the sound of the footsteps of men running in the corridors. Then the door to our cell opened and my cell mates came in one after another, still panting from running too fast.

I asked, "What's happening?"

They told me, "The commandant and a lot of soldiers came to the yard and started kicking us and beating the prisoners with the butts of their guns. It was chaotic. The commandant was shouting and cursing and saying that they would deal with the people's enemies and take care of them.

"Some guys couldn't run very fast and fell down. They were trampled, kicked and beaten, and threatened to be shot with machine guns."

The prisoners were herded into their cells. Then, there was an eerie silence. I heard no more sounds of movement. We all waited to see what was going to happen next.

The Thought of Being Tortured

During the time that we were in Pul-i-Charkhi Prison, we had seen a lot of people brought to the prison, tortured, and eventually executed. We had witnessed the slaughter and killing of many prisoners right in front of our eyes. It was very hard for us even to think about what was in store for us. What did the bloodthirsty commandant Said Abdullah and his partners plan to do to us? Again, I thought of the sheep in the slaughterhouse lined up for the chopping block. But what could one do under such circumstances? Keep up your morale, go to the chopping block with your spirits high, and try not to lose your mind! But the prospects did not worry me much. Strangely enough, I did not think much about myself.

I was praying all the time: "O God, please save my kids and family. Don't let anything bad happen to them!" At times of calamity or in the midst of disaster, praying and thinking of God is comforting and helpful. It revives hope.

Earlier, some of the prisoners who had been tortured told me that they had done two things that were helpful in reducing pain during torture: reciting verses from the Holy Quran, and continuing to shout and scream as loud as they could. But to tell you the truth, at this moment, all that I was doing was saying my prayers.

I Am Beaten and Tortured

Time seemed to drag on. At about nine o'clock, I heard the sound of footsteps. There seemed to be several people walking in the corridor. They stopped in front of our cell. Once the door flew open, several soldiers, with guns in hand and led by the commandant himself, burst into the room, all the while repeatedly shouting to me: "Minister of Mines, give me your radio!"

I kept on saying, "I don't have a radio!" Said Abdullah and the soldiers kept beating me and my cell mates Karim Ataii and Ghausuddin Fayeq with their fists and gun butts and kicking us with their boots. I had become a punching bag. Fortunately, the frail former prime minister, Noor Ahmad Etemadi, was spared. All I could remember was trying to protect my head. My glasses had fallen down somewhere, so I could not clearly see objects at a distance.

There was a swarm of soldiers beating me down to the floor and dragging me into the corridor. I kept falling to the floor and trying to get up. The soldiers kept on beating me, dragging me along the floor and pushing me through the corridor. They pushed me down the stairs to another, bigger corridor on the first floor and then toward the commandant's office. While running and falling, I saw a person lying

233

curled up on the floor. I thought that he had been killed. I stooped down to see who it was. Governor Roshandil looked up at me and motioned me to go ahead. He was alive. Soldiers came from behind and pushed me on. I kept going toward what seemed like the head offices of the prison.

There, the commandant was standing. He spoke to the soldiers. Two of them grabbed me and pushed me into a room, which, I pretty soon found out, was where they tortured the prisoners.

My mind was not functioning properly, but I thought to myself, *I am in the human grinding machine.* The commandant and his assistant came into the torture room and told the soldiers to stretch me out on the floor. After doing that, they tied wires to my toes and fingers. The commandant said, "Minister of Mines, where is the radio?"

I said, "We do not have a radio."

He told his assistant to turn on the electric machine and give me shocks.

With the shocks, I kept bouncing up and down on the floor. I felt that an extreme pressure was building inside of me until I passed out.

They gave me more shocks and kept on asking, "Where is the radio?"

I faintly responded, "We don't have one." They kept on delivering the electric shocks more and more until I was unconscious.

When I came to, they repeated the shocks all over again. I could hear the commandant telling his assistant, "What kind of a guy is this? We give him more shocks, and he's smiling!" Then, he would say, "Give him stronger shocks." He said this repeatedly; I could hear him when I regained consciousness.

I thought, *This guy must be a sadist.* I was benefiting from the advice of previously tortured prisoners on how to feel less pain, but I was not smiling. I was grimacing, showing my teeth in pain, which made the commandant think that I was smiling.

Said Abdullah was indeed a bloodthirsty sadist.

I thought to myself that he would probably not stop giving me shocks until I was dead. I thought that he must have gotten some information about our radio from his spies among the prisoners. Since we were sharing the daily news with the other prisoners, maybe a cell mate had inadvertently told someone that we (or the minister of mines) had a radio from which we got our daily news.

Finally, I told the commandant, "We had a radio once that belonged to Juma Mohammadi. He took it with him when he was released from the prison. We don't have a radio anymore." I thought to myself that this half-truth might satisfy Said Abdullah so he would stop torturing me. In this way, his spy's information would be confirmed and my statement that we did not have a radio would be validated, given that the guards had thoroughly searched my cell and did not find any radio.

I really do not know how my mind worked at such a critical time to find a solution that would satisfy the commandant, but my instinct to ease the pain and to struggle for survival may have, at times, given me a subconscious solution.

Sure enough, my statement did work. The commandant stopped giving me shocks. By this time, I was nearly dead anyway. The soldiers threw me onto the floor inside a dark hole; since I was motionless, they probably thought that I was dead. While I was lying there on the dirty floor of a dark basement hole, I saw that it was pitch-black. I could not see anything, but I thought, *I am alive!* It felt better than being in the torture room!

I do not know how long afterward it was when the soldiers came into the hole, picked me up, and took me back to the torture room. From there, they dragged me to the hall in front of the commandant's office.

I saw some other prisoners lined up in a circle, all waiting their turn to enter the grinding machine. I was not sure that my cell mates could endure the stress of a long period of torture like what I had gone through. If they admitted that we had a radio, then our goose would really be cooked. Each one of us would contradict the other, and we would all be proven to have told lies. I was unable to walk, so I crawled and managed to get myself to where Fayeq, pale-faced, was standing.

I tugged at his trousers and said, "We had a radio. It belonged to Muhammadi. He took it with him when he was released." Then, I crawled to where Ataii was standing. I wanted to repeat to him what I had told Fayeq, but it was not necessary because, at that moment, the commandant ordered the guards to herd us back to our cells. The torture session had ended. Fortunately, my cell mates were not tortured, at least not for the time being.

We were back in our cell no. 14 by about eleven o'clock that night.

An examination of my body showed some bruises, scratches, and burns, but I did not mind those, as I was content to be alive.

I was not aware of having suffered any permanent damage from the beatings and torture inflicted on me that night.

I had no means to evaluate any long-term damage that I might sustain in the future.

It looked as though the Soviet experts had trained the Afghan Communists quite well. Their guiding rule was to prolong suffering and agony: terrorize, beat, and torture, but do not let the prisoners die until the time comes when you decide to get rid of them. At that point, kill them fast.

Going Down Fighting

Tuesday, March 13, 1979 (Hoot 23, 1357)

Early in the morning, the prison commander ordered all the prisoners to come down to the backyard. The guards herded us downstairs and out of the block, making us form a straight line in front of two wooden tables. All around us and on rooftops, soldiers with machine guns were standing guard. Said Abdullah, his assistant, and several staff members were standing behind the tables. There were some objects on the tables. The commandant began speaking. "The government of the People's Democratic Party of Afghanistan is fully aware of all the things that our enemies are doing in the country.

"We know what is going on in this prison," he said. "We know that there are certain reactionary elements who are planning to disrupt the order of our authority. Do you think that we did not know about the radios that you had in your rooms? We did not find a radio in the minister of mines' room, but I have information that he had appointed an unqualified boy, the son of an influential person, to a big job in the Ministry of Mines and Industries." He lifted a piece of bent and twisted red plastic high above his head and announced, "We found this radio in the woodstove in the room of Gul Ahmad Noor, Modir Faqir, and Aziz Ludin. They were trying to burn it."

He lifted another object and said, "We found this radio in Roshandil and Taj Mohammad's room. Israrullah Badakhshi has admitted to burying a radio. And Maiwandwal's group, which was transferred to Pul-i-Charkhi, also brought their radios with them.

"If we catch anyone who does not obey our rules and orders," he declared, "we will empty a whole machine-gun magazine into his belly."

The commandant said some more things that I do not remember very well, but one thing he said kept puzzling me. I kept wondering, *To whom was he referring when he said that I had appointed someone to a big job?* That type of thing did not fit my work ethic. I never appointed "an unqualified boy" to do a big job. Who was this person to whom the commandant was referring? And who was the influential father? This whole accusation did not fit in with the hiring methods that I adhered to at that time. Employment in my ministry was based on specific qualifications:

1) A minimum degree of education: a high school diploma for passing the twelfth-grade examinations.
2) Meeting the criteria of provincial quotas, which were determined on the basis of population. Each province had a quota, a predetermined number of people who could be employed for government staff positions. Thus, people from provinces in the far corners of the country had an opportunity for employment equal to those from provinces that were closer to the capital.
3) In addition to needing a twelfth-grade diploma, applicants had to pass a literacy and education-level examination given by an independent commission.
4) Those who were applying for technical or professional jobs had to have diplomas and degrees from accredited educational institutions.

These rules and regulations were designed to give everyone equal opportunity for employment in government jobs. So, what the commandant was saying was not true and could not be true. I thought, *Why did he say it? Maybe there is some personal reason or grudge behind his statement.* Of course, Said Abdullah's judgment was not of great value, since he was indoctrinated by Communist recruiters into hating anyone who was influential or rich or who worked in the previous governments. This slur on my professional ethics continued to puzzle me for several years until I finally figured out the reasons behind it.

The person to whom Said Abdullah referred was the son of General Serajuddin Khan, who headed the military division in Herat Province when I was the governor there. The general's wife was Said Abdullah's aunt, so he was related to them through his mother. While one sister was the wife of a general, the other (his mother) was married to a perhaps less important man (his father), so he himself had a lower social status than his cousin, the general's son.

This had resulted in Said Abdullah's holding a grudge, which was coupled with his indoctrination by Communist recruiters who persuaded him to hate his own family, his relatives, his clan, and his origins.

Communist indoctrinators in Afghanistan made extensive use of the element of hatred to recruit young people into joining either Khalq or Parcham. I had well-documented information that these young recruits were trained to spy on their own families—father, mother, and siblings. However, the hate element that was recommended by Soviet agents as a foundation for indoctrination later became the source of disenchantment among the traditional Afghans. It contributed heavily to the popular revolt against the Communists and their subsequent downfall.

One cannot use hatred and destructive methods and expect to gain friends.

Many years after this incident, I met the person to whom Said Abdullah had alluded. I told him about that day in the prison and the commandant's comments. He told me, "You never gave a point-blank order for me to be employed in the Ministry of Mines, like, 'Hire this person for this position.' The order that you gave for me was conditional, depending on my qualifications, my education, the provincial quota, my passing the tests, etc. The job that I finally got was not a very big job, anyway. It was actually below the level of my qualifications."

Personally, I learned from all this that plans and programs which I design and work on should always be built on facts. This is a rule that I give to the people whom I have the privilege of training.

My motto is, "Never make your plans and programs on the basis of unverifiable assumptions." To put it positively, "Always make your plans and programs on the basis of verifiable assumptions." (My motto applies to small as well as large projects. Many programs that I know of went awry, did not result in preconceived objectives, and eventually failed, because they were based on unverified assumptions.)

Tuesday, March 13, 1979 (Hoot 22, 1357)—the Same Day

Two more prisoners were brought to Pul-i-Charkhi: a Mr. Karim and a Dr. Wais Sulaiman, the latter a member of the extended royal family.

A Parchami minister of the PDPA government, Nezamuddin Tahzeeb, was also brought to Pul-i-Charkhi Prison.

March 17–18, 1979 (Hoot 26–27, 1357)

In two days, between six hundred and a thousand prisoners in seventy-five vehicles with guards in blue military uniforms, and a number of civil prisoners from the Parcham faction of PDPA, were brought into Pul-i-Charkhi Prison.

Also, Latif Tikadaar, a wealthy contractor, was brought into the prison on March 18. The prison command made an exception to the rules for this rich man. They allowed him to bring all his bedroom furnishings to the prison. He was living at his leisure and in luxury.

Friday, March 23, 1979 (Hamal 3, 1358)

Three busloads of prisoners—about 120 people—were brought into the prison. Forty prisoners were taken on one bus to the Polygon for execution.

Monday, March 26, 1979 (Hamal 6, 1358)

About a hundred prisoners from the south block were taken out for execution.

Saturday, March 31, 1979 (Hamal 11, 1358)

Three prisoners, the grandsons of Mia Gul-jan, were brought in to the prison. Also, Sulaiman Layeq was brought back to the prison. Judging from the distribution of food in the prison, I discerned that the total number of prisoners in the south block was forty-two hundred.

Wednesday, April 4, 1979 (Hamal 15, 1358)

Three brothers and sons of Noorgul Zazi were taken out during the day for execution.

Thursday, April 5, 1979 (Hamal 16, 1358)

Toryalai, General Arif Khan's nephew, went blind. He could not see anything.

Tuesday, April 17, 1979 (Hamal 28, 1358)

The Air Defense Unit Battalion as a whole was brought to the south block of Pul-i-Charkhi. Four officers from this group were brought into the prison and then taken out for execution.

Sunday, April 22, 1979 (Saur 2, 1358)

Fifteen prisoners from the south block were taken out to the execution grounds and killed.

Saturday, April 28, 1979 (Saur 8, 1358)

The prison staff brought twenty to thirty people into Pul-i-Charkhi and then took them out of the south block for execution.

Monday, April 30, 1979 (Saur 10, 1358)

Twenty soldiers were brought into the south block.

Tuesday, May 1, 1979 (Saur 11, 1358)

Thirty soldiers were brought into the south block.

Friday, May 4, 1979 (Saur 14, 1358)

At about 8:30 in the morning, the delivery of prisoners' items from family members outside the prison was stopped.

Saturday, May 12, 1979 (Saur 22, 1358)

About 170 persons were brought from Badakhshan to the south block and then were taken out for execution at night.

Monday, May 14, 1979 (Saur 24, 1358)

About three hundred men from the Fourth, Eighth, and Fifteenth Divisions of the Afghan army were brought into Pul-i-Charkhi.

Thursday, May 17, 1979 (Saur 27, 1358)

Seven sons and seven women from the family of Representative Azam Shinwari were brought to the west wing of political block no. 1. They had been imprisoned for a period of ten months in some other prison before being brought to Pul-i-Charkhi.

Friday, May 18, 1979 (Saur 28, 1358)

About thirty people were brought into the south block during the day.

Saturday, May 19, 1979 (Saur 29, 1358)

The minister of the interior, Lieutenant Colonel Sher-jan Mazdooryar of the tank corps, and the commandant inspected some of the cells inside Pul-i-Charkhi Prison.

Tuesday, May 22, 1979 (Jauza 1, 1358)

Said Abdullah, the commandant of Pul-i-Charkhi, checked the names and made a list of prisoners in every cell of the prison.

Sunday, May 27, 1979 (Jauza 6, 1358)

Twenty-three people were brought into the south block.

Tuesday, May 29, 1979 (Jauza 8, 1358)

A Dreadful Night

This was *a dreadful Tuesday night.* The prison lights were turned off. We heard the sound of heavy machinery and three buses and a tank coming from the main gates into the courtyard in front of the commandant's office.

Our lookouts on the top floor saw that three to four prisoners at a time were being escorted to the prison's main office by soldiers who carried machine guns and walked in front of and behind the prisoners. As I noted before, 145 prisoners from the Ikhwan (Muslim Brotherhood) had been brought to Pul-i-Charkhi on Tuesday, August 8, 1978. A week after that, on Wednesday, August 16, 1978 (Asad 25, 1357), 30 prisoners from this group, including Faizani and General Mir Ahmadshah, were taken out at night and killed at the Polygon execution grounds across the river.

The prisoners whom the soldiers were bringing out tonight appeared to be some of the 115 of Faizani's group, which remained in the south block. These prisoners were now taken to an outside door behind the commandant's office and then led through a door and into a room that was set up to prepare the prisoners for execution. Each prisoner, his hands tied behind his back, was blindfolded and then guided through a corridor in front of the commandant's office. Once out in the front yard, these men were led up ramps and loaded onto buses that had been waiting there for them.

The high, barred window in my cell faced the front courtyard. By putting an object under my feet and standing on it, I got a glimpse of the front yard.

I could hear the footsteps of prisoners as they walked up the ramp, and I was able to count the number of prisoners who were being loaded onto the buses.

At about 9:30 that night, there was a lot of commotion in the prison. We heard the sound of men running and shouting on the first floor. Machine guns were fired inside the prison and outside in the yard. The sound of machine guns inside the prison came from smaller-caliber Kalashnikovs (AK-47's).

The shots fired in the front yard sounded like those of the type of heavy-caliber machine gun that is mounted on weapons carriers, tanks, and four-barrel anti-aircraft guns.

After a few minutes, we heard voices from one of the windows in the officers' sleeping quarters. They called out to the prison guards and soldiers who were standing on armored machinery, saying, "O soldiers, do not be deceived by the Communist heathens and traitors who are selling our country to the Soviet Union and its operatives. They are deceiving you and will later kill you all. Join us and other mujahideen to liberate our land from these traitors. This is the time when we all should unite!"

We could hear a chorus of voices from inside the buses.

The prisoners who had been loaded onto the buses were singing hymns and prayers: "Allah-u-Akbar, Allah-u-Akbar. Allah-u-Akbar, Allah-u-Akbar. Laa-Ilaha-Illallah-u-Allah-u-Akbar. Wa Li'llah-u-l'Hamd." (Translated, this means, "God is great" [repeated three times]. "There is no other God but God. God is great, and praise be unto Him."

Mass Murder

The Communist soldiers showered the buses with all the bullets they had, but the chorus of these hymns and prayers was repeated over and over again for several hours, until it gradually got weaker and weaker and finally faded away.

The call for patriotic unity from inside one of the rooms also continued for a long time. But the Communist soldiers threw grenades through the broken windows and into the rooms. The shouts from therein gradually faded away; after a few hours, we could not hear them anymore.

Killing those men with bullets and grenades may have stopped their chorus on that tragic night, but the sound of their cries never stopped reaching the ears of an unfortunate nation that had fallen prey to and was being crushed under the wheels of heavy war machinery, including the chains of T-62 tanks of the Soviet expansionist move that had begun trampling and gobbling the free people of the region.

All the time that this nightmarish tragedy was going on, we prisoners could hear what was going on inside the prison and outside in the front yard. But we were unable to do anything. The lights were off and the doors were locked from the outside. It was a sickening feeling.

I could not even peer out into the front yard in front of my cell. My cell mates would pull me down, shouting, "It's useless! You'll be killed! They're firing on the buses and the prison from all directions!"

They were absolutely correct, but what can one do in an abnormally disastrous and mind-boggling situation except be there and bear witness to a calamitous tragedy?

We eventually learned the cause for this night's slaughter. The last group of prisoners who were taken into the execution-preparation room had jumped the soldiers guarding them and succeeded in grabbing their weapons. The soldiers had panicked and run out, shouting. The armed prisoners had rushed to commandant's office to take or kill him. Said Abdullah, who was really a coward, had run away and hidden himself under one of the guard's beds in the basement of the prison block. That is how the commotion, running, shouting, and firing of machine guns in the prison had begun that night.

The armed prisoners, having found themselves outnumbered, had entered an officer's dormitory and locked the door. Since they had assault rifles, no one was able to come close to them. Instead, soldiers who had come to take the prisoners to the execution grounds had opened fire with whatever weapons they had at their disposal. Light and heavy machine guns were fired at the window of the room where the armed prisoners were, and at the buses loaded with the prisoners who were already blindfolded and bound. The calls for unity that we had heard came from the armed prisoners in the officer's dormitory, the ones who were finally silenced by the grenades thrown inside.

The chorus of prayers that came from the helpless prisoners trapped on the buses was silenced only by bullets. The incessant sound of machine guns being fired at them on the front yard of the prison did not stop until 2:30 in the morning. In the end, the buses were like sieves with bullet holes oozing blood out onto the ground. We prisoners who remained alive had witnessed another of the most tragic events in modern Afghan history.

The killers then proceeded to hide the evidence of the mass murder they had committed. It took them until 5:30 in the morning to bury the evidence in the front yard of the prison. That whole morning, we prisoners were not allowed out to clean up.

Can atrocities of this magnitude and the history of an unfortunate nation be hidden from humankind? I wondered when justice would be served to the perpetrators of such murderous deeds.

Wednesday, May 30, 1979 (Jauza 9, 1358)

One person was released from political block no. 1 on this day.

Sunday, June 3, 1979 (Jauza 13, 1358)

Fifty-six prisoners were taken out for execution during the day.

The Honorable Muballigh, one of the Shia sect's prominent lecturers and preachers, was executed with this group today.

Thursday, June 7, 1979 (Jauza 17, 1358)

Mr. Hanif Gharwal and Mr. Mawlana, the father of Saif-ur-Rahman, who walked with a stick, were released from the prison. Both were from Maiwandwal's group. The rumor was that they had agreed to cooperate with the Khalqis who were now in power among the leadership of the Communist government.

Wednesday, June 13, 1979 (Jauza 23, 1358)

One person named Shahzada was released from the prison.

Wednesday, June 20, 1979 (Jauza 30, 1358)

Two hundred people were brought to the south block. Among this group, Dr. Abdul Karim Zarghoon, head of the Indira Gandhi Children's Hospital,[23] and one Yairghal, both of these men Khalqis but Taraki loyalists, were brought to political block no. 1. Also from this group, five were imprisoned in the east wing. Five others were taken to the third floor of political block no. 1.

On the same day, about seventy of the imprisoned soldiers were released from the south block of Pul-i-Charkhi Prison.

Saturday, June 23, 1979 (Saratan 2, 1358)

Six women who belonged to the Parcham faction of the PDPA were brought to the west wing of political block no. 1.

Monday, June 25, 1979 (Saratan 4, 1358)

One hundred people were brought to the south block, and five Parchami women were brought to the west wing of political block no. 1.

---

[23] An early member of the PDPA central committee who had quit the party.

Saturday, June 30, 1979 (Saratan 9, 1358)

Brigadier Generals Babri Gul and Sultan were released from the prison on this day.

Wednesday, July 4, 1979 (Saratan 13, 1358)

Sixty people were brought to south block, and twelve were brought to political block no. 1.

Thursday, July 12, 1979 (Saratan 21, 1358)

Thirteen women prisoners were brought to block no. 1, and eight hundred soldiers were brought to block no. 3. Also on this day, sixty students from the military school were brought into the prison.

Tuesday, July 24, 1979 (Asad 2, 1358)

The women and children of the Mojadidi family were released on this day.

Sunday, July 29, 1979 (Asad 7, 1358)

About six hundred soldiers, some of them wounded, were brought into the prison.

Wednesday, August 1, 1979 (Asad 10, 1358)

Twelve women, wives of soldiers and officers, and their children were brought in to the prison.

Tuesday, August 7, 1979 (Asad 16, 1358)

One hundred seventy-one soldiers of the rank of corporal were taken out of the prison.

Tuesday, August 21, 1979 (Asad 30, 1358)

Prime Minister Etemadi

Former Prime Minister Nur Ahmad Etemadi, who was with us in cell no. 14, was taken out in the middle of the day. About midday, one of the guards had come to our cell and told Mr. Etemadi that he was being released. The guard said, "I will be waiting in the corridor for you to pack your belongings."

At that time, I was alone in the room with Mr. Etemadi; our other cell mates had not come back from their washup session. I asked the guard, "How will Mr. Prime Minister get home from prison at this time?"

He said, "Someone has come after him."

I asked, "Who is that person?"

He said, "I don't know. He is a tall, dark fellow and has brought a small red car." I sensed that Mr. Etemadi was worried. I was, too (and so were our cell mates, when they returned).

While Etemadi was gathering his belongings, he asked me, "Mr. Assifi, what do you think?"

I said, "It is a bit unusual for prisoners to leave the prison at this time of day, but I hope everything will be well. Maybe the commandant has asked someone to come and pick you up to take you home." Then I added as casually as I could, "By the way, we need to agree on some *signs* between us. When you get home, will you ask your wife to cook some rice and send it to me in a small container on the next day when families bring clean clothes for their relatives?" Mr. Etemadi had some plates and eating utensils, so I added, "I'm going to keep a few of your utensils. In order for me to know that you've arrived home, first there will be the rice. Second, whoever brings the rice should tell the guard who is to carry it to us, 'Mr. Etemadi wants the remaining items that he left behind.' *With these two signs,* we will be further assured that you have arrived home."

Mr. Etemadi said, "I'll remember what you said." He then said good-bye to the three of us in the cell and asked us to pray for him. We said good-bye to him, prayed for him, and wished him a safe arrival home.

Also on Tuesday, August 21, 1979 (Asad 30, 1358)

Ninety-three soldiers were brought to Pul-i-Charkhi Prison.

Friday, August 24, 1979 (Sunbula 2, 1358)

This was the day when we all got our bags with clean clothes, the ones that our families brought to us in prison. According to the sign that I and Mr. Etemadi had agreed on, we should have also gotten a container of rice—but there was nothing from Mr. Etemadi in the packages that were brought to me and my cell mates. I thought that maybe Etemadi had either forgotten about it or did not have anyone to bring it to us. In any case, our signal had not been used.

So, through the secret communication channel that my wife and I had established, I sent a message to Fariha, asking her to go to Mr. Etemadi's house, ask his wife if he was at home, and let me know her answer on the next delivery day.

By then, I was quite worried, but the only thing that I could do was wait for the next delivery day, which would be Friday, September 14, 1979 (Sunbula 23, 1358).

Sunday, August 26, 1979 (Sunbula 4, 1358)

Fifty soldiers were brought to Pul-i-Charkhi Prison on this day.

Tuesday, August 28, 1979 (Sunbula 6, 1358)

Two more women prisoners were brought into Pul-i-Charkhi. At this time, there were about fifty women political prisoners in Pul-i-Charkhi Prison.

On this day also, Officer Asif and Officer Ishaq, two former prisoners, were brought back to the prison. Officer Asif was tortured many times. He was electrocuted with wires attached to his genitals. Asif was very sick, and the guards brought him to my cell. He had a problem of continuously discharging semen and was nearly dying. I gave him all the vitamins that my family had sent me. Also, my cell mates and I gave him a greater share of our daily food ration, but it was no use.

On the same day, August 28, the guards brought twenty-seven members of Parcham to the prison. These prisoners were first taken to the south block, and from there they were moved to political block no. 1.

Among them was Samad Azhar, a notorious police officer who had sabotaged previous non-Communist governments on many occasions. Samad Azhar was rumored to have been responsible for the murder of former Prime Minister Mohammad Hashim Maiwandwal in Dehmazang Prison during Daoud's presidency. At that time, false reports were circulated, trying to make it look as though Mr. Maiwandwal had committed suicide.

The Tafsir

Abdul Ghafoor Parwani, the mathematics teacher and textbook author who had been brought to Pul-i-Charkhi from another prison in late November 1978, had been executed.

Sidiq Wahidi, a top-notch Afghan police officer whom I had known for a long time, found out about Parwani's execution and gave me the sad news. However, Wahidi also said that Mr. Parwani had left behind in his cell an English-language *tafsir*—a detailed commentary on the Holy Quran—written by Yusuf Ali, a well-known scholar and professor of languages at Cambridge University.

Mr. Wahidi said that he would let me read it for six hours every day. He added that four of us would secretly rotate the tafsir among ourselves during the twenty-four hours of each day. I said that would be beautiful and asked, "Who are the four?"

He said, "You, me, Ravan Farhadi, and Sabahuddin Kushkaki." (Sabahuddin had once been the minister of press and information.)

Wahidi told me that my time would be in the morning, if that was okay with me. I said, "Yes, of course, it's a very good time for me."

This was a wonderful opportunity for me. I could study the tafsir during the best time of day. I had not even dreamed that I could have such an opportunity in prison.

Fortunately, this chance came to me at a time when the prison rules were a bit relaxed. Still, we had to be extremely careful to pass the tafsir among ourselves discreetly, take precautions while reading it, and do our best not to expose our reading program. Our reading and rotation program went quite smoothly and without any mishap. Prison was a place where we had almost no way to fill or spend our time, even with our learning exchanges.

This tafsir study was a very beneficial occupation; reading the tafsir gave me an opportunity to become a better Muslim. Not only did we spend our time usefully, but, as the saying goes, we also paved our way for the Last Day of Judgment.

With their newly acquired power, Communists in the government made facetious remarks to the effect that they were giving some people an opportunity in prison to become reeducated and learn the fundamentals of Marxist–Leninist socialism.

But, as it turned out, the blessings of the Almighty worked in such a way that at least some of us were given an opportunity in prison to become better educated in our own religion. I had a lot of time to study the verses of the Quran. Thinking deeply on their meaning gradually opened the way for my vast understanding of the true meaning of these verses and their interpretation by using scientific principles. The more I studied, the more I understood my own religion.

Friday, September 14, 1979 (Sunbula 23, 1358)

Sixteen prisoners identified as Pakistani nationals were brought into Pul-i-Charkhi.

This Friday was the day for the exchange of packages between the prisoners and their families. We all got what we were waiting for—except nothing came from Etemadi. I went to my cell and began searching for a message from my wife. I found it. She had informed me that she had visited Mrs. Etemadi, who told her that Mr. Etemadi had not come home and that she did not know where he was. This information was very saddening to me and my cell mates. If Mr. Etemadi did not get home, where was he?

This was why we had not gotten our first signal: the rice.

Regarding our second signal, a strange thing happened during the previous week. Sometime in the middle of the week, one of the prison guards came to our cell, stood at the door, and said, "The commandant says you should return Etemadi's things that are still with you."

This was very strange. I asked the guard, "Is Mr. Etemadi asking for them?"

He said, "No. Someone else is in the commandant's office asking for them." Because we had not received the first signal, we suspected that Etemadi was not at home. Was he alive or not? The following possibilities occurred to us:

a) Etemadi was alive; he had sent us signal 2 to tell us that he was still alive, although not yet home.

b) He was alive, but not free. He had been forced to tell his interrogators about his conversations with his cell mates, specifically those of the day when he left the cell. He had to tell them something, so the information about signal 2 was forced out of him.

c) The prison command had installed listening devices in our cells; they had bugged our cell. This, however, was less likely than (a) or (b).

But we were unable to find any trace of Mr. Etemadi or learn anything about his whereabouts. We were forced to make the conclusion that he had most likely been killed.

As we all knew, Mr. Etemadi was one of the most important prisoners in Pul-i-Charkhi Prison at that time. He had been prime minister during Zahir Shah's time. During his term of office, relations with Soviet Union were good. He was even honorably recognized by the Soviets. Before his prime ministry, he served as foreign minister. As a career diplomat, he had held many important posts in the foreign ministry and served as ambassador to Pakistan, Italy, and the USSR.

So, why did the leadership of the Communist regime decide to kill him? I myself think that perhaps Mr. Etemadi played an important role in a broad-based Soviet-guided government led by Parcham, which was what the Soviets apparently wanted.

Hafizullah Amin, who had quelled a revolt by the Parchamis and their cohorts, eliminated Taraki, took over the leadership of the PDPA, and expected that he would be leading the country in the future. He did not want any potential collaboration with his Parchami competitors. Perhaps he didn't want any competition from a distinguished non-Communist collaborator, either. He may have been aware that the Soviets wanted to get rid of Mr. Etemadi. Or perhaps Mr. Etemadi had refused to cooperate with them. I can only speculate.

Sunday, September 23, 1979 (Mizan 1, 1358)

Four hundred soldiers were released from Pul-i-Charkhi Prison on this day.

On this Sunday night, I had one of my usual premonitions: I dreamed that I saw my wife walking in the air and coming toward the block where I was imprisoned. She was wearing a camel's-hair topcoat that fluttered in the breeze.

Sunday, October 7, 1979 (Mizan 15, 1358)

Sardar Ahmad Ali Khan, the minister of court during Zahir Shah's time, passed away on this day. The prisoners in political block no. 1 all gathered in a room that was supposedly a library (it had government propaganda pamphlets in it) to pay their respects to him as an exemplary prisoner.

He had really been a father figure to all the prisoners in political block no. 1. Even the Parchamis and the Khalqi Tarakists who had been imprisoned by Amin's government gathered in the "library" to pay their respects to this fine gentleman.[24]

In the past, Parchamis and Khalqis habitually used bad names and curse words for the king and the people who worked for him.

Now that they were in prison, their tone was different. In death there is mystery.

His death had dissolved, or at least neutralized, most of the grudges and hatred that had been instilled by Soviet operatives into the naïve and easily pliable minds of less-educated young Afghans. Their slogan was, "Hate and kill to get the power into your hands. Then when you get it, give it to your big Soviet friends, who will be your eternal friends and bosses and lead you on the way to eternal utopia."

---

[24] The honorary title "sardar" can be used for a dignitary, a nobleman, or a gentleman of fine qualities, as well as for a prince.

Monday, October 8, 1979 (Mizan 16, 1358)

Family Visit

Some of the guards came to my cell and told me that there were some people in the commandant's office who wanted to see me.

I was really shocked. At first, I worried about a frightening dream that I had had a couple of weeks before, and I hoped that the guards had not brought any of my family members to the prison. Then, I thought of the way in which Mr. Etemadi had been taken out in the middle of day. (We still could not find any trace of his whereabouts.)

With a heavy heart, I stood up and followed the guard down the corridor and toward the stairway. Walking close to me, he said, "I think some members of your family are here to see you."

I wondered, *Is my dream coming true?* In my heart, I kept praying, *O God, please save my family. Do not let any harm come to them!*

I followed the guard through a big hall on the first floor, passed the prison command offices on the left, and entered through the last door on the right into another big room full of officers' cots.

In one corner at the end of the room, my mother, my wife, and my son were sitting. Facing them on the opposite side were one of my aunts, my cousin, her husband, and another, older woman.

In a state of incomprehension, I kept saying, "Why have you come? You shouldn't have come. Please, leave as soon as possible."

I did not want them to be there. This was the room wherein, on the "dreadful night" in May, several prisoners were killed by the Communist soldiers who threw hand grenades through the windows. Looking around, I could still see the marks of shrapnel on the walls and ceiling. Yes, this was one of the rooms of the slaughterhouse!

All these thoughts were going on in my mind, so seeing my family there in the same room was mind-boggling and quite upsetting.

Family visits were never allowed in Pul-i-Charkhi Prison. This visit was the first and last during the period I was there.

Of course, from my family's point of view, they were visiting a dear one. I must have looked distraught and emaciated with my hollowed cheeks. I was wearing a chapan and shabby clothes. But my family was happy to see me alive. After a few minutes, two more prisoners—Khalil Karzai, the old woman's son, and Sultan Aziz Zikria—were brought into the room. At that moment, we almost had a family reunion.

But I was still in a state of shock. All I wanted was for my family to leave the stifling and blood-soaked environment of the prison safely. I felt a little better when they got up to leave, got into their van, and drove away toward the big outer gates of the prison. At that time, the guard took me back to cell no. 14.

I prayed again and said, "Dear God, thank you."

The Fifth Coffin

After mid-September 1979, the government television and radio stations announced that a number of prominent PDPA members had been killed while defending the party. They showed an official funeral procession with an honor guard. In the film that we prisoners saw on TV in the corridor of our floor, five flag-draped coffins were shown. However, only four names were mentioned as people who were honored in the procession.

In the morning, we asked each other who was in the fifth coffin. At about that time, the government announced that President Nur Mohammad Taraki[25] was sick and that his deputy, Hafizullah Amin, had assumed the chairmanship of the PDPA. (In fact,

---

[25] To this day, I still do not know who was in the fifth coffin. Was it Taraki?

around this time, Amin had had Taraki killed.) The same night, twenty-seven members of Taraki's family, including his wife, Punba gul (her name, translated, means "the flower of cotton"), and his brother were brought into the west wing, the female section of block no. 1.

My guess was that during Taraki's visit with Soviet higher-ups in Moscow, before he came to Kabul, he had hatched a plan to kill Amin. The plan was that Amin would be apprehended or killed when he welcomed Taraki at Kabul Airport.

However, an Amin confidante who had been in these meetings informed him about the plan. Consequently, Amin was not present when Taraki landed at the airport. Taraki and the Soviet ambassador had gone to the president's office and called Amin for a meeting. Amin and his armed friends went to the meeting prepared for a showdown.

Then, a scene like one in a cowboy movie played out. The result was that several prominent PDPA people were killed, Taraki among them. Was he in the fifth coffin?

Monday, October 8, 1979 (Mizan 16, 1358)

On this day, Dr. Mir Ali Akbar and General Shahpur Ahmadzai were taken out of the prison and executed. Also on this day, twenty-eight men and women, members of Taraki's extended family,[26] were brought into Pul-i-Charkhi Prison. Those of us who were in the prison kept wondering how it was possible for the government to put Taraki's wife and his brother into Pul-i-Charkhi Prison if Taraki was still alive. There were apparent discrepancies in the announcements.

---

[26] Taraki was killed on the night of October 8–9, 1978.

Said Abdullah's Knifing

Although I do not remember the exact date of this incident, it is important that I mention it. We prisoners were engaged in our afternoon cleanup outside. Most had finished up and were walking in the yard when we heard a loud noise: machine guns being fired in the adjacent block, no. 2. At first, it sounded as if the gunfire was inside the block, but then we heard some noise from the yard. We all knew that something had happened in block no. 2, but we could not guess what it was.

The guards ordered us to go back to the block. Our top-floor lookouts informed us that there was commotion in the yard outside block no. 2. Some cars and military jeeps and soldiers were seen coming in. Later on, a weapons carrier came in, and then an ambulance. Then, somebody said that he had seen Asadullah Sarwari's car come into the block.

The next day, another officer came and gathered the prisoners in the yard, introduced himself as Captain Zahir, and told a story about some prisoners who had acquired a knife and refused to go to the commandant's office for investigation. When the commandant came to take them himself, one of the prisoners who had the knife attacked and wounded him. "The sounds that you heard," he explained, "were from the gunfire that the guards opened on the one who had the knife and would not let go of it. Said Abdullah was taken to a hospital, but he will come back as soon as he recovers. I advise the prisoners to stay calm and not to worry," Zahir told us. "The prison operation will go on as before."

When he finished speaking, our group broke up and started guessing at the outcome of these events—and what improvements, if any, we might expect. Someone said that he knew the new commandant and that Zahir himself had been a prisoner in Pul-i-Charkhi at some time before. Since our experience in the prison was that things got worse with any turn of events, we did not really expect any improvement at all. We waited for more information to percolate out from the various sources that we had acquired up to this date.

Eventually, we learned that a large group of about seventy or eighty prisoners had all occupied one of the large cells. They knew that they were going to be killed any day. So they talked among themselves and decided to create a situation in which they could attack the commandant.

First, they planned to buy a stabbing knife, the kind that is used in knife fighting. They each chipped in some money and gave it to one of the guards they trusted. They asked him to go to Kabul and then go to the old bazaar and get them a *jawhardar chaquu*—a kind of knife that makes wounds that never heal. (I really do not know how these knives are made, but I have heard many stories about them.)

After the prisoners got the knife, they discussed how to get the commandant into a situation that could lend itself to their plan. A prisoner named Zalmai (I am not sure that this is his name), who had been in the armed forces, was familiar with martial arts and was an expert in the use of knives. He volunteered to do this job. Of course, it was not an easy thing to do.

After some time, the execution order for this group arrived in the office of the commandant. Said Abdullah planned to have the prisoners brought to that office through the back door as usual, tie their hands, blindfold them, and take them to the buses that were waiting to take them to the killing grounds.

The commandant sent some soldiers to block no. 2 to fetch the prisoners in groups of three or four and place them under an armed escort of special guards. Usually, the killing jobs were done at night, but this time it was in daylight to make it appear that it happened after a routine investigation.

Said Abdullah had told the guards to tell the prisoners that they were going to be asked some questions in some sort of an interview. When these soldiers came to fetch the prisoners, they prisoners refused to go to the commandant's office, telling the soldiers to tell the commandant to come himself for the interview.

Hearing this, Said Abdullah, who was a proud killer, got very angry and told the soldiers, "I'll go and show them who is the boss here!" He then went to prison block no. 2, accompanied by several armed soldiers.

He entered the room and called out, "Who are the people disobeying my orders? Okay, I came here myself. Show yourselves to me and say what your complaint is."

The prisoners said in unison, "We didn't understand what the soldiers said, and we don't object to going to your office." The commandant stood by the door, with one pistol in his holster and another pistol in his hand, and ordered, "Okay, let's go."

There were two armed guards inside the room with him and several more outside. The prisoners stood up and started to leave the room in single file, passing in front of Said Abdullah to go out the door. Several of them passed in front of him and went out. Zalmai, who had volunteered to do the stabbing, moved as though to go out of the room, but then he suddenly turned around, grabbed Said Abdullah from behind, and started knifing him in the belly and chest. Zalmai was very strong; he held the commandant with one hand and kept stabbing him with the other. He pulled Said Abdullah into a corner of the room where the soldiers could not shoot at him without hitting the commandant first. The commandant cried out in pain and tried to get free of Zalmai's grip, but he couldn't. Zalmai kept stabbing and twisting the knife into his belly and chest.

The commandant cried out, "Don't kill me! I am a Said, and Saids are the progeny of Prophet Mohammad! For the sake of the Prophet, please don't hurt me!" Zalmai kept on stabbing, telling the commandant how many people he had killed and saying that he was a traitor to his country and his people—and to Prophet Mohammad.

The commandant then slumped to the floor. That is when the soldiers opened fire on Zalmai and several other prisoners who were standing close by. The soldiers outside the room started firing at the prisoners who were outside in the yard.

That is when we heard the sound of the assault guns. When we heard the gunfire, we had all been walking outside in the yard. We waited to find out what had happened and to learn whether the commandant was hit, wounded, or killed. I remember that Dr. Abdullah Omar, a colleague and the former minister of public health, came close to me and said, "What do you think, Assifi? Has the commandant been killed?"

I said, "No, I don't think so. It would be a very easy death for him to die so soon. I believe that the worst death for these Communists will be when they are named as traitors by their own party. They have committed so much torture and have killed thousands of innocent Afghan people. I don't think that the commandant will die so easily!"

Dr. Omar said, "I asked if you know what really happened, and now you are telling me your theories about justice and what *should* really happen."

I said, "Well, you asked me a question, and since I didn't know the real answer, I answered you according to what I believe."

Eventually, we heard that although Said Abdullah survived, he was so badly injured that he was taken to Moscow for surgery and treatment. He spent several months in Russia. When he came back, someone who had seen him said that he looked like a walking dead man and had a tube sticking out of his body for the discharge of material from his intestines.

Zalmai and all his friends were killed, but they had accomplished an impossible mission: *they had turned Commandant Said Abdullah into a walking dead man.*

Invasion

Tuesday, October 9, 1979 (Mizan 17, 1358)

On this day, government television and radio stations made an official announcement regarding the death of Taraki.

Tuesday, October 16, 1979 (Mizan 24, 1358)

The families of Watanjar, Asadullah Sarwari,[27] and General Gulabzoy[28] were all brought to Pul-i-Charkhi Prison.

Friday, October 19, 1979 (Mizan 27, 1358)

A number of important people were taken out of political block no. 1 and executed on this date. Eidi Mohammad Khorsand was one of them. Several others—Dr. Zarghoon, Dr. Karim Yorish, Rasta Khiz, and Yerghal—were Tarakists from the Khalq faction. Maulana Hedayat was an important Islamic scholar at the Ministry of Justice who had learned that his son was also a prisoner and asked the guards to transfer the young man to block no. 1; a few hours after father and son were united, the father was taken out for execution.

Also on October 19, eleven people from block no. 2 were taken out at about 10:30 at night and executed. General Issa Khan and Safar-Jan, both from Nuristan Province, were included in this group.

---

[27] Sarwari, the feared and hated "King Kong," was involved in Taraki's Soviet-backed plot to kill Amin, as were other Taraki-faction Khalqis. When the plot failed and Amin had Taraki killed, Sarwari had to take refuge in the Soviet embassy, as did Watanjar and Gulabzoy—who were also implicated in the plot—leaving their families to be jailed in Pul-i-Charkhi.

[28] Lieutenant General Sayed Mohammad Gulabzoy, the air force commander, was a key figure in the 1978 coup. A Khalqi with direct Soviet ties, he, too, was involved in the Soviet plot to get rid of Amin and, like Watanjar and Sarwari, had to take refuge in the Soviet embassy.

Monday, October 29, 1979 (Aqrab 7, 1358), and Tuesday, October 30, 1979 (Aqrab 8, 1358)

Dr. Akhtar Mustamundi and Hakim Hazrat-Mir Agha were both taken out, but then they were brought back to Pul-i-Charkhi Prison on the same day.

Azizullah Wasefi, the former minister of agriculture during Daoud's time, left the prison in the morning and came back at night. When I visited him, he was very much upset, but he wouldn't tell me where he had been.

Since the Early Part of December 1979: Air Traffic over the Prison

We could see more air traffic over the prison, which was on the path of Kabul Airport's landing route. As time went on, the volume of air traffic increased and heavier military transport planes flew over Pul-i-Charkhi. For three to four days and nights, an air bridge was formed. Heavy four-propeller and jet-engine airplanes flew over the prison every three to five minutes.

Some time earlier, the prison administration had begun work on the shower rooms in our corridor. I noticed that plumbers were working in our block. Once, I saw an old plumber laying water pipes in the corridor. I looked for an opportunity to talk to him when the guards were not around. Finally, I had a chance to go over and speak. I asked him why so many military planes were flying over Pul-i-Charkhi. Had he been to the airport and seen what was going on? The old man had been told not to talk to any prisoners, but, looking around and not seeing any guards, he answered me. "Yes, I was at the airport. As far as I could see, there were thousands of troops and a large number of weapons carriers and small tanks there." He added, "I'm afraid it looks really bad!"

Monday, December 24, 1979 (Jadi 3, 1358)

I asked some air force officers who were among the prisoners, "Can these planes carry tanks?"

The answer was, "Yes, they can carry smaller tanks."

So the Soviets had brought not only troops by air, but also weapons carriers and small tanks—and that was what the old plumber had seen at the airport.

Thursday, December 27, 1979 (Jadi 6, 1358)

It was dark outside. We could hear the sound of machine guns and cannons firing around the prison. When the prison lights were turned off, it was dark inside, too. Some time ago, I had been transferred to another, larger cell on the second floor with different cell mates. We began to hear the sound of machine guns in the backyard. I told my cell mates that we should all lie down on the floor to avoid being hit by stray bullets or possibly by tanks firing at command posts on the periphery of the prison compound—and maybe even the prison block that we were in.

At about that time, two scared young boys, the sons of Mia Gul-jan, a holy man, came into our cell saying that they would feel safer if they stayed with us.

I told them that it was okay, that they could come in and lie down on the floor as we were doing. The noise went on for some time; finally, it quieted down. A while later, we heard people talking outside in the yard. It sounded like they were talking in another language—maybe Russian.

We stayed on the floor and waited, not moving at all. We were all listening, trying to understand what was going on. Every one of us was alone with his own thoughts. Sometime after midnight, a prisoner came to our cell and said that there were no guards anywhere on our block.

A while after that, another prisoner who had tried to go downstairs and into the outside yard told us that there were Russian soldiers standing at the entrance of the block; they had motioned to him to go back inside.

Judging from all that had transpired up to that time, we came to the conclusion that the Soviets had attacked, taken over, and were in control of Pul-i-Charkhi Prison. In other words, we were now in the hands of Soviet military forces.

I wondered, *What next?* The next morning, we could move around in the block and even go outside to clean up. Some of the guards were back, but things seemed to be lax. Already, we were hearing new rumors.

Someone said that the night prior, as soon as the Soviets took control of the prison, they released four or five Parchami women from the west wing of our block and took them into the city on weapons carriers and tanks.

We heard that the Soviet special forces had attacked the Chilsitoon Palace, which Hafizullah Amin had made his residence, and that Amin, some members of his family, and his security guards had been killed. Rumor had it that on the same night, Babrak Karmal broadcast a speech from Tashkent (but he claimed that he was in Kabul). In that speech, he had announced his takeover of the government and the PDPA.[29]

Friday, December 28, 1979 (Jadi 7, 1358)

Members of Parcham and all their friends were released from Pul-i-Charkhi Prison on this day. I heard that they numbered about five hundred.

Monday, December 31, 1979 (Jadi 10, 1358)

The Khalqi members of the PDPA politburo who had supported Amin, and other friends of Amin, were brought into Pul-i-Charkhi Prison.

---

[29] The rumors about Amin's death and Babrak's speech turned out to be true.

Friday, January 4, 1980 (Jadi 14, 1358)

Amin's Daughters Are Brought

On this date, the wives and daughters of Aminist Khalqis were brought into Pul-i-Charkhi Prison at night. Among these were two daughters of Hafizullah Amin. One of the guards told me that Amin's daughters had been badly molested by the Soviet soldiers. They were in terrible pain and bleeding. They could not even walk by themselves. "So," the guard told me, "when they were in need, two of us supported them beneath their arms and took them to the latrines in the yard. We waited for them and then brought them back to their room."

Sunday, January 6, 1980 (Jadi 16, 1358)

Two Thousand Prisoners Released

About two thousand prisoners, including seventy-three prisoners from political block no. 1 and eighty-one prisoners from the south block, were released. However, members of the royal family, President Daoud's ministers, some generals, and a number of prominent people such as former parliamentarians—altogether about fifty-five people, including me—were not among the prisoners who were released on this day. Rumors had already spread in Kabul that all political prisoners were going to be released from Pul-i-Charkhi Prison on this day. My wife, my parents, and others in my family were expecting that I would be released and come home.

When I did not come home, my family was extremely saddened. They gave up hope and thought that I might never be released and come home.

Thursday, January 10, 1980 (Jadi 20, 1358)

One hundred and fifty-two prisoners were released. Roshandil Wardak from political block no. 1 was among them.

Friday, January 11, 1980 (Jadi 21, 1358)

At about nine o'clock at night, the newly appointed commandant of Pul-i-Charkhi Prison, Zahir, called the remaining fifty-four political prisoners in block no. 1 to meet with him in one of the larger rooms in the second floor of our block.

He announced, "Your group is going to be released tomorrow. In the meantime, tonight, we will move you to block no. 2, and in the morning you will be released from there." He added, "I want you to pack whatever belongings you have. We will give you an hour to pack up."

In recent days, we in political block no. 1 had seen several groups of prisoners released, but since we were not included in any of those groups, we had assumed that we were not going to be released at all. Moreover, we had also witnessed many prisoners who were taken out of the prison and never made it home.

The thought that most of us had was that the guards were actually going to take us out of the block, but then they would take us to the execution grounds, as they had done with hundreds of prisoner before us. Therefore, we decided to stay in the block we were in. If their plan was to kill us, then we would put up a fight to the end.

We would create a huge commotion. There would be lot of noise from guns and bombs inside the block, and a lot of blood would be splattered all over the floors, walls, and ceilings. Maybe somebody outside the prison, someone in Kabul, in Afghanistan, or even in the wider world, would hear of it.

In this way, our lives would not have been lost in vain, and our blood would have made little crimson rivulets flowing into gutters, ditches, and then rivers. Our lives would not have been lost for nothing, and our sacrifice would make a mark in human history for future generations to learn from: not to let dictators and potentates take hold and play with the destiny of nations.

We told Commandant Zahir that we had all decided not to move out of the block tonight. If we were to be released in the morning, then we would go from here. In this way, it would be less of a bother. Commandant Zahir saw that we were absolutely determined not to leave the block and go to block no. 2. He therefore agreed to our staying put. When leaving, he called to a man named Zamaryalai to pack his items and come with him. Zamaryalai obediently got his stuff and followed Commandant Zahir out of the room.

I had seen this guy before. He was one of the Parchamis. He used to come and sit some distance away from the circle of chess players. No one spoke to him because, his being a Parchami, we considered him to be one of the people who belonged to the PDPA and was responsible for the Communist coup, the torture, the killings, and the mess that we were all in.

But earlier on the night when Commandant Zahir told us about our release and the plan to move us to block no. 2, Zamaryalai came to where I was standing, introduced himself, and said, "Mr. Assifi, I know that you all are going to be released tomorrow. I also know that I will not be released at all."

I said, "Who are you? And how do you know?"

He said, "My name is Zamaryalai, and I was one of the earliest founding members of Parcham." He added, "Mr. Assifi, if one is a member of a party and then decides not to be a member, can he do so?"

I said, "Well, I don't know about the rules of your party, but ordinarily, becoming a member and then deciding not to be a member should be a matter of a person's volition."

He said, "I am Babrak Karmal's cousin. At the beginning, Babrak and I began standing on stumps at Kabul University and lecturing against the government. We invited students to join the Communist movement. I was a member of the central committee of Parcham and one of its founding leaders. Then, as time went on, I became disillusioned with the movement and finally announced my resignation." He added, "From that time on, the party was very angry with me. It now considers me a traitor to Parcham. That is why I will not be released."

I asked, "What was the reason you left Parcham?"

He said, "I had my own reasons. Plus, I didn't agree with Babrak's taking directives from non-Afghan sources."

Well, when Commandant Zahir told Zamaryalai to follow him, he was indeed separated from our group of prisoners. One of our friends had gone outside for personal reasons. When he came back, he told me, "The reason the commandant told us to go to block no. 2 is because they were trying to make room for a large number of new prisoners who were being brought to our block tonight." He added, "All the big rooms on the first floor are filled up with a lot of new prisoners, ones I've never seen before."

I had to see it for myself. I called one of the guards and told him that I needed to go outside. He said, "Okay, come on out." I went out. Coming back, I went to the large rooms on the first floor. I looked inside room after room. Sure enough, they were all full of new prisoners. The new captives all were young, twenty-five to thirty years old. They looked pale and showed signs of having been in prison for at least a month.

In one room, I saw Zamaryalai spreading his blanket on the floor among the other prisoners. I went over to him and said, "You were right. Do you need anything? I have some money."

He said, "No, thank you. I have money." So, one of the things that I witnessed at that time was that while the new Babrak regime and the Soviets were putting on a show for the outside world by releasing some well-known prisoners, they were actually, unbeknownst to the outside world, imprisoning more people. This was the real story of how the Soviets and their group of East European Communist satellites worked. They always put on an outside show for the gullible West.

In the morning, our observation scouts on the top floor of our block told us that they were seeing minibuses and several television vans with dishes on top. These had moved into the inside yard of block no. 2. The buses were brought inside the prison but were parked in the passageway between blocks.

We Are Released

It seemed that Commandant Zahir's announcement was right. It was probably the first time that the word of a Pul-i-Charkhi commandant was really true.

We the prisoners who had been told to expect release had already packed and were ready. The guards escorted us to the first floor of block no. 2. From there, we walked in single file out to the entrance of the block, where we were individually interviewed by international television crews and journalists who had gathered there.

I was confronted by a journalist with the BBC or some other international television station while a cameraman took pictures. The journalist asked me several questions that I don't remember now, but one of his questions, and the answer I gave, still lingers in my mind.

He asked me, "Why have you been in the prison so long?"

My main interest at that moment was to board the bus that was waiting, get out of the prison, and, hopefully, get home and join my family as soon as possible. I wanted to get the interview over fast, so my answer was, "It's due to the garbage-can factor."

He asked, "What do you mean?"

I said, "Well, it's like this. The garbage that you threw in the can a few days before? When you clean the can, it comes out last."

Then I started toward a bus that was in the passageway outside in the yard of block no. 2.

The film showing us walking out of the entrance of block no. 2 and being confronted by a number of international TV and radio journalists and observers who had been invited to report on our liberation was quite a big show—a show put on by the PDPA and their Soviet benefactors to impress the world. They wished to show how nice the newly installed Karmal government was. This show, in their minds, may have, to some degree, been useful to provide justification for the invasion of a sovereign country by an all-too-powerful neighbor, the USSR.

I boarded one of the buses and sat somewhere in the midsection. Other prisoners kept on coming in. Pretty soon, the bus was full.

Two armed soldiers were standing in the bus, one in front and the other in the back. Before the bus started moving, the soldier in front said, "Please close the windows, and do not speak to anyone on the outside when the bus comes out of the prison gates. When we get to the city, tell the driver where you want to dismount. The driver will stop the bus for you to get out." We waited a while longer until the other buses were ready.

Then, the buses moved out slowly, going through the main gates of the prison.

As soon as the buses were outside the prison's front gates, I could see that there were thousands of people waiting there to see their loved ones.

There was a rush to the buses. Hundreds of people were running alongside and banging on the windows, calling out names and shouting, "Did you see so-and-so?" "Where is so-and-so?" "Is he alive?" "Is he in these buses?"

It was a very sad and chaotic scene. So many people had lost loved ones and were looking to see whether their relative or friend was on one of the buses, or if we had seen him, or if he was still alive.

The soldiers were shouting, "Do not open the windows!" But for us former prisoners, it was impossible not to help these people in some way.

Out of many names that the people from the outside were calling to us, I recognized only one. I called back to the fellow running beside the bus, "Yes, he's alive and is released. He's in one of the other buses, maybe two buses in front of ours."

One man who was running outside the bus was so agitated that I opened the window for him. He was so frantic that he jumped up and got himself into the bus through the window, at which time he kept begging me to let him know if the person who he sought was released, alive, or still inside the prison.

The soldier in our bus came toward this man to beat him up. I got up and begged the soldier not to hurt him. I told the soldier, "He is desperate, and we should have mercy on him. He has done what he has out of love and caring for the one that he has lost." I told the guy who had climbed in, "The people in the bus all heard you, and no one recognized his name. You'd better get out of this bus and look for him in the other buses." He climbed out of our bus and ran toward the other buses. Given the commotion outside, I did not see where he went.

The scene that we witnessed outside of Pul-i-Charkhi Prison showed us that the scale and number of people who had been lost to their families was large.

How many were still inside the prison? And how many had been killed? Remember that this scene was occurring outside just *one* of the prisons in Kabul.

Getting Out

Slowly, the buses pulled away from the crowd and started moving toward the Pul-i-Charkhi bridge across the Kabul River. After crossing the bridge, the buses started moving west on the road to Kabul City.

I did not want to look toward the military base at my right. I knew that so many people had been killed on those grounds, and it was painful to look in that direction. At this moment, I was looking straight ahead toward Kabul, where my apartment was.

The bus driver called out, "Please let me know where you want the bus to stop for you so you can get home."

That sounded like music to my ears. But I myself was not a good sight to behold. I had lost a lot of weight. My cheeks were hollowed, and my face was pale from malnutrition. For weeks, everyone who saw me invariably exclaimed, "Oh, you look so thin! Are you okay?" I was wearing a tattered old chapan, loose, baggy clothes, and heavy old boots made in the Ahoo factory across the river from where I lived with my family.

After half an hour, I called out to the driver to stop for me. He stopped the bus, and I got out.

I started walking toward my apartment in the Micro Rayon apartment building complex. I did not have a suitcase, only a cloth sack in which I was carrying my belongings. Since I was not included in the release of prisoners a week earlier, my family did not believe that I would be released. My son, Tamim, and a close friend of my family, Said Yusuf Agha, had driven as far as the entrance of Pul-i-Charkhi. They could not get any closer because there was a mass of people outside the gate, but when the buses exited the outer gates, they followed the bus I was in all the way back to Micro Rayon apartment buildings.

I walked from the street to the apartment building. My wife saw me from the balcony of our apartment. She and our two young daughters came running downstairs to greet me. A little later, our son and our friend made it home. And then my mother and father joined us.

I need hardly describe the joy and happiness that this brought to me and all my family. We had a minicelebration going in our apartment, then and for days after. Other relatives and friends joined us as time went on and as the new situation allowed.

There were clouds casting shadows of uncertainty and gloom all around us. Kabul was not the city I had known. It had become one big prison. I had lost the sense of belonging in my hometown.

Prison Kabul

The atmosphere of Kabul was very tense. There were Russian tanks and weapons carriers patrolling the streets all over the city. A curfew was enforced after 8:30 at night. After that, we could no longer hear voices outside or ordinary traffic noise in the city, only the clink-clink of Soviet tanks patrolling the streets close by. People were not allowed to tune into radio stations broadcasting news and music from outside the country, even in their homes. There were spies everywhere. The PDPA regime was recruiting and training young boys and girls to eavesdrop on neighbors and even on their own families.

Spies were rewarded on the basis of their loyalty to the Communist Party. Loyalty to the party was given precedence over loyalty to one's own family and friends.

I could not recognize the town where I had grown up. I did not feel at home anymore. A sense of belonging and recognition depends more on the people that you know, your friends and family, not on mountains, buildings, monuments, and landmarks. I had a feeling now that I no longer knew this place. I had lost the sense of my belonging to Kabul. Kabul was not the same place in which I had grown up. It had been turned into a big prison.

I wrote a poem to express how I felt:

> O my beautiful Kabul, what happened? I don't recognize
> you anymore.

Where are the people? Where are our friends? I don't see
them anymore.

Your grass is yellow, trees are drying up, but your
mountains are standing;

Your daughters and sons are fighting tyranny and will
keep on standing.

When you were free, I loved your cool breeze in late
evening and early morning.

The musical sound of bells on goats, donkeys, and camels
kept ringing.

Young men riding donkeys, playing flutes, and singing
"Shamali Lala Zar Ast,"

Hauling milk, cheese, fruits and veggies, wood, and
charcoal to your markets.

O my Kabul! Where are your beautiful people and my
old friends?

What happened to your crowded bazaars where friends
could meet friends?

I don't see shopkeepers haggling with bargaining buyers
anymore.

Your unpaved streets, rutted by horse-drawn gawdi
carriages, have been rutted more,

Trampled by cannons and tanks, rockets from jets of
Soviet air fleets;

Where are the old-model, third-hand cars and buses that
roamed your streets?

Your citizens are terrorized by the Soviet army and
military might;

Your sons and daughters, forced to serve the party as spies
and fight.

Where is our neighborhood mullah who sang "Azaan" for
worship?

Now neighbors fear neighbors. There is no more
brotherhood or friendship.

My neighbor said to me, "My son was taken to serve the
party. I fear

He will then be in the service of evil, terror, and murder.
I fear.

> Will he then be killed in pain, with his picture on his
>   grave, as I fear?"
> O Kabul! Where is the busy humming of your bustling
>   town?
> Where does the crash of thunder and the bristle of lightning
>   shine?
> Where is justice, where is liberty, and where is my
>   freedom?
> O Kabul! I loved your warming sun and your clear blue
>   sky,
> Your lovely moon and glittering stars shining in a clear
>   night sky.
> Your refreshing seasons of the year gave us plenty of fruits
>   and veggies.
> Your springtimes gave us fresh, cool water and air, with
>   berries and cherries.
> Your summers gave us wheat, corn, apricots, peaches,
>   and plums.
> Your autumns gave us rest from summer's warmth, with
>   grapes and melons.
> Your winters brought icy air and snow from the sky,
>   covering mountain peaks.
> For justice and liberty, your sons and daughters will fight
>   and speak,
> Though they may be tortured, terrorized, trampled, and
>   crushed.
> O Kabul! Your sons and daughters will not let you be a
>   big prison!

Upon seeing my family again, it was as though I had been given a new life. I hugged them over and over again. For a while, my senses could not comprehend that all this was real and not a dream. When I heard their stories about how they had survived and tried to get by, I was worried.

Their experiences and the conditions in which they were living, under a Communist regime and Soviet occupation, were quite nightmarish.

All these so affected me that I almost forgot my own tragic experiences in Pul-i-Charkhi. Putting together my family's experiences and mine, it became apparent to me that the situation was impossible for us to live in and survive.

One factor in our favor was that my wife, my mother, and my father were not only very intelligent but also emotionally and mentally strong. Nevertheless, I would have to find a way to get my family out—out of Kabul, out of the country. As a good engineer, I knew that when confronted with a problem, the first thing to do is to make a survey of all the circumstances, as much as one can. Next, one should conceptualize and make a plan of action on the basis of verified assumptions.

After I emerged from mental numbness and started to think about getting my family out of Communist Afghanistan, I concluded that any plan I was going to make should be built on verifiable assumptions. But how could we make a plan of action to save ourselves if we did not have any control or any ability to verify our assumptions?

Although some well-informed people had warned me not to contact too many people in my once-beloved city, I ignored this caution and spent a lot of time walking around Kabul and talking to people in both the old neighborhoods and the new ones.

I wore clothes that would not be too noticeable or distinctive among ordinary folks (except for my eyeglasses, which always gave me away; but without them, I cannot see things at a distance). I did all this on foot.

It provided me with good exercise, although it was not very healthy because of the ever-present dust in Kabul streets. I wanted to observe how the people of Kabul were doing. What was their reaction to a Communist government and to the presence of Soviet troops among them, in their city? I went everywhere—to shopkeepers, tradesmen like tinsmiths and iron smiths, carpenters, tailors, used-clothes sellers, tea merchants, *naan buyiies* (bakeries), etc.—and said to these people (referring to Communist promises), "You must be happy now that you have a government of workers and toilers. They are from among you and are working for you." Their answers always surprised me.

They would say, "Brother, before this, we had one loaf of bread. Now, our ration has been cut down to half a loaf." And they would go on to say, "Brother, these people said all those things to get power in their hands. They are not working for us. They are working for themselves and will keep power at any cost to the Afghan nation."

My survey of ordinary people in Kabul showed that an absolute majority hated the Communists and their government. They vehemently hated the Soviet troops. They were extremely angry with the Soviets for patrolling the streets of Kabul during the daytime as well as during the curfew period at night.

Sometimes, I rode Kabul city buses to get to distant neighborhoods.

I would always see Soviet army weapons carriers and tanks on patrol or parked on city streets. I was astonished that when the people in the bus saw them, they always raised their hands in prayer and sang loudly in unison, asking God for help in defeating the Soviet troops and the Afghan Communists and destroying all of them and all their war machines.

A majority of people in the bus sang their prayers out loud, unafraid of Communist government spies and Soviet agents amongst them. One thing that always surprised me was that all these expressions of hatred and disgust were made very openly and frankly. It seemed that these people did not mind, or were not afraid, that some spy would report them to the local party headquarters or the Communist government intelligence services, KhAD and AGSA.

My personal survey made it obvious to me that the people of Kabul had made up their minds to fight this regime and the Soviet military forces. This result corroborated the observations I had made in Pul-i-Charkhi: this was the reason that a large number of people were brought into that place for torture and execution every day and night.

I learned from this that Afghans may be poor and backward, but they are truly endowed with national bravery and spiritual strength!

There was a war going on between the Afghan Communists, their Soviet masters, and the people of Afghanistan. The shackles of imprisonment and bondage had to be broken.

From all this, I came to the conclusion that the Communists and their Soviet masters were going to be defeated and that the Soviet army would definitely leave Afghanistan. The question was, how soon?

When Communists took over the government, there was a sudden shift in rules of employment, promotions, and other job opportunities. Now, all appointments and promotions were decided on the basis of Communist Party interests. All privileges were granted on the basis of party membership. There were no exceptions; these rules were absolute.

As soon as they seized power in the 1978 coup, the party organized Communist committees at all levels among the people. These committees were meant to control all aspects of community life in the cities, the villages, and the rural areas of the country. Government employees were at the forefront of this process, and the new rules permeated all sectors of society.

The PDPA operatives were being trained by their Soviet counterparts. After all, the Soviet Union was the flag-bearer, and its rulers were the absolute masters of Communist ideology and its governance methods all over the world. There was supposedly no question regarding the operational efficiency of this system. But so far, the result of these operations in Afghanistan was not as successful as it was assumed to be.

The Afghan Communist regime's response to this failure, as is usual with most bureaucracies, was to increase the intensity of pressure to meet the stated goals—by means of terror, torture, and eventually execution, like what I had witnessed in Pul-i-Charkhi Prison.

But the intensified pressures had not produced the desired results; this eventually resulted in the invasion of a neighboring country by one of the most powerful armies in the world.

Once huge bureaucracies, civil or military, are mobilized and set in a direction of any kind, their course cannot be altered without the exertion of a large counterforce. It is easier to increase or decrease the intensity of those pressures than to change a bureaucracy's course.

This phenomenon was seen in Soviet actions in Afghanistan, which were followed by the release of some well-known prisoners, I included, following the Soviet invasion. The Soviets had a formula in mind for the organization of an acceptable government in Afghanistan that would, they thought, pacify the country.

This was the formula they preferred. Having pressured the antagonistic Khalqi and Parchami factions into a degree of unity as the PDPA, the Soviets planned on the more pliable Parchamis' forming a pseudo-broad-based government (including a hodgepodge of non-Communist elements) under the nominal presidency of Nur Ahmad Taraki, who was formally Khalqi but relatively obedient to Soviet direction, and the primary actual leadership of Babrak Karmal, a longtime Soviet agent guided and controlled by Moscow.

But the Khalqi strongman, Hafizullah Amin, Karmal's tough competitor, wanted the Afghan government to be formed under his own leadership and that of the Khalq faction of the PDPA. Although presumably supported by the Soviet Union, Amin, who had extensive army support, was less willing to take Soviet direction. He wanted to run the show his way.

So, in September 1979, Taraki, at Moscow's suggestion, tried to have Amin killed. He failed, however.

Amin ousted Taraki and took over. A few weeks later, he had Taraki killed.

The Parchamis had tried to organize a coup to regain their leadership of the PDPA. However, Amin and his cohorts learned about the coup and quashed it before it got started. That is why so many leaders of Parcham (and a number of non-Communists who were cooperating with them to get rid of Amin) were caught and brought into Pul-i-Charkhi as prisoners. All this explained some of the changes I saw and experienced in Pul-i-Charkhi Prison. But that was not the end of the story. Actually, it triggered a completely new phase. When the Parchami were unable to get rid of Amin, the Soviet army invaded Afghanistan, killed Amin and his friends, and took full control of the country themselves, installing their preferred Parchami, Karmal, as a puppet.

At this moment, the Soviets had full control of Afghanistan and could do whatever they wanted. However, the Soviets wanted to form an Afghan government that would appear acceptable and would put an end to the nationwide resistance to the Communist takeover.

The formation of a government under Soviet leadership with full support by Parchamis and Khalqis was a preliminary requisite. However, previous rivalry and, in some cases, animosity between these two factions had to be handled with tighter Soviet discipline. Increased tension between these two necessitated a firmer Soviet hand, driving Afghanistan's control under increased Soviet command. The following examples clearly illustrate this phenomenon.

An acquaintance of mine who was working at the Kabul radio and television station called me one day and said, "Listen to the eight o'clock news tonight." A few minutes before eight, I turned the TV on, but there was no interesting news worth listening to. After about fifteen minutes, this person called me and said, "I will come later and tell you what happened." When he came later, the story that he told me was very interesting.

He said that as an announcer, a printout of the eight o'clock news was given to him. There were six appointments of people to important jobs. These were made by presidential decree, signed by Babrak. "That is when I called you to listen to the news tonight," he said.

"However, about five minutes before news time, some armed Soviet soldiers came into the room, took the sheet away, and put a new sheet in front of us, one that did not have the news of the appointments on it."

I asked the names of the people who had been newly appointed to the important jobs. He told me, and I noticed that the people in question were either PDPA sympathizers or non-Parcham or non-Khalq members.

I waited to hear community rumors about repercussions following these appointments. The following are things that I heard through the grapevine:

1) The newly appointed mayor of Kabul had called the municipality secretary's office, introduced himself as the new mayor, and asked if the secretary would send a car that the mayor needed for some work. The secretary had told the existing mayor about this new appointment, and that mayor had told the secretary to send a car. Then, he had made a call to the Russian embassy for a "going-away meeting" with Ambassador Fikrat Ahmadov. At the meeting, the ambassador had asked him where he was going. He responded, "I have been replaced, by Babrak's decree, by someone else." The ambassador told him to go on and continue his work as the mayor, saying, "I have not approved this appointment."

2) Mr. Rahimi, then the deputy minister of mines, had announced in the director's meeting that I had been replaced by way of Babrak's appointing another person to my job. But my friends from nine thousand kilometers away did not allow this to happen.

These two examples demonstrate that although the Soviets had installed Babrak as the new president, they had not authorized him to make important decisions.

The formation of an "acceptable" Afghan government reemerged in a metamorphosed form. The Soviets had absolute control with the presence of their army and air units and a full force of operatives of all kinds.

Soviet-Controlled Hodgepodge Government

The Soviets could expand the hodgepodge of sympathizers and even non-Communists attached to the government, and they could include in that government some individuals whom they had, so to speak, reeducated in Pul-i-Charkhi Prison for almost two years.

The Parchami leadership was instructed to begin active organization of this new "broad-based" government, which, as envisioned, would appear to be supported, and thereby legitimized, by prominent, respected non-Communists. They thought that this would pacify the Afghan people and satisfy the rest of the world. And that is when the tentacles of the Communist operatives began infiltrating Afghan society and particularly the prospective hodgepodge elements.

In my work as governor of Herat Province, I had become acquainted with the area's history. Herat was already a great city when Alexander the Great came through. For centuries, it was a world-class center of culture, literature, poetry, miniature painting, calligraphy, philosophy, and Sufism. Plus, it is the birthplace of great scholars.

In my work in that province, I came to know many people. I have long had much respect for Heratis. If anyone introduced himself as a Herati, I would naturally offer him the courtesies that are customary in that part of the world. When I came out of Pul-i-Charkhi Prison, many Heratis came and paid their respects to me as a past governor of that province.

I had been told that since the Soviet invasion, some men were actively serving the Communist government. Therefore, I had been warned to be careful with the people who came to visit me at home. But my family's apartment was in the middle of a very crowded part of the city, and many people came to say hello. Given Afghan tradition, it was very hard for me to refuse to see people who came to our home as guests.

There was one man who came to visit many times. His name was Khushdil-i-Siah, and he always brought along sweets from Herat. According to Afghan custom, one cannot refuse a box of candy that a guest brings to one's home. This man told me that in the old days, he used to smuggle sheep across the open border to Iran for sale. (Afghan mutton is very popular in Iran.) But he told me that he had since repented and no longer smuggled (which means that he had probably made a lot of money and now was sitting on the stash he had made). Anyway, I told him that he should not bring candies to us anymore.

After that, he came without the candy—but he kept on coming. He always told me, "Qader says hello, and he wants to meet with you one of these days."

I asked him, "Who is Qader?" (It's a popular name, so it could have been anybody.)

"Well," he said, "Qader is my son-in-law, and he is from Herat, you know."

I immediately realized whom he was talking about. His Qader was the Soviet-trained air force officer who had attacked the Kabul Airport and taken over the air force planes that bombarded the presidential palace on the first day of the Communist coup against President Daoud. Those were the planes whose rockets nearly hit me when I was walking in front of the palace that day. Qader was one of the key figures in the Communist coup, but he was associated with Parcham. When he was the minister of defense, he was imprisoned in Pul-i-Charkhi by Hafizullah Amin for organizing and being actively involved in the Parchami coup against Amin and the Khalqis. He was one of those of whom many knew but never saw. After the Soviets installed Karmal, Qader had been released from prison and returned to a high-level position.

To my dismay, I realized who Qader was, who Khushdil-i-Siah was, and why so many visits and so much candy. I put two and two together, coming to the conclusion that Parchamis and their Soviet bosses wanted to include more of the hodgepodge sheep so as to give an appearance of legitimacy to their PDPA government. And, quite aptly, Khushdil-i-Siah had had good experience with carrying sheep across borders. After some time, and as I had suspected, Khushdil told me that "they" had set up a meeting for me with Qader and his friends. There would be a car with guards coming to fetch me for the meeting.

He then added, "Governor, this is going to be a very friendly meeting." He said this with a sheepish smile.

The guards and a car came, and they took me to the big hall (the Salam Khana) at the old palace, which they were now calling the people's palace. I found a big meeting going on. Many there were from the group of distinguished non-Communists whom I had known in Pul-i-Charkhi.

Our hosts were trying to organize committees. When I refused to join any of the committees, someone told me, "Hey, guy, they'll take you back to Pul-i-Charkhi, and you may not come out alive this time!"

I said, *"Whatever will be, will be."*

Farewell, Homeland

When I returned home, I told my wife, "I don't think that we can survive in this country anymore! We should get out as soon as we can."

But getting out of Afghanistan at that time was not easy. We faced several obstacles. For example, permission to leave the country would have to be given by the government, but this was an absolute impossibility for us.

The government had their eyes on me to serve as one of the hodgepodge group to form a showcase government that the people of Afghanistan would eventually accept. Therefore, getting exit permits for me and my family was not possible.

My father's health was not very good. His chronic asthma often acted up in the dusty atmosphere of Kabul, and he needed special injections and periodic hospitalization. There were no medical facilities or nursing homes in Kabul then, so whenever he needed an injection, I would bring the neighborhood nurse or a doctor to my parents' home. If the injection was needed at night, this was difficult because of the 8:30 p.m. curfew. I could not bring any help or take my father to a hospital emergency room, so my mother and I were forced to give the injection ourselves.

My son, Tamim, had been in his last year at the College of Engineering of Kabul University at this time. But on the day after I was released from Pul-i-Charkhi, he left Kabul secretly with a relative to make his way to United States.

The night before he left, he told me, "Dad, I took care of Grandfather and Grandmother, my mother, and my sisters all the time that you were in prison. Now that you're out, it's your turn to take care of them."

Since my family could not possibly get permits to leave, our only alternative was to leave Kabul and Afghanistan without permission. This meant that we would have to use the routes that were not under the control of the Communist regime and the Soviet army.

To get out that way, we would have to go with guides and, with the help of freedom fighters, make our way through rural areas, mountains, and valleys, avoiding the cities and towns. In other words, we would have to *walk* out of Afghanistan.

This was very dangerous, as it posed the risk of getting caught or killed by government or Soviet forces. It also meant passing through areas that were under siege or attack by these forces.

Tamim had gotten out of Afghanistan this way. I could also go by this route. But I could not take women and children with me. I could put myself in danger's way, but not my wife and our two younger daughters. (Fortunately, our oldest daughter, Giselle, was in England, where her maternal grandfather had sent her for medical treatment.) Trying to find a solution, I studied the problem and consulted with friends who had relatives who had successfully made it out of Afghanistan.

Medical Passports

Finally, my wife and I concluded that we could perhaps get medical passports for our two little girls, five-year-old Shamila and six-year-old Madina, and one for Fariha to accompany them. Then, we could get special visas from the government to permit them to go to another country for medical treatment. If my wife and the girls got out of Afghanistan on a medical excuse, then I could walk out of Afghanistan with the help of freedom fighters and join them later, wherever they were. I discussed this plan with my parents and with some trusted close relatives and friends. They thought that it would be feasible, but only if the medical visas were given for a free country, not for travel to the Soviet Union or one of the countries in the Soviet bloc.

I started working out this plan in detail. First, I had to get justification for a claim that the girls needed medical treatment outside the country. Such medical permissions were given only if the treatment was not available or possible in Afghanistan.

To get this justification, we needed a lot of help from friends and medical doctors in local hospitals, especially those in the children's hospital, where the girls had been treated in the past. All medical facilities and hospitals were in the hands and under the control of the Communist government.

However, most of the medical and clerical staff and doctors were not Communists. Hopefully, they would cooperate in facilitating our plan. For this, we had to rely on the cultural characteristics of the Afghan people.

Afghans are known for their hospitality. If anyone comes to an Afghan home and seeks refuge, he or she will be accepted as a guest and taken care of until the time comes when he or she chooses to leave.

Afghans, no matter how poor they are, will share whatever they have with anyone in need who comes to their house. Afghans will go out of their way to help anyone who asks them for help. Afghans will fight for the rights of property, dignity, and the honor of any member of their family, extended family, clan, or tribe, even if it requires personal sacrifice. As a former public servant, an engineer, the head of an important office, an administrator, a governor, and a cabinet minister, I was recognized and accorded full courtesy and respect everywhere I went. I enjoyed the full cooperation of the people working in public and government offices and businesses in the country (except for really devoted Communist Party members and PDPA operatives). It was an amazing feeling to be the recipient of the benefits of all those wonderful Afghan qualities mentioned above.

When I told the children's hospital staff and doctors that I needed a justifiable reason for getting medical passports for my daughters' treatment outside the country, the people involved said that they would take care of it, telling me not to worry. And they went ahead and did it. They made special dossiers for each of my daughters, got them approved by the special committee composed of Afghan and Russian doctors, and then wrote the necessary letters of recommendation to the passport offices to have passports and visas issued for the girls' medical treatment in India.

This really sounds like a fairy tale, especially because, lo and behold, all this was done under the nose of Communists in the government and the party. When I asked one of the doctors at the children's hospital and on the special committee how it was done, he said that they had looked in the hospital files, found the girls' medical records of past treatment, and completed those files with what was necessary to get the exit permits.

When our request for medical passports and exit visas was received in the passport offices, I received a call from Mr. Hakim, a Parchami official who was a tribal relative whom I had met in Pul-i-Charkhi

Prison. He asked me, "Are you requesting medical-treatment passports and visas for your daughters and wife to go to India?"

I said, "Yes. Is there a problem?"

He said, "No. I'll call the passport offices and tell them to expedite it."

As I have said, tribal relationships are important in Afghanistan, especially among Pashtuns and, in this case, even under a Soviet-controlled Communist regime. (However, this may have been done with tacit approval from the government.) The medical-need passports and exit visas were issued by the government offices. This completed the first part of our exit plan; the possibility that my wife and daughters would get out of Afghanistan was coming close to reality. Once they were safely in a free country, I would go ahead and make my own plans to walk out of my homeland. Until then, I did not want to attract the attention of government intelligence offices.

We Needed Money

We needed money for our escape, first for the expenses of Fariha and the girls, and eventually for mine, too. My wife started to sell our belongings—furniture, carpets, and the rest of what we had in our apartment. Of course, this did not earn us much money. Through the grapevine, perhaps, our friends and relatives learned that we were selling our things for travel expenses (for the girls' medical treatment, of course). Word got around. One other thing that we could sell was our old Volkswagen bus. Last but not least, we could lease out our apartment, in which case (in the Afghan system) we would get the lease money up front. As I said before, one of the things that we had going for us was that Afghans are an amazing people.

When I was in Pul-i-Charkhi Prison, I had known two merchants. We called them the Akhund brothers. One day, our apartment doorbell rang. One of our daughters went to the door, came back, and said to me, "There's a man standing out in the corridor, and he says that he is the son of Akhund Sahib. He says that he wants to see you." The atmosphere of Kabul was very tense, and we were very careful not to meet with people we did not know. I went to the door and, indeed, saw the son of Akhund Sahib standing there.

He said, "My father told me to see you and ask you if you need any money or anything else. My father has given me an order to see if we can help you with anything that you may need." I told the young man to come in and, as was customary, offered him tea. In order to get better acquainted and reach a comfort level with him, I asked how his father and uncle were, whether they were still in Kabul, and so on. He said, "My father owns a pharmacy on Maiwand Boulevard called Sardar Hashim Khan Darmaltoon. He would have come himself to see you, but he was very busy with customers, so he decided to send me first." Well, I knew exactly where Sardar Hashim Khan Pharmacy on Maiwand Boulevard was, so my comfort level rose a bit more than when I had first seen the young man.

He said again, "My father says, 'If Mr. Assifi needs anything, we would be very happy to help.'" He continued, "My father says, 'Although Mr. Assifi has previously worked on important jobs, I know that he does not have much money. Since he is reputed to be one of the most honest people in Afghanistan, he therefore would not have much money.'"

"Well," I said to the dear young man, "I'm okay, and if I need money I'll give a call to your father, Akhund Sahib, and ask him for it." Then I added, "By the way, we have an old Volkswagen bus. I want to sell it. Do you think you could find a buyer for me?"

The young man said, "Yes, I could certainly help. Where is the bus? Is it possible to look at it?"

I said, "It's down in front of the apartment building complex. Let me take you there and show you." We went outside, and I showed him our old VW bus.

He said, "Yes, I'm familiar with these cars, and I could give you a price, tell you how much you could sell it for."

I asked, "How much?"

He said that we could get 100,000 to 120,000 afghanis for it (an afghani is a unit of Afghan money; $1.00 = 55 afghanis).

Well, I knew that this young man was doing what his father had told him: he was actually helping me financially. I didn't think that the VW bus was worth that much; I had bought it at a customs house auction for fifty thousand afghanis. But anyway, I thought that it was a very good deal. At that time, the exchange rate for one US dollar was fifty-five afghanis, so he was offering me about two thousand dollars for my VW bus.

The next day, the son of Akhund Sahib brought 120,000 afghanis to our apartment in a paper bag. He said, "Here is the money, but you can use the bus as long as you need it. I will take care of the paperwork for it. When you are ready to go and you don't need the bus, just call me or my father, and we will come and take it from you. Otherwise, we don't need the car right now."

"Well," I said, "let me give you a receipt for the money, with the stipulation that it is for the price of the VW bus that I have sold to you. I'll sign all the papers when you have them ready. By the way, son, tell your father 'thank you' from me." Remember that at that time, I was just a man who had been released from prison. I did not have a job or any influence within the then-government. In fact, the government was looking for an excuse to send me back to prison. So this gesture showed how nice the Akhunds were.

Now that my family had some money and the necessary paperwork, passports, and exit and entry visas for my wife and daughters to go to New Delhi, we did not want to wait too long for them to leave, because the passports and exit visas could be rescinded.

My Wife and Daughters Fly Away

At that time, two airlines, Ariana and Indian Airlines, were flying the route from Kabul to New Delhi. One of them flew the route twice a

292

week, and one of those flights made a stopover in Peshawar to pick up passengers for India. We chose this flight, and I got the tickets. Although my wife's and daughters' tickets said New Delhi, our plan was that they would get off in Peshawar and stay in Pakistan until I could join them. So, their date of departure was set. I contacted my wife's cousin Naim-jan, who was working in Pakistan on one of the United Nations projects near Peshawar. I asked him to meet my wife and daughters at the Peshawar Airport and take them to a safe house either in Peshawar or wherever else he could make the necessary arrangements.

Finally, the date of their departure arrived. My wife and I were both excited and concerned, seeing as many things could go wrong. We had heard that the Communists refused to let some passengers enter the airport or else refused to let some people board a flight for which they had reservations and tickets. Sometimes, they had even entered a plane and ordered passengers to get off.

I drove Fariha and the girls to the airport. They did not have much baggage, only a small briefcase and a handheld women's toiletries case. Because my face was familiar to some Communist officials and airport police, I tried to avoid being seen with them in the airport; with some government people, my close association with my own family could have caused some unforeseen problem. While taking all these precautions, I was praying in my heart for their safe journey. I kept on praying while they boarded the plane. The plane taxied, took off, and started its flight to Peshawar. From then on, I was anxiously waiting for the good news that my wife and daughters had arrived and had been escorted to a safe house.

After a day or so, I got the good news. Now my family was out and free. My wife later told me, as we had planned, that as soon as the plane landed in Peshawar, she and the children got out and went into the airport, where she told the airport security officers and gendarmes that she and her daughters were seeking asylum and would like to be escorted to a safe place in the airport.

After they were safe, Fariha called her cousin, who was waiting for her call.

Naim-jan soon arrived at the airport with a car and drove my wife and daughters to a house where he was staying. Later on, Fariha learned that the house was frequently used by Afghan freedom fighters, so she decided that it would be better for she and our daughters to stay in a motel in Rawalpindi, which is very close to Islamabad, the capital of Pakistan. After I received the good news of their arrival and finding a safe place to stay, Fariha and I set up a new channel of communication.

To finance our plan, we still needed to lease out our apartment. I had told some friends to let me know if they heard of anyone who might be interested. Finally, I found a chap named Rahim Naebkhel. I talked to him, and we agreed on a price and the terms of the lease. But someone told me that in order to lease out your apartment, you had to get permission from the government office of Micro Rayon. So I went to the office and found out that before they would give me permission to lease, I needed to pay off the remainder of the purchase price of the apartment, which I had purchased from the government on the basis of payment in installments. Once I paid off the remainder, they would issue a deed of ownership. After I had that deed, I could apply and get permission to lease it.

Rahim and I talked it over. He agreed to pay all the money for the lease up front. He also promised to help get the paperwork for the ownership deed done in a legal office. I would then pay off the rest of the apartment purchase price, the government office would issue the ownership deed, and I would apply for permission to lease it out. The government would get its taxes and fees from all these transactions.

But first we had to make something called a common law agreement for the lease, in the presence of neighbors and community elders who would sign as witnesses. After making this agreement, I would go ahead, pay the rest of what I owed for the apartment, and get the ownership deed—which I did.

Up to that time, I had paid about 60 percent of the total purchase price of the apartment. Now, I paid the remainder from the money that Rahim had paid me up front. After a couple of weeks, I was issued an ownership deed. This part of the process went smoothly and without any problems.

Leasing Our Apartment

However, when I applied for permission to lease out the apartment, my application got bogged down in the deputy minister's section of the Office of Public Works.

The deputy kept shifting the application from one corner of his desk to another. Every time I talked to his secretary, the secretary said that the deputy minister did not have time to do it. And this kept dragging on.

Ironically, I knew the deputy from long before. His name was Tayeb. I was very well acquainted with him. He used to work for in the office of the Helmand Valley Authority (HVA). At that time, he had gotten a scholarship from HVA to study in the United States for a few years. I would never have guessed that someday Tayeb would be working for a Communist government of Afghanistan. I asked someone, how come? That person told me that Tayeb's older brother, Sultan Ali Keshtmand, was a very big shot in the Parcham faction. Keshtmand was deputy prime minister in Babrak's PDPA government and a member of the politburo. (He had been one of the Parchamis imprisoned by Hafizullah Amin in Pul-i-Charkhi after Parcham's attempted coup.) I visited Tayeb a while after I submitted my request for a leasing permit. Not only was he courteous to me, but he also got up from his desk and took me to a far corner of the room to talk. There, he said, "Mr. Assifi, my brother says that you want to get a permit for the lease of your apartment because you are going to leave the country."

I said, "Mr. Tayeb, how can you, of all people, say that I'm going to leave the country? You know very well that I have worked very hard and very honestly for more than twenty years in the service of this country. When your older brother and his friends came into leadership and power, the first thing they did was put me in Pul-i-Charkhi Prison for almost two years. I was tortured and waiting to be killed almost every day in that place. Do you think that a person of my academic caliber and work experience should stay in this country for the purpose of being in prison? Don't you think that it would be better for me to leave this country and put my knowledge and experience to the service and benefit of myself, my family, and the community in which I will be living?"

Since I had known Tayeb a long time ago in Helmand, I was very frank with him. Somehow, I did not feel that he would tell on me or report what I had said to him to the secret police or the intelligence services of the PDPA, even though he was the younger brother of Keshtmand, who had betrayed his own homeland and sold it to his Russian friends.

Tayeb did not say anything in response to what I said. The next time he spoke, he said, "I'll try to get this thing done for you, and I'm sorry that it has taken so long." But Tayeb still didn't do it, and I had to wait.

A few days later, I returned to Tayeb's office and asked his secretary if my request had been taken care of. He said that it was still on Tayeb's desk. I really did not know what to do except to keep going back and inquiring.

One day, I was sitting next to the secretary's desk in the outer office when a man named Akbar-jan, a military officer in Herat Province whom I knew from my work there, came in with someone and was going into Deputy Tayeb's office when he glanced back and saw me. He rushed over to me, exclaiming, "Oh, Mr. Assifi! Why are you sitting here? This is not a place for a person of your stature to be sitting, in an outer room with all these people around!"

I said, "Akbar-jan, it doesn't matter. I'm waiting for Deputy Tayeb to finish approving a request that I've made for leasing my apartment."

He said, "Well, is that all? Wait a minute, and I'll take care of it for you." Saying that, he stepped into Tayeb's office. Akbar-jan came back after about five minutes, holding my request form in his hand. He gave the paper to the secretary and told him, "Please, take care of this for Mr. Assifi, and call him when the request is approved by the minister of public works." Then he came over to me, took my hand, and escorted me out of the secretary's office.

I asked, "Did Tayeb sign the request?"

He said, "Yes, of course."

I asked him what he had done to get it signed. He said, "I asked the fellow that you saw entering the deputy's office with me to write the approval of your request himself. Tayeb, seeing that the president of the Micro Rayon apartment complex did it in his own handwriting for the approval of the minister of public works, went ahead and signed it without any hesitation." Then he said, "I'll tell you why. Tayeb is a Parchami. The minister of public works is a Khalqi, and he won't approve anything that is written by a Parchami. But if the president of Micro Rayon approves it in his own handwriting, then the minister recognizes his handwriting and approves it without thinking twice. Since I know all these guys, I immediately realized what Tayeb's problem was. That's why I asked this Khalqi guy to write it, and then asked Tayeb to sign it." Then, Akbar-jan added, "Khalqis and Parchamis don't get along well and don't cooperate with each other in most items of work that involve them both."

While I had been trying to get permission to lease out the apartment, I was in Tayeb's office one day when the secretary showed me an order that the former minister of public works, Dastagir Panjsheri, had given regarding my family's apartment when I was in Pul-i-Charkhi.

The prison commandant's assistant had called me to the office. He gave me an official request to relinquish the ownership of the apartment so that the government could give it to the Soviet advisors who had come to assist them.

Although I was under their knife in the prison, I nevertheless responded, saying that after serving Afghanistan for more than twenty years, all the property that I owned was this apartment, and I would not in any way give up my right of ownership to the government.

When they didn't get me to agree, the man who was then the deputy minister of public works, Mr. Firoz, sent soldiers to our apartment, called my wife to his office, and told her to leave the apartment, which was to be used by "Soviet friends." My wife responded just as I did. Deputy Minister Firoz told her, "We know that your father-in-law owns a house. You can leave the apartment and go and live with your in-laws."

My wife replied, "Their house is theirs, and our apartment is ours. There is no room in their house for us. You have force that you can use to kick us out of our apartment, but then I'll take my kids and live in a tent in front of the apartment building."

Deputy Minister Firoz persisted. "Your father-in-law is old, and he'll die very soon. You can go and live with your in-laws."

She answered, "Mr. Deputy, how do you know who will die first, my father-in-law or Mr. Firoz?"

He got mad and told the soldiers, "Kick this impertinent woman out of my office!"

Then, his office wrote a proposal to the then-minister, Dastagir Panjsheri, giving an account of all that had happened and asking for an order to confiscate our apartment. Panjsheri scribbled an order under the proposal: "Leave them temporarily. The father-in-law is an old man. When he dies, the Assifis should be made to leave the apartment."

Now neither Panjsheri nor Firoz was working in the Office of Public Works. Akbar-jan's maneuver had worked. Tayeb's secretary called me after five days and said, "Your request has been approved. Do you want me to send it to you, or do you prefer to come and get it?" I told him that I would pick it up myself.

Once the paperwork was finished, Rahim Nawibkhel and I exchanged the necessary documents. He told me that he was not in a hurry and would come to the apartment whenever I told him. He also told me that he was the subgovernor of Shinwar (a southeastern province bordering Pakistan). If I wanted to go to Pakistan, he said, then he would personally take me across the border. I told him that I did not have a plan at that time.

Now I had the money we needed. My family was waiting for me in Pakistan. But my father's health was not good, so I decided to wait until he felt better. However, my father was getting information from people he knew, and he kept telling me to get out of the country as soon as possible.

He told me that my life was in danger, and that there was a possibility that they might take me back to prison. Finally, I told him that I would leave only if he and my mother promised to join us wherever we were. I told him, "Father, if you promise to join us, I'll leave—that's the only way."

He finally agreed, saying, "I promise that your mother and I will join you, provided that my health permits me to do so."

I needed to get our money safely out of Afghanistan and converted into an international currency. One of our relatives, Hemayat-jan, was a businessman who had a shop that specialized in wool yarn imported from all over the world. I asked him, "When you order your imported goods, do you send payment from Kabul to a foreign country?" He said that, yes, he always did that; in his business, it was essential.

He did it all the time through export–import banks or sometimes via the *hawala* system of money transfers, depending on which was convenient or available at the time. So a transfer he made would not arouse suspicion. I asked him, "If I give you some money, can you send it to my oldest daughter who is in England?" I gave Hemayat-jan some of the afghanis that I had at that time.

He counted them and said, "At the current rate of exchange—which is fifty-five afghanis to the dollar—this will be about twelve thousand dollars. To whom shall I send it?"

I said, "To our daughter Giselle in England," before I gave him her address.

A few days later, Hemayat-jan told me, "I have confirmation that your money has been transferred." I could not independently determine whether Giselle had received the money. We were not allowed to call each other by phone, and a letter or aerogram took several weeks to arrive. Besides, all letters and aerograms were opened at the post office. Officials would open and read it, and then close it very crudely before the postman brought it to our apartment. Many outgoing letters were never sent out, and many incoming letters were never received by the addressee. But my wife could contact Giselle.

Anyway, the first part of the exit plan, getting my wife and younger daughters out of Afghanistan, was done. Getting some money and converting it to foreign currency had been accomplished, too. But the most difficult part was yet to be done. I needed to make a detailed and practical plan for my own exit from the country.

A Strange Encounter

Soviet troops and army tanks, weapons carriers, and military jeeps could be seen at any time and almost everywhere in Kabul, as they were continuously patrolling the city, day and night. One had to keep away from the places one frequented. At night, no one could go out, drive a car, or walk in the streets after the 8:30 curfew. The Soviet patrols would shoot without asking questions.

Hemayat-jan's older brother Bashir-jan was shot and killed by Soviet soldiers one night after closing his business, when he was going home in his car. For several days, his family, friends, and co-workers did not know what had happened to him.

However, during the day, I continued with my daily exercise walks through the streets of Kabul, although I tried to avoid going to those areas where I knew I might encounter government police or military officers and personnel.

One day, I was walking along Maiwand Boulevard in the direction of the Pamir Cinema. I usually walked at a fast pace, looking ahead in the direction I was going. I arrived at the roundabout of the Maiwand Martyr's Monument, where the road is a traffic circle. I was in a ten o'clock position on the sidewalk and going west when I saw two military jeeps across the circle from me, traveling in an eastward direction. They suddenly stopped with a screech.

The doors were flung open. Four uniformed soldiers, guns in hand, got out of each jeep. An Afghan officer wearing a peaked army cap climbed down from the front seat of his jeep and came toward me.

I told myself, *Tawab, you made a mistake walking on the streets of Kabul. Some folks warned you not to do it, but you ignored their advice and did it anyway. Now the Communists are going to take you back to the prison, and it is all your own fault!* I stopped and was transfixed by the scene unfolding in front of me. I did not move; I just stood there looking. Other people on the sidewalk had all stopped and were looking at what was happening in front of them.

The officer kept coming toward me. Then, when he was about ten feet away, he stopped and gave me a military salute, clicking his heels and touching the peak of his cap. I was frozen; I kept looking at him, not understanding the meaning of his salute. He bent his head slightly in courtesy and said, "Mr. Minister, I am Shoaib." At that moment, still frozen, I did not recognize his name.

He repeated, "Mr. Assifi, I am Shoaib, your friend from Pul-i-Charkhi."

Then, seeing that I still did not recognize him, he took off his cap and said, "Look at me. I am Shoaib. Don't you recognize me?" Then I recognized Shoaib; he had indeed been one of my friends in Pul-i-Charkhi.

But how could I have recognized him here? The circumstances in which I had known him in the prison were totally different from the scene that had unfolded in front of me here. My initial shock changed into distress, given what I was seeing.

I frowned at Shoaib and said, "A curse on you! Why are you wearing that military uniform?" He crossed the curb and came closer to give me an Afghan hug. I was reluctant to receive the hug because of the uniform he was wearing. As he embraced me in a hug, with his mouth close to my ear, he said softly, "I am still a freedom fighter. I wear the uniform so no one knows."

I relaxed and said, "I'm glad to see you, even in the uniform of the culprits, for the sake of knowing what you are actually doing."

He said, "Mr. Minister, when I saw you walking on the sidewalk, I had to see how you were doing. Besides, I have some interesting news that I am sure you would like to hear. The news is that Said Abdullah, the commandant of Pul-i-Charkhi, was executed several days ago. Do you remember that he was knifed in block no. 2 of Pul-i-Charkhi?"

I said, "Of course, I remember."

Shoaib said, "He survived the knife attack, but after that he was really crippled and disabled. Then the Parchamis tried him for killing several members of Parcham in Pul-i-Charkhi. He was pronounced guilty by the special military court, cited as disloyal and a traitor to the Communist Party, the PDPA, and sentenced to be executed as a traitor to the party.

"I heard when they were going to execute him," Shoaib went on, "and I made sure to be present at that time. They brought him to the execution place. There were a number of Parchami officers present there. They read the sentence of the special court aloud. Said Abdullah was falling at the feet of each one of them and begging for his life, saying that he was a very loyal servant of the party and they should not punish him.

"When he fell at the feet of the officers and begged them to forgive him, they kicked him in the face and called out loudly, 'You are a traitor to the party and to the cause!' He went around begging, and everyone kicked him in the mouth.

"Then they made him stand against a pole, tied his hands, covered his eyes, and shot him with a machine gun. Then, to make sure that he was dead, they shot him with single bullets to his head."

I said, "The other officers who were present there, they all have the blood of thousands of innocent Afghan people on their hands. When will justice be served?"

Shoaib said, "When I saw you on the sidewalk here, I wanted to come and salute you. I had to give you the news of Said Abdullah's execution. I am sorry that I stopped you at such a place, but I had to tell you." He then took a few steps backward, gave me one of his military salutes, turned on his heel, walked back to his vehicle, and climbed in.

The soldiers all got back into their jeeps, drove away, and left me going on my way. I never stopped my daily exercise walks as long as I was in Kabul.

Exit Plans

All the while, I was making plans for my own escape from Afghanistan, with the final goal of getting to America, which involved many elements that I had to think through carefully. It had to be practical, ensuring (as far as was possible) that I would come out safely and not get hurt, caught, or killed. No such plan was easy to make or carry out.

I had to deal with many unknowns. In other words, I had to plan on the basis of many unverifiable assumptions. This was totally against the principles that I had been trained to use, those that I had always preached to the engineers whom I mentored and trained to carry out sound projects.

But this was not a plan for a road, a bridge, a canal, a water project, irrigation and agricultural resource development, a reservoir, a dam, or a powerhouse, which I had made many times in my professional career. This was a matter of life and death—my life and my death. I was fully aware that the Communist government's intelligence agencies, advised by their Soviet counterparts, were not sleeping. As we all knew, the Soviets had very efficient spy organizations in the Soviet Union and all other countries under their control or influence. In the case of Afghanistan, they were physically present all the time. Their intelligence organizations and staff had their ears and eyes open, observing all events that countered their interests and joint endeavors. And I already knew that they wanted to use me. So, I had to very carefully evaluate all of my assumptions, even though all of them may have been unverifiable.

Therefore, I had to make a lot of preparations for the pre-implementation phase of my exit plan.

I also kept in mind some folklore based on human experience—what I call words of wisdom.

1) First, Murphy's Law: "If anything can go wrong, it will."
2) Second, the Fox's Tail: "The fox fools the hunter with its tail: it shakes its tail in one direction and goes a different way."
3) Third, "Never assume that going around that bush is safe. There may be a sleeping tiger behind it."

I did not make only one single plan of exit. I made several plans, following the example of the Fox's Tail. In matters of life and death, overplanning is okay. One problem that I had in all of my plans was that my face was recognizable all over the country. Before I was imprisoned, I was a well-known person; my picture was displayed in papers and magazines. Therefore, it was very likely that I would be recognized on whichever route or means of transportation I took.

Maybe I was suffering from false pride, which would not allow me to change my face so it looked different. This was a handicap, but I went ahead and made my plans for different routes, anyhow. Each of these plans was discussed in detail and agreed on with the trusted people who would be assisting me in implementing that plan, including means of transportation, detailed routes, and the date and time for each section of the trip.

I made exit plans for five different routes, via Iran or directly to Pakistan:

1) Kabul to Herat by airplane, bus, taxi, or truck, and then across the Iranian border. The total distance had to be split into sections, going to the Kabul, Kandahar, Girishk, Dilaram, Farah, or Herat border with Iran through either Ghorian or Islam Qala. For each segment of the journey, the specific contacts and means of transportation were decided on.

2) Kabul, Kandahar, Helmand, or Nimroz to the Iranian border. Since I had worked for seventeen years in this area, I was very familiar with different routes and also with the people. I had contacts in every part of this region. In effect, I could consider it my home country.

3) Kabul, Kandahar, or Spin Boldak to the Pakistan border and Quetta. This seemed the most like the Chaman route, and I planned it in great detail. The person who was going to help me get across the border to Pakistan on this route visited me in Kabul. We discussed and settled many details. When he left, he took back with him a metal trunk containing the clothes that I would need to travel onward to the United States.

4) Kabul, Ghazni, or Katawaz to the Pakistan border. One of the well-known freedom fighters in that area came to Kabul himself; we discussed my plan and worked out all the details of the trip using this route. He suggested that I drive my VW bus to the Katawaz area and, from there, across the

border into Pakistan. He told me, "You'll need a vehicle to get around in Pakistan. Otherwise, you'll have to hire taxis for transportation, and it will cost you a lot of money."

5) Kabul, Jalalabad, Nangarhar, or the Free Tribal Area into Pakistan. This was the main route—the shortest and most direct—between Kabul and Pakistan, but I couldn't use the main roads because they were used by military vehicles all the time.

A while after my wife arrived in Rawalpindi, she sent me a message through a cousin of an old acquaintance of ours who was staying at the motel in Rawalpindi Fariha and our daughters they were living. The acquaintance's name was Satar-jan, and his cousin Adila-jan, the wife of our old acquaintance Mohammad Mirza, was also staying there with her kids. Satar-jan came to my home and told me that my family was fine and that they were living in the Gatmel Motel, which was frequented by Afghan refugees. The motel was near the home of Pakistan's president at the time, Zia-ul-Haq. When he went by on his way to his office, he would sometimes stop and say hello to the children there. It appeared that the motel belonged to the British before they left the Indian subcontinent in 1947. In its backyard was an English cemetery.

As it happened, Satar-jan traveled back and forth between Rawalpindi and Kabul almost every week, and he became our courier.

Sometimes, I gave him money to take to my wife in Rawalpindi when she sent word that she needed it. Satar-jan was a good and honest man. As time went on, he gained the trust and confidence of many of us while performing his courier duties. His home village was Qala-i-Ghazi, close to the Kunar River in Nangrahar, halfway between Jalalabad and Torkham, a town on the Afghanistan–Pakistan border.

I asked him whether the route via Jalalabad to the Pakistan border would be safe for me. He said, "Yes, of course. I have helped several families travel from Kabul to Pakistan quite safely."

I decided to take the Nangarhar–Jalalabad route to get out of the country. All the routes that I had planned were feasible, but the Jalalabad route was the fastest. I thought that the faster I got out would be best. I asked Satar-jan to sit down with me and help me make a plan to get out by that route. He gave me all the details of the trip from Kabul to Rawalpindi, and he promised to take me all the way to Rawalpindi and the Gatmel Motel himself. I decided that I would base my escape on the knowledge and experience of Satar-jan.

Not many people knew the details of my plans, not even my close relatives. The people who were involved in the other plans would occasionally contact me and ask when I was going to move. I would tell them, "Please wait a while, because I still have problems before I begin the trip." Then I would say, "I'll inform you at the last minute when I decide to move." Satar-jan and I had made our plans, but we had not decided on a date.

Unfortunately, my father's health was still not very good at this time. His doctors advised me and my mother to hospitalize him in Wazir Akbar Khan Hospital, which was about four miles from my parents' home. I stayed with him all the time that he was in the hospital. After about ten days, he was discharged, as his health had much improved and was now quite good.

By this time, all the other necessary arrangements, like the VW bus transfer and the lease of my apartment, were completed. I had told Rahim Naebkhel to move into the apartment, saying that I could not stay there myself because, given my father's ill health, I had to be with my parents at the time.

When my father was discharged from the hospital, I spoke to the local nurse whom my family had known for many years and arranged for her to come to my father's home when she was needed to give injections. I also spoke to a local doctor and arranged for him to come to my parents' house maybe once every three to four days to make sure that my father received the medications he needed. Actually, this fellow was not a real doctor. He was a doctor's assistant, but, under the circumstances, he was the best that I could get—and he could serve. (In fact, one time my father had had an attack after the curfew, and the doctor couldn't come. With my mother's help, I had administered an injection into my father's vein myself. I had seen doctors and nurses do it and, that way, had learned how it was done.)

It was the beginning of July 1981, the month of Ramazan,[30] when Muslims fast from dawn to sunset. In the month of July, the days are long and Kabul is warm and dry.

At this point, my father and mother told me that it was the best time for me to leave Kabul. They had heard through their contacts that something might happen in the country.

One evening, Satar-jan came from Rawalpindi. My father had been out of the hospital for a few days and was feeling better. Satar-jan said that the freedom fighters had sent word today that they would allow passenger cars and buses to pass freely through the Mahipar and Tangi Abreshum Gorge passes between Kabul and Jalalabad. He said, "Mr. Assifi, I have come to take you tomorrow if you decide to go with me." I made my decision to go!

"Where can we take a bus for Jalalabad?" I asked.

"Those buses take passengers from near the Summer Stadium, near Eidgah," Satar-jan said.

My mother spread a bed in the living room for Satar-jan, and he spent the night with us in my parents' house. We got up early, quite some time before sunrise. Satar-jan and I would be fasting, so we had *sahari*[31] before leaving. I said good-bye to my mother and father. My father gave me two lemons to take with me on the trip. He said, "If you get very thirsty, squeeze some lemon juice in your mouth. It will help quench your thirst."

---

[30] The holy month of fasting, called "Ramadan" in Arabic-speaking countries, and "Ramazan" in Afghanistan.

[31] During Ramazan, sahari is the last meal of the night, before fasting resumes at dawn.

Good-Bye, Kabul

I wore loose, baggy clothes and a cotton waistcoat that had some pockets. I was carrying a small plastic bag in which I had a towel, a bar of soap, and a pair of rubber flip-flops, if I needed to wear them for washing purposes. I had asked Satar-jan how much it would cost me for the trip expenses; he said maybe about five thousand afghanis. I took ten thousand afghanis with me to repay Satar-jan for all the costs that he might incur during the trip and to have a few afghanis for myself.

A Dangerous Trip

I did not carry anything with me, no papers, no ID, nothing else whatsoever. If I was searched, no one would find any identification on me.

Satar-jan and I walked to the place where passenger buses, taxis, and cars were parked and waiting. He told me, "I'll take care of all the arrangements wherever we go. You don't have to speak at all. If you have to say something, speak in the Pashto language."

I thought to myself that there were four things that might give me away: one, my recognizable face; two, the eyeglasses that I always have to wear; three, my Pashto with my Kandahari accent; and four, a chance meeting with some former employee who was a Communist. Then I told myself, *Hey, boy, you can act like someone else and speak Pashto with a Nangarhari accent. And don't forget that your grandmother on your father's side was from Surkh Rud in Nangarhar.*

Well, it would all boil down to having some good luck and trusting Satar-jan's smarts not to expose me to those situations that would give me away.

Satar-jan spoke to the young man who was the driver's agent and got me a seat smack in the middle of the bus. The bus was soon packed with passengers—men, women, and children. Fortunately, there were no goats or sheep on this bus, as they were being hauled in trucks or maybe on very old buses, older than the bus we were riding in.

After about ten or fifteen minutes, the bus started moving. Someone called out to the driver, "Why are you carrying so many people in a bus this size?"

The bus driver shouted, "Sir, once the bus moves and shakes, you will be jam-packed more comfortably."

At this point, I was not concerned about being squeezed in. What I was thinking was, *What lies ahead? What will confront us on the trip?* The bus kept moving toward Pul-i-Charkhi on the road to Jalalabad. It passed the bifurcation point where the bridge road crosses the Kabul River near Pul-i-Charkhi Prison.

I could see the high walls of the prison from a distance. To my distant left, I saw the military barracks and the Polygon, where I thought the Communists were still killing hundreds of people, day and night.

Then, the bus came near the entrance of the Mahipar Gorge. Here, there was a lot of military equipment—tanks, weapons carriers, soldiers' tents, high antennae, and a control gate patrolled by Soviet soldiers. The soldiers signaled for the bus to stop, ominously pointing their machine guns at us. There were many other buses and trucks stopped there, some going in the same direction as we, and some in the opposite direction, toward Kabul.

Soviet soldiers spoke to the bus driver, and then several of them looked at the bus from all sides. One or two looked into the bus and at the passengers. There was total silence and tension among the passengers. Then, one of the Soviet soldiers came to the door beside the bus driver, opened it, and looked into the bus and at the people in the front seat.

Before he closed the door, the driver touched his left palm to the soldier's right hand. I saw that he gave him a packet of some sort.

The soldier then looked in at the front of the bus, turned around, closed the door, walked away some distance, and waved his gun at the driver to pass on.

I could hear a sigh of relief from the passengers (including me) after the ordeal that we had just gone through.

The bus started moving slowly toward the Kabul River Gorge and the entrance to the Mahipar Gorge. The high, steep mountains on both sides of the pass looked empty and desolate, but as we moved into the gorge, we could see, high on the rocks above, freedom fighters who were waving at the bus to pass on. They would not allow the government military or Russian convoys to pass without firing at them and attacking them on all sides from the mountain cliffs. Even for civilian passengers, they would allow free passage only a few days of the week. They let the word get around to inform private passenger vehicles that it was safe for them to pass on such-and-such a day. But as soon as they saw military jeeps, trucks, and convoys trying to take advantage of that time, they opened fire, not allowing them to pass.

As my bus approached the diversion weir of the Mahipar power tunnel, I could see some military sentries posted there; however, they did not stop the bus, so it kept on going farther into the Kabul River Gorge. From there on, the gorge narrows down to the Mahipar Falls. The bus passed through several tunnels and very narrow roads between steep cliffs. At some critical locations, I saw freedom fighters standing on top of huge rocks and waving to the bus driver to keep on moving.

Throughout this period, the freedom fighters and the Afghan people waged war only against the Communist government and the Soviet invader forces and their military machines. Nothing belonging to the people of Afghanistan was destroyed or damaged, so it was not necessary to keep any security staff at bridges and other structures. The bus kept on through the Kabul River Gorge, which became wider as we approached Sarobi, the site of the German-built hydroelectric dam that provided power to Kabul. Before we reached the Sarobi bazaar, I saw another control point where many military machines were parked.

Soviet Russian soldiers were patrolling the area. Ominously pointing their guns at us, as before, they signaled for the bus to stop. It stopped at the control gate.

The Soviet soldiers started to scrutinize the bus from all angles.

Then they looked inside, peering through the windows at the interior and the passengers. Then, again, one of the soldiers opened the driver's door and looked inside; once again, the driver gave him a packet. After that, the soldier waved his gun at the driver and signaled for the bus to move on.

As we passed on through the deep canyon, again I could see the freedom fighters standing on the high cliffs and rocks on either side and waving the bus to go on without stopping.

Later on, I asked the driver, "What did you give the Soviet soldiers in the little packets?"

He answered, "I prepare these packets before we start the trip. We put *chars*[32] in them. The Soviet soldiers love it."

The next checkpoint was at Daronta. There were two locations controlled by Soviet troops: one at the Daronta bridge and the other at the Daronta Dam and Nangarhar Canal intake structures, parts of an irrigation project. The procedure at these locations was like that at the other checkpoints we had passed. Fortunately, it all went well. The bus driver had learned by this time how to deal with Soviet soldiers and sentries.

Some distance after we passed the bridge over the Surkh Rud River, and shortly before we reached Jalalabad, Satar-jan asked the driver to stop.

---

[32] Chars is hashish, marijuana, or a combination of both.

Skirting Jalalabad on a Gawdi

Satar-jan and I got out, and the bus went on its way. Satar-jan said, "We have to go the rest of the way by gawdi. It isn't safe for us to go into the city of Jalalabad."

After a while, a horse-drawn gawdi came along. Satar-jan haggled with the driver and settled on a price. The two of us got in and started moving. But before we reached the city, Satar-jan ordered the driver to take a side road to the right, and then another.

We kept on traveling on side roads that totally skirted the city, until we were all the way on the other side of Jalalabad. We were close to the paved road, but there were no buildings or houses anymore. Satar-jan asked the driver to stop, and we got down.

This place had tall ash trees. In between them there were irrigation ditches flowing with cool water. Satar-jan asked me to come with him to a cluster of trees, where he found a good spot with nice, cool shade, and advised me to stretch out and rest. He said that he would go to find another means of transportation. Then he disappeared. I found a good spot at the side of the irrigation ditch, took my shoes off, put my feet in the cool, running water, and washed my hands and face. I had a towel and a cotton cloth in my plastic bag; I laid them on the ground, lay down, and waited for Satar-jan to show up again. I thought to myself, *When Satar-jan comes back, he will have some means of transportation for traveling the paved road nearby. To get to the road, I will need to jump over a pretty good-sized ditch.* In order not to be recognized by anyone on the road, I thought it would be wise to take off my glasses. Then I thought, *When you take off your glasses, you won't be able to see what's in front of you. You won't even be able to see the side of the ditch to jump from.* I thought that I would definitely fall in the ditch, and that would not be a good sight. At this time of my life, I was in pretty good physical condition and could jump far and high, but if I couldn't see, what would be the consequences? If I fell in the ditch, my clothes would get wet, but it wouldn't matter because it was quite warm and my clothes would dry very fast.

There was occasional traffic on the road, but not many people crossing in that area. With the Soviet troop presence in Afghanistan, people had withdrawn into themselves and retreated to their homes. We did not see tradesmen or farmers moving about in much of the area.

A Government Project Pickup

After an hour, Satar-jan showed up. He called to me to walk to him on the paved road. He said that he had found a means of transportation. I got up, picked up my things and my plastic bag, and followed him to the road, where I saw a Russian-built pickup waiting for us. Some people were already in it. The back of the pickup had a black tarp that looked like a tent covering it.

I remembered to take off my eyeglasses and put them inside my waistcoat pocket. When I came to the irrigation ditch, I told myself, *Come on, boy, you can do it.* Satar-jan jumped. Following his lead, I walked up to the ditch and then jumped. I did not fall in; in fact, I think that I overjumped it, because I found myself running on the other side.

Satar-jan motioned for me to come to the back of the pickup. There, I saw people sitting under the tarp on benches along the sides and around some tall milk cans in the middle. Satar-jan climbed in, and then he helped me get in and find a seat on one of the benches along the side. I could see through the rear window of the cab that there were two military officers in uniform sitting in the front seat next to the driver. As I later found out, this was a pickup that carried milk from the Nangarhar Canal Project farms to the city of Jalalabad.

Nangarhar Canal Project

I knew a lot about the Nangarhar Canal Project. It had been built by the Russians as a showcase of Russian prowess in planning and building irrigation, agricultural, and water projects. It was meant to show the Afghan people that the Russians were better than the Americans who had helped develop the Helmand Valley Project in southwestern Afghanistan.

The Soviets were indoctrinating a lot of young minds in Afghanistan through a very efficient propaganda machine that they had developed and implemented in many schools and government offices. The so-called progressive elements in the country especially had put themselves at the service of Soviet interests. (One of the main Soviet objectives was to misinform the people of Afghanistan about anything that had to do with or was related to the United States of America.) The Helmand and Arghandab Valleys Project, an Afghan project with which the United States had assisted and provided advisors for, was therefore a primary target of the Soviet propaganda machine. I had spent about seventeen years of my young life in operating and developing that project. The Soviets began the planning and construction of the Nangarhar Canal Irrigation Project as a showcase of Soviet superiority and prowess in technology, engineering, agriculture, etc. However, after a few years, the people and the government of Afghanistan realized that this project had many problems, ones that originally had not been envisioned.

One of the important points was that the land developed in this project cost a great deal. At one time, when I was still in Helmand, the Office of the Deputy Prime Minister called me to Kabul and assigned me to do a comparative analysis of the Helmand Valley versus the Nangarhar Canal Project. I traveled to the site of the canal project and met with Hakim Khan, an old acquaintance, who had at one time been the deputy director of the Helmand agricultural department. I studied the canal projects in detail, prepared a comparative analysis report, and submitted it to the Office of the Prime Minister.

In my conclusions, I praised the engineering design and construction of the canal, its laterals, and the irrigation distribution systems of the project. In these aspects, it was a world-class job.

But there were two major differences between the two projects:

1) In the Nangarhar Canal Project's developed lands, agriculture was to be carried out by way of a government-run state farm system, while the Helmand project's developed lands

were all distributed to landless farmer-settlers from all over Afghanistan.

2) The cost of land that was completed and ready for agriculture in the Nangarhar Canal Project was more than seventy thousand to eighty thousand afghanis per jerib,[33] whereas the most costly land developed in Helmand (land in the Marja region) was about nine thousand afghanis per jerib. In short, the cost of developed land in the Nangarhar Canal Project was seven to eight times greater than that in the Helmand Valley Project. Also, an area of the Nangarhar Canal Project was developed for olive tree production and was associated with an olive oil extraction and processing plant. Since olive oil had not previously been a significant product of Afghan agriculture, this caused a lot of operational and olive-specialty-personnel problems later on.

3) An area that was designated for a pump irrigation system was never operational because of a shortage of power generation in that area.

4) The Helmand project was reputed to suffer from a salt problem, but after the development of drainage systems, it became one of the agriculturally most productive lands in the country.

The milk pickup started to move. Because of the tarp, I could not see out of the sides, only from the open back. Once someone raised the side tarps, I could see where we were going.

The first part of our journey was through some agricultural acreage in the lower valley lands of Nangarhar. Then, we came to a location that someone said was close to the canal siphon, crossing some irrigation ditches and flood channels and gullies. The end of the siphon was on higher ground, an area of the upper desert lands where some farmland had been developed for the canal's agricultural systems.

There was a security post with a very heavy military presence here, before the road went on to the upper desert lands. I saw a Soviet

---

[33] A jerib is about half an acre.

control gate and Soviet soldiers patrolling the area. They pointed their guns at our pickup to stop it. There were many buses and trucks parked on both sides of the road.

The inspection process here took much longer than at the other posts we had encountered so far in our journey from Kabul. Here, there were some civilian personnel who came and gave us the up-and-down look. One of them spoke to the passengers in the pickup. They even spoke to me. I responded in carefully Nangarhari-accented Pashto. Finally, after an hour, the Soviet soldiers were satisfied. They waved their guns and signaled the driver to go on.

The pickup truck started to move slowly up the hill. It gained speed when it came to the level ground of the desert. In the distance, I could see the embankment of the Nangarhar Canal. After twenty minutes or so, Satar-jan told the driver to stop. Once the truck stopped, Satar-jan got down and asked me to get down, too. Getting down from the back of the pickup was awkward. I gave my plastic bag to someone sitting there and asked him to hold it for me. When I was down, he handed it back to me. I thanked him for his help. Later, Satar-jan laughed and told me that the fellow was a Parchami.

The pickup truck drove away. Satar-jan took me to a low spot, where I could see an irrigation culvert under the road. The water was flowing out into a ditch. A little way down on either side of the ditch were some tamarind bushes. Satar-jan told me, "There is a little spot with some shade in there among the tamarinds where you could lie down and wait for me to get some means of transportation to get us close to our qala."

Qala-i-Ghazi

There was no traffic—and no people—in this spot. Cool water was flowing in the ditch. I put my bag down, sat near the water, and washed my hands, face, and feet. In the July heat, it felt really good to clean myself up with fresh, cool water. The sound of water flowing in the ditch was pleasant. Not even a fly was to be seen. I looked in the direction from which the water was flowing. I felt sure that there were some farms down there.

After an hour or more, I saw an old truck coming up the dirt road toward the place where I was resting. The truck stopped. I saw Satar-jan jump out, shake the dust from his clothes, and come toward me. He smiled and said, "Well, I have some means of transportation for you." I saw that the truck was trying to turn around. A young boy, about seven or eight years old, was calling to the driver and giving him directions for turning. The boy's face, hands, and clothes were all black with soot and grease from working on the truck.

I could not understand how this broken-down old truck could actually move. It had high sides made of wooden planks that had once been painted with a design that might have been flowers and a wild-eyed tiger staring out, ready to jump at any moment. The bearded driver stood because there was no seat for him to sit on. He was probably about fifty years old, but I could not distinguish his face from his beard and clothes, as everything about him was black. I came closer to the truck and saw that it was a large Mercedes-Benz, maybe from the era when the company had just started to manufacture diesel trucks. Credit had to be given to that old marvel of mechanical engineering, to this blackened driver/mechanic, and especially to the young grease boy, who was soot-black from head to toe.

I asked Satar-jan, "Where did you find this contraption?"

He said, "I went to the village of Ghazi Abad, but I couldn't find any other vehicle. I went into a shop and saw these two guys repairing this truck. I asked the older man, 'Can this truck move?' He said, 'Of course it can.' So, I told him, 'Come on, drive me to the main Jalalabad–Pak border road and back, and I will pay you Iftar[34] money.' Since the truck made it to this place, it can take us to the village. Come on, let's go."

---

[34] Iftar is the evening meal that breaks the daily fast during the month of Ramazan.

I climbed up into the truck to where the front seat may have been at one time, grabbing some iron angle bars for support. The truck started forward, with every part of it moving a separate way. I held onto the bars, which, I assumed, were ultimately tied to some steel member of the truck structure.

As the truck moved along, I had a feeling that the floor I was standing on was not secured to the front of the truck. It felt like I was skating on ice. I kept holding onto the only thing that I thought was connected to the main structure of the truck, which was moving to an unknown destination, one that only the grease boy and the driver knew. If someone had seen us from the back, they would have thought that we were doing a Hawaiian dance. (I beg your pardon, but I believe, in the midst of drastic situations in life, a little bit of humor is not that bad!)

I could see some mud walls and trees in the distance. Before we reached the village, Satar-jan told the driver to stop and then asked me to get down from the truck and follow him. Getting down from that truck was not easy. One had to be a gymnast or a daredevil to do it.

From here on, Satar-jan and I walked across the desert, about forty-five degrees from the easterly direction. In the far distance, I could see a mud-walled qala, some more mud houses, and scattered trees in the compounds.

Satar-jan said, "This is my ancestral qala. It's called Qala-i-Ghazi. My ancestors were freedom fighters and fought the English troops when they invaded Afghanistan a hundred years ago, going toward Kabul." He said that they fought the British both ways, coming in from India and marching toward Jalalabad on their way to Kabul and, later, coming out on their way to leave Afghanistan.

I said, "Oh, so that's why they were called *ghazi*! (*Ghazi* means someone who fights an invading army that has come to conquer his or her country).

We came closer to the mud walls, skirted them, and went behind them, where there were more mud houses of this small village.

Satar-jan showed me the high wall and towers at the corner of one compound and said, "That's where our qala is. But first, I will take you to the *masjid*[35] so you can rest there until after the Iftar, breaking the Ramazan fast."

The mosque was small and shaded by big mulberry trees. We went inside. There was no furniture of any sort, except *booriyaa* (straw mats) spread on the floor. I would need to wash before praying and eating. Satar-jan said, "There is an irrigation ditch outside where you can wash your hands, and there is a well where you can get water with a rubber bucket made in the village." (Village bucket-makers peeled the inside woven rubber out of old truck tires and made buckets from it. Cobblers made rubber flip-flops and slippers from the same material.)

It was still daylight, so I was still fasting. I stretched out on the floor on one of the mats and rested there for a while; I may have dozed off. Satar-jan, who had gone to his family home, came back and shook me to wake me.

I awoke and went out to wash up. I got a bucket of water from the well, washed my hands, face, and feet (a formal ablution), came back to the masjid, and sat down at one side. A villager came in and spread a large cloth on the floor in front of us. He then put some flat loaves of homemade oven-baked Afghan bread (naan tandoori) in front of me and all around the eating cloth. (I cannot say *tablecloth,* because there was no table.) There is a tradition in villages in Afghanistan: the village people take turns every day bringing bread and other food for travelers, guests, poor people, and the mullah of their masjid to break the fast and eat.

In Ramazan, the time to break the fast—literally, "breakfast time"— is after sunset, when the darkness begins to rise from the eastern

---

[35] Mosque.

horizon. The village mullah, if available, or one of the knowledgeable elders of the village, stands outside and says the Azaan (the call for prayer) in a loud, melodic voice for all to hear. Some villagers come to the mosque for congregational prayers and maybe to eat a little fast-breaking food there before going back to their homes to dine.

Fast-Breaking Food

I was honored to be one of the guests on this occasion. It really felt good, and the food was very tasty.

Satar-jan was sitting next to me and acting as host, inviting me to take food from different bowls and plates. In the Afghan village tradition, one does not have separate plates or use forks, knives, and spoons to eat. The flat bread and one's right or left hand are one's respective plate and utensils. Everyone reaches into the big plate or bowl of food and takes some with their fingers or a spoon, if available. I got a big spoon, reached out, and put some food on a large piece of bread in front of me so as to eat from it with my fingers.

I had depended on forks and spoons for a long time, so my finger eating was not perfect or neat. But no one looked at me because they did not want to embarrass me. I remembered how my father used to say that food tasted much better when he ate with his fingers. I would say, "Father, I wash my hands with soap and water before I eat food. But if I eat with my fingers, then I have to wash them again with soap and water; otherwise, there would be a lot of grease on my fingers."

"Well," he would say, "you can't have all the luxuries of life without doing a little more work for it." So for my father, eating with his fingers was a great luxury. He enjoyed eating that way whenever he had the chance.

After we ate and said our prayers, Satar-jan told me that I should go with him inside the qala and rest for the night. We went out quietly in the darkness, entered the qala, and went to the back, where there was an orchard. In the middle of the orchard was a platform-like area shaded by an arbor of grapevines with small irrigation ditches all around. There were two or three *charpayees* (wooden beds crisscrossed with stretched straw ropes for a mattress) with wool blankets and Afghan-style long, round pillows. A few kerosene lanterns hanging from posts shone some dim light so we could see a little bit of our immediate surroundings. A transistor radio was blaring some sort of local music. Satar-jan pointed to one of the beds and said, "You can rest on that bed." Our hosts brought pots of tea and milk and some cookies and lumps of sugar for us. There were no other guests but me. Satar-jan kept going in and out of the *saracha*[36] to the main qala's mud buildings. I was really relaxed at this moment.

A little later, however, I noticed that men who had guns hanging from their shoulders had come into the orchard where we were. They kept coming in and then vanishing into the orchard, where I couldn't see them anymore. It seemed to me that there was a large number of them. Well, I was a guest in Satar-jan's home qala, so I figured that nothing would bother me. When Satar-jan came back from some errand, I said, "I saw a lot of men come in. Who are they?"

"They are here for your protection," he said. "They are all freedom fighters. There are sixty of them here with their guns. They will be positioned behind the walls all around this compound."

"Well," I said, "could we offer them some tea before the sahari?"

He laughed and said, "No, they are on duty and won't drink tea at this time." He then turned on the transistor radio to the Kabul radio station, saying, "Let's hear the propaganda news from the government."

At the end of the news broadcast, the announcer said, "We have sad news that thieves and robbers and troublemakers have assassinated Qamar Gul, the famous female vocalist who used to sing on government television and radio stations."

---

[36] A saracha is a unit separate from the qala, made to receive guests, where they can also spend the night.

Day Two at Qala-i-Ghazi

I thought that Satar-jan and I would have sahari and then leave this place for our trip across the valleys and mountains of the regions that are known to Afghans as the Afghan Free Tribal Areas and to Pakistanis as Administered Tribal Territories. But it was still dark when Satar-jan woke me and said, "Let's go." I looked at my watch; it was two in the morning. I got up, put on my old walking boots, picked up my plastic bag, and followed after him. We followed a footpath through the wheat fields, heading in an easterly direction. I could not see anyone, but I had a feeling that the guards who had been with us the night before were accompanying us at a distance. After about twenty minutes, we came to a river; I could hear the running water.

Swimming across the Kabul–Kunar River

I estimated that we were at a section of the Kunar River some distance below its confluence with the Kabul River. There were tall bushes, tall weeds, and tamarind bushes near the riverbank. It was dark, so I could not see the opposite bank of the river.

We came to a point on the riverbank where several people were standing. One man had entered the water about knee-deep and was holding a *zhaala* float. Zhaala floats are made of sheepskin or calfskin, which is puffed up with air and looks like an misshapen air bag or balloon. A number of these inflated skins are tied together by weed-straw ropes and covered with clean tree branches to form a sort of platform or float. People sit on these floats and ride down a river, navigating with wooden poles to get to the other bank. In other words, zhaalas are microferries used to carry people across flowing river water. The man who was standing in the water here was running a small business of ferrying people across the Kunar River.

Some zhaala operators may have a rope or cable stretched across the river from bank to bank; the zhaala operator holds onto the rope and pulls on it to get his float and passengers across the river. At this location, there was no rope to pull on. We had to float down and across the river.

I asked Satar-jan, "Would it be okay with you and the zhaala operator if I swam across the river?"

He said, "No, this a swift river and you could drown by swimming in it." I am a very good swimmer. I took lifesaving classes, I am licensed, and, when I was at Cornell University, I worked as a lifeguard at Beebe Lake for a whole summer. And in truth, I had not bathed for two days, during the time I had been traveling in the heat of July. I had accumulated lot of sweat and dust on my body that I wanted to wash off.

I said, "I'll swim alongside the zhaala. If there is trouble, I can hold onto it."

Satar-jan said, "Okay, but please swim close to the zhaala."

I took off my clothes (except for my underwear briefs), put them in my plastic bag, and gave the bag to Satar-jan. Then, he and two armed security men got on the zhaala and started floating away. I swam next to them.

When we got to the other side, I got out of the water feeling exhilarated. I put on my clothes and started up one of the footpaths leading from the riverbank to the higher ground above. Satar-jan stopped me, saying, "We'll wait here till we have word that our transportation is here."

Soviets Attack Goshta

After a few minutes, a young boy, about fifteen years old, came running to us. He said that the Soviets had attacked the village of Goshta and were bombarding it from the air. The pickup that was supposed to come for us could not make it; it was stuck in the fighting. Truck traffic was halted.

Satar-jan said, "Let's wait here a while. Then we'll go ahead on our own. Maybe on the way we will find some kind of transportation to help us get where we want to go."

So we waited for a few minutes. Then, I, Satar-jan, and the two security guards started walking toward the mountains, heading away from Goshta. Dawn was breaking. In the distance, we could see jet planes swooping down on the town. Black and gray smoke was rising here and there. We could also see helicopters circling in the sky. The Soviets were attacking the village of Goshta in full force. Obviously, we could not go there.

Satar-jan said, "Well, it's a long way to our destination, but we don't have any alternative. So we'll walk there through the mountains."

An Old Pickup Truck

We started walking toward the mountains. After about an hour, we came upon a Toyota pickup in a gully, packed full of passengers. There were women, children, and men all over the overloaded pickup. Satar-jan asked the driver why they were waiting. The driver said that his pickup engine got hot, so he was waiting for it to cool down. Satar-jan asked, "Can you carry us, too?"

The driver said, "No, we can't take all four of you."

Satar-jan said, "How about two of us?"

The driver said, "If you guys can squeeze yourselves in, I don't care." I don't know what Satar-jan told the driver after that, but the driver asked one of the men who was sitting in the front seat to give his place to me and go sit somewhere in the back of the pickup.

After doing this, the driver raised his hands in a gesture of prayer and called out loudly, "Let us all pray to get to our destination without any mishaps!" Everyone in the pickup raised their hands and said the prayer in unison. The pickup started moving in the direction of the mountains. Its engine kept missing but still managed to carry its heavy load. The pickup went in the gullies and sometimes on flatter ground. Generally, the slope of the ground increased mile by mile. I was expecting the engine to stop at any moment, but it kept on going. I was amazed that it wasn't boiling over.

I couldn't decide on what kept the old pickup chug-chugging along. Was it the Japanese genius for making engines, or was it the prayers of the driver and passengers seeking help from the Almighty? Finally, I settled for the validity of both.

The driver did not stop the pickup again. We kept on going uphill. After about two hours, we arrived at a group of buildings at the foot of the mountains, something like a customs house with large storage warehouses. But these did not look like government-built warehouses. They had probably been built by people who didn't want to pay customs duties on the items they traded in, otherwise known as smugglers. As far as I was concerned at that moment, I really did not care.

Donkey Ride

Satar-jan told me, "From here on, we'll have to walk. I have two bags that I left in one of these warehouses last week. I am going to go and get them, and I'll hire an animal to haul the bags." After some time, he came back with two medium-sized travel bags that he was transporting for some other people. He also had a man in tow who was pulling a donkey. Satar-jan said, "This man will help us with the donkey and the bags, and he'll also be our guide for this stretch of our journey." They loaded the two bags, one on each side of the donkey like saddlebags, and tied them down with ropes.

Satar-jan said, "The first part of our trip today is going to be up this very steep hill. I think it would be better for you to ride the donkey for that." To tell the truth, I really did not care what means of transportation was afforded me at that time. I told Satar-jan that I could much better walk up the hill, but he would not listen. So I mounted the donkey before we started up the hill.

This was not as easy as it had seemed at first. The big problem was that I kept sliding off the donkey. Donkeys do not learn to keep their backs level while they are going up or down a steep hill, and this hill was very steep. As the donkey went uphill, his back was parallel to the angle of the slope. In all my life, I had failed to learn "monkey business," and now I was failing to cope with "donkey business." I kept sliding off the back of the donkey. Finally, Satar-jan consented to let me walk up the hill on my own feet.

Farm Tractors

We hiked up that hill and then went further through other hills before we finally came to more-level ground. There, we found two farm tractors waiting, crazily loaded with people. Once again, there was no room for us. The ploughs had been extended, raised above the ground, and covered with wood planks and old carpets to make a sort of platform. A large number of people were sitting on that and on every other feature of the tractor. They were on top of the ploughs, on top of the front bulldozer blade, on the mudguards, on top of the engine hood, and anywhere else that one could imagine.

Satar-jan spoke to the tractor driver and then told me to sit on top of the right rear mudguard. He added, "When the tractor is moving, you can hold onto those two steel bars sticking out." I don't know where Satar-jan and our guide sat or stood on the tractor. I also don't remember what happened to the donkey. There must have been about thirty people loaded on each tractor. No one had a camera to take pictures. The whole thing looked kind of funny, but the situation did not allow anyone to laugh. It was not funny at all. We were all running away, trying to escape from our own homeland.

We expected to be attacked by Soviet jets and their deadly Hind helicopters at any minute during our journey if they spotted us. The tractors moved along ravines and gullies, climbing down the slopes and up again, zigzagging their way and always moving without any pause. It was a sorry sight, but the glimmer of hope—that we might make it to a land free of Soviets and their Communist protégés—made us all endure every hardship the occasion presented.

After about two hours, the tractors came to a stop on top of a hilly area. They were unable to go any farther. All of the passengers got down and continued their journey on foot.

There were women and children in the group. They were moving a bit slowly, so Satar-jan, I, and the guide who had been helping us with the donkey and the bags started walking at a faster pace than the others.

Russian Toy Bomb

Our guide knew the way. He walked a bit ahead of us. After about an hour, we three were quite a bit ahead of the rest of the group that had come with us on the tractors. When I looked back, I saw that we seemed to be alone.

I could not see any others walking behind us. Along the way, I had noticed carcasses of animals—sheep, dogs, or, in one place, what looked like a jackal or a small wolf. I asked our guide, "Am I imagining things, or there are a great many animal carcasses scattered around this place?"

He said, "You're not imagining. These are carcasses of animals that were killed by Russian bombs."

I asked him, "What do you mean by 'bombs'? Did the Soviets bomb this area? It doesn't make sense. Why would they bomb such a remote area on the hilltops?"

He said, "This is on the route of many refugees going from Afghanistan to the Free Tribal Areas and Pakistan. Also, this route is frequently used by freedom fighters when they're traveling back and forth between Afghanistan and Pakistan. At first, the Soviets sent planes and helicopters to bomb and attack the travelers. However, they found out that they could not stop the traffic of people and animals that way, seeing as the number wasn't small and the people didn't come only sometimes. The foot traffic was more like a river flowing all the time. Refugees did not know where they would camp or finally settle, but when the Soviets bombed their homes and villages, they had to save themselves from being killed. So, at such a time, they moved to a safer area. People would travel at night or scatter so that they were not a definite target.

"So then," the guide continued, "the Soviets started dropping a lot of small plastic bombs[37] that looked like green leaves, children's toys, and things like that. They plastered the whole area with these toy bombs. People walking did not know what they were. They picked them up to look at them, or they stepped on the ones that looked like leaves in the grass. When refugees were getting out of Afghanistan, they brought their livestock and animals with them. The animals stepped on the plastic bombs that looked like leaves and got killed. There are maybe several million Afghan refugees in the border region and farther inland in the Free Tribal Areas and Pakistan."

Our guide continued speaking. "The Soviet policy of killing the Afghan population caused this mass movement of people. The Soviets tried many killing methods but could not stop the movement of people. The spreading of toy bombs is one of those Soviet killing methods, and the carcasses that you see are real."

"The toy bombs have broken the legs and hands of many children, and also killed many children," he said. "Children pick them up to look at what they think is a toy. But the toy bomb blows up in their face and kills them, or at least maims or cripples them. The world knows about this tragedy, but no one does anything about it. Maybe they are indifferent about what happens to our people!"

Our guide told me to be careful where I was walking, and to carefully look ahead to where I was going to step. He said that I should stop if I noticed any unusual object in the path.

I said, "Okay."

---

[37] These mines were eventually reported by French doctors and humanitarian NGOs, at which time they became known to the world. The green plastic ones were called "butterfly mines" and were dropped by the millions. In grass or shrubbery, they were effectively invisible. The toy mines were disguised as dolls, watches, pens, toy cars, etc.

"Stop! Don't Move!"

Suddenly, the guide shouted, "Stop! Don't move!" He was looking at me, and he repeated, "Don't move!" I froze and stood still in my place. Then, he came walking slowly toward me, carefully looking where he was stepping, and reached me from the side and a little behind. He held my arm and repeated again, "Don't move!" Then he said, "Now walk back slowly—but while you're doing that, don't twist your foot on the ground!"

He guided me carefully backwards about ten feet and then said, "Come on, let's get behind this rise and lie down at the bottom." He shouted to Satar-jan, saying that he should do the same. All three of us went behind a clump of tall weeds and bushes. The guide said, *"Keep your heads down."*

Then, he started throwing large pieces of gravel and rocks at the place where he had ordered me to stop. He said again, "Keep your heads down," and kept on throwing stones.

Suddenly, there was a loud boom! Blue-gray smoke rose from that spot. He said, "That was a bomb, and I'm very glad that you didn't step on it! We could have lost you!" It took me a few moments to fully comprehend what had happened. When I heard the explosion and saw the smoke rising, I realized that this guide had saved me from a terrible accident. And this had happened when I was feeling good, when I felt like I was walking on air, going toward a safe place to meet my wife and daughters!

The guide went over to where the bomb had been, stooped down, picked up something, and brought it for me to see. It was a twisted piece of green plastic. Maybe before blowing up, it looked like a leaf or part of a rubber tree.

I wanted to take the object in my hand and look at it closely. The guide told me, "Don't. It will burn your fingers. It probably has some acid on it. Usually, after these things are blown up, the remains burn people's hands when they touch it. You know," he said, "several times, people have used flocks of sheep, maybe two or three hundred of them, to pass on this track and blow up the bombs. This area has been demined several times. But still some bombs remain, like this one that you nearly stepped on."

We started walking again. While I walked, I kept thinking that in these last few years, I had many times come close to being killed, as close as the width of a hair; but somehow, I had been saved. What was it? Was it chance? Happenstance? Good luck? Or maybe it was because when I was leaving Kabul and saying good-bye to my mother and father, they said prayers for me: "May you get safely to your destination, and may God keep you from any harm that may come on your way. God be with you. *Insha'Allah!*"[38]

We are the beneficiaries of our mothers' and fathers' goodwill and good prayers—from the womb, throughout childhood, when we are growing up, when we have learned what is good and bad, and forever thereafter, here on earth and hopefully in heaven.

Out

I, Satar-jan, and our guide started walking again. After about half an hour, we came to another steep slope. In the distance, at the foot of the hill, I could see two buses.

We walked down the hill to the buses. They already had some passengers sitting inside, and the drivers were waiting for the seats to fill up. Satar-jan and I said good-bye to our guide and boarded a bus wherein several people were already sitting. Others arrived and boarded our bus, but five or six seats remained unoccupied. After a while, it was clear that no more people were coming.

The bus driver was still waiting for the empty seats to be filled. I knew that all the passengers from the tractors had arrived and that there would be no more coming for the time being. I told Satar-jan that I did not think any more passengers would show up, saying

---

[38] "God willing!"

that we were waiting in vain. Then I said, "Tell the driver to go ahead and move. I'm ready to pay the cost of the remaining five seats." The driver wagged his head from side to side in a gesture of agreement[39] before proceeding to start the engine and get the bus on its way.

An hour later, we arrived at Charsadda, a large town bustling with business, traffic, and busy people who mostly spoke the Pashto language. I was now out of Afghanistan. The bus stopped at a location where I saw other buses, taxicabs, and taxi vans parked, all of them in the business of serving passengers who came from various parts of the surrounding area.

Satar-jan told me that we would get out here and rent another vehicle to take us to Rawalpindi. It was still daylight, and Satar-jan and I were both fasting.

He found a van that was almost full of passengers, so it was not very long before it started to move. Satar-jan had already put his two bags and my plastic bag in the top compartment of the van, which started speeding its way toward Rawalpindi. We did not go into Peshawar. Instead, we skirted the city so that we would not be delayed by its heavy traffic.

Anyone could guess my state of mind at that moment. I had successfully escaped Prison Afghanistan, and I was euphoric in my anticipation of seeing my wife and children after more than four months. The van was briefly stopped twice by highway security police for traffic and load checks. In my state of mind, I had no sense of time.

---

[39] In Europe and America, this is a negative gesture meaning "no," but in parts of Asia and the subcontinent, it has the opposite meaning: "yes" or "okay."

Reunion with My Family

In a few hours, we arrived at the Gatmel Motel in Rawalpindi. The area around the motel was very green, with trees everywhere. The driver stopped the van at the gate, and Satar-jan and I got out. Satar-jan was familiar with the motel; he had visited his cousin there. I followed him. We entered through the main entrance and then went through a wide corridor and into the backyard, where most of the motel rooms were located. Most of the guests in this motel were Afghan refugees waiting to find a way to leave and join their families elsewhere.

Many children were playing in the yard. Most of them stopped playing and looked at us. Suddenly, two little girls, my daughters, Madina and Shamila, saw me and came running. They hugged me and shouted to their mother to come and see—their father was here! My wife came running out of the motel room. We hugged and embraced. It is not hard to guess our state of mind at that moment. It was one of the happiest moments of my life.

The other children had gathered around us. Hearing the excitement, many of the other guests came out of their rooms to welcome me and tell me that they were very happy that I had made it safely out of Afghanistan. My wife said, "Let's go to the room. I have some food prepared so you can break your fast." By now, the sun was setting in the west; it was almost time for the Iftar meal. I wanted to wash up before joining my wife and kids to eat.

Satar-jan went to his cousin's room to break the fast and said he would see me in the morning.

The quarters that Fariha had rented were very small—just one room and a bathroom, Pakistani style. That was all we could afford at the time. We were on the run, but we were happy to be alive, healthy, and together.

Later on, my wife brought me up-to-date on what she and our daughters had been doing since they reached Pakistan. The second day that they were in Rawalpindi, she had gone with the kids to the American embassy in neighboring Islamabad and met with the American consul.

The consul had advised her to go to the UN Refugee Office and register our names there as refugees applying to go to the United States. He advised her that claiming refugee status would be better for us than asking for political asylum. Fariha had not wasted any time; she, too, had spent time in the United States and was fluent in English, so she filled out all the necessary forms for us. They were all ready, except my signature was needed on some of them. The American consul had also advised her to stay put and keep a low profile, saying that it would be dangerous for her husband if the Kabul government found out that his wife and children had already left the country and were waiting for him in Pakistan (instead of going to India for medical treatment).

We made an appointment with the UN Refugee Office, went in, and signed all the forms that my wife had already prepared. We were informed that there were two more steps we had to take. The most important one was that we had to be interviewed by a US Immigration and Naturalization Services (INS) judge. He would be the one to approve our qualifications as refugees. Second, we needed to be sponsored by someone in the United States who would assume the responsibility of providing for us until we found jobs to support ourselves. Fortunately, we had a very good sponsor. My wife's brother, Dr. Shir Ali Miskinyar, was a plastic surgeon in Garden Grove, California. He and his wife, Makai-jan, had agreed to sponsor us and let us stay in their home until we found jobs. They sent the necessary documentation.

Everything was ready, so we waited for the Immigration and Naturalization Services' judge's interview. We finally got an appointment, and all of us went together. After interviewing us, the judge told us that he thought we were most qualified. So we had the approval of the INS judge. The UN Refugee Office told us that they would process our papers and inform us of our departure date. They also told us that Catholic Community Churches had agreed to pay our airfare to California on the condition that we repay the cost as soon as I found a job. We gladly agreed. From then on, we waited to hear when we would go. Since Fariha had already done the paperwork for all of us before I arrived, we only had to wait another two and a half months.

Visiting Refugee Camps

While we were waiting, I went around Pakistan to see for myself how the millions of refugees from Afghanistan were doing. I visited several refugee camps near Peshawar and farther west, near Quetta in the state of Balochistan. I also visited some of the freedom fighters who came from Afghanistan to get arms and then go back to Afghanistan to fight against the troops of the Soviet army and the Communist regime.

It was generally known that after the Soviet invasion, the United States began providing financial assistance and weapons to Afghan freedom fighters (some called the fighters "the resistance" or "mujahideen").[40]

Since Afghanistan is a landlocked country, such aid had to go through Pakistan. However, the CIA, which, under US law, was the channel for that aid, did not give the funds and arms directly to the resistance organizations. Instead, the aid was supplied to the Pakistan army's Inter-Services Intelligence (ISI) organization, which distributed the arms and money to the leaders of the seven

---

[40] The freedom fighters could properly claim the title of mujahideen because religious authorities like Pir Sayed Ahmad Gailani, Sibgatullah Mojadidi, and others had declared the struggle to be in the defense of Islam, seeing as the Communist regime had taken steps to undermine religious devotion.

resistance parties[41] recognized by ISI and the Pakistani government. The ISI then distributed it to the mujahideen affiliated with those parties.

The fighting men everywhere told me that a lot of the aid money and arms disappeared at ISI before any was passed on to the parties. A second big loss occurred when the aid was passed from the parties to the fighting men. At each transfer of funds and arms, big losses occurred. By the time anything reached the actual fighting men, 70 percent to 80 percent or more had been lost.

Several freedom fighters in different camps showed me very old, rusted British army rifles that were totally frozen and useless. The Pakistani government got new guns, including machine guns from

---

[41] The seven parties were Mahaz-i-Milli Islami Afghanistan (National Islamic Front of Afghanistan [NIFA]), a pro-royalist, pro-Western group headed by Pir Sayed Ahmad Gailani, who also led the Qadiriyya Order of Sufism; Jamiat Islami Afghanistan (Islamic Society of Afghanistan), headed by Professor Burhanuddin Rabbani, who had ties with the Muslim Brotherhood (Commander Massoud in the Panjshir Valley was affiliated with this group); Jabba-i-Milli Najat-i-Afghanistan (National Front for the Rescue of Afghanistan), a pro-royalist group headed by Professor Sibgatullah Mojadidi, the chief survivor of the Mojadidi clan who was out of the country when the men of that family were murdered; Harakat-i-Inqilab-i-Islami Afghanistan (Movement for the Islamic Revolution of Afghanistan), headed by Maulawi Mohammad Nabi Mohammadi, an influential theologian and member of Parliament; Hezb-i-Islami Khalis (Islamic Party, Khali faction), headed by Maulawi Mohammad Younos Khalis, a respected Pashtun mullah, university lecturer, and editor who went onto the field of government; Hezb-i-Islami Hekhmatyar (Islamic Party, Hekhmatyar faction), headed by Gulbuddin Hekhmatyar, an Islamic extremist and a highly controversial figure who attacked Soviet and Communist units and rivals; and Ittihad-i-Islami Baraye Azadi Afghanistan (Islamic Union for the Liberation of Afghanistan), a small group headed by Abdul Rasul Sayyaf, a member of the Muslim Brotherhood who was funded by Saudi sources and was closely associated with Wahhabis and Salafis.

the United States, but it kept them and, instead, passed on to the Afghan freedom fighters the old, rusted guns left over in Pakistani military warehouses from the days of the British colonial time, which had ended in 1947.

They told me, "It's like fetching water from the well or a river using a bucket with a hundred holes in it, but the Pakistani government has a barrel under the bucket."

$2.7 Billion Afghan Refugee Cost

At one time, I found out that the Pakistani government was receiving about US$2.7 billion annually for the cost of leasing land for refugee camps and other costs associated with supporting what eventually numbered several million Afghan refugees. This sounded incredible to me. I was grateful to the Pakistani government for allowing Afghan refugees to stay on government-owned land, and I knew that there were expenses involved. But I did not know that Pakistan was charging the United States and the United Nations so much money every year for their hospitality.

Quetta and Chaman

I made a trip to Quetta, where I visited several refugee camps. From there, I went to Chaman on the Afghan border to pick up my old trunk, which contained the clothes I could wear in America and which I had previously sent on ahead.

I spent several days in Quetta as the guest of Habib and Khalil Karzai, to whom I was tribally related. Khalil had been with me in Pul-i-Charkhi Prison, and we had become quite well acquainted. When I thought I would leave Afghanistan via the Kandahar–Spin Boldak route, one of Khalil's tribal relatives had come to Kabul, helped me with the plan, and taken the trunk back to Chaman. He told me that he would keep it safe for me and that I could pick it up once I escaped.

Khalil and I went to Chaman, to the qala of Hayat Khan, who was an important leader of the Achikzai Pashtuns. We stayed overnight. Ismat Achikzai, Hayat Khan's son, threw a big Pashtun-style feast in my honor, to which he invited many mujahideen leaders. (Ismat Achikzai was himself one of the leaders of the freedom fighters in this region.) I was distantly related to the Achikzai tribe.

As I have noted, among Afghans and especially Pashtuns, tribal relationships are very important. That is why Ismat threw such a big feast in my honor.

The next day, I returned to Quetta with my old trunk; everything in it was intact.

A Kidnapped Russian Specialist

When I was back in Rawalpindi, one day the motel manager came to me and said, "There are some people here from the British embassy in Islamabad, and they want to speak to you." I went to his office, where two men from the British embassy were waiting. They introduced themselves to me and said that if it was okay with me, they would like to have me go with them to the embassy in Islamabad, as they wanted to consult with me about some important matter. So I went with them.

On the way, I was thinking to myself that at one time, the British ruled this area, when it was a colony and part of the old India. From here, the British had conducted several wars against my ancestors in Afghanistan. I thought, *Well, I'm sure that they are not conducting any war against the Afghans now. Now the Brits are our friends against the Soviets, who are the invading enemies of the Afghans. Therefore, we are friends, on the same side. I'll help them as much as I can.*

When we arrived at the embassy in Islamabad, I was greeted by someone from the British intelligence office. We went into a room where two other men were waiting. They got up and shook hands. One of them said, "Mr. Assifi, we are very happy that you arrived safely in Pakistan. I understand that you were the minister of mines and industries in Afghanistan before the Communist coup. I assume that you know most of the Russian advisors and high-level technical people who worked in your ministry."

I said, "Yes, you are correct," and asked how I could be of any help.

He said, "Do you know a Mr. Akhrimiuk?"

I said, "Yes. He was the top technical advisor and the head of a team that was assigned to work with us with respect to geologic and hydrocarbon projects that the Russians were assisting Afghanistan with."

He asked, "How important is this guy?"

"He was their top advisor," I said. "Very competent and a highly qualified person. He is very important."

He asked, "Would you recognize this man if you saw him?"

I said, "Yes, of course. He doesn't look like a typical Russian. He looks like a professor from an American or British university." The man then went ahead and showed me a picture. I said, "That's him. What's the problem?"

He said, "The mujahideen have kidnapped him, and they have him in one of their prisons somewhere—we don't know where."

I said, "Oh! How did they do that?"

He didn't answer my question, but he said, "Some freedom fighters have been caught by the Communist government and the Soviets. They have them jailed and probably will kill them if nothing is done. The mujahideen have been planning for some time to kidnap an important person so they can use that person to bargain for the exchange of a number of mujahideen who are currently in government and Soviet prisons. The more important the kidnapped person is, the larger the number of mujahideen they can demand in exchange. They want forty mujahideen in exchange for Akhrimiuk.

"Representatives of mujahideen approached us for help in this regard. We didn't know this man and couldn't help them. We found out that you were here, so that's why we asked you to come here and help."

I said, "Well, I'll help you in any way that I can, but I can't help you make an evaluation of equivalency for the exchange of prisoners. I know that the life of one freedom fighter is very important to me, and I would not exchange it for ten of the people who invaded our country. But as to how important this person is to the Soviets, in terms of an exchange, I couldn't make an intelligent guess. If we look at it from the point of view of technical worth, the Soviets have many qualified people at their disposal. But if this man is related to an important person on the basis of party or personal relationship, then he could have a lot of political pull or weight in their bureaucracy. He could be worth more than forty mujahideen."

Then I added, "Britain has very good intelligence services. Maybe they could help?"

The two men looked at each other. One said, "That will take some time. Thank you very much, Mr. Assifi, for giving your time and coming to the embassy to help us in this matter. If there is anything that we can do for you, please do not hesitate to call on us." Then, they drove me back to the motel.

I visited as many places as I could while I was waiting in Pakistan. This period provided me with an opportunity to learn about the war and the mujahideen, and about the issues regarding the aid—from the United States and other free countries—that had been extended to assist in the Afghan struggle for freedom and the Afghan war against the Soviet Union and the Communist government it had installed in my home country.

I also learned about the people of Pakistan: how nice and generous they were to the Afghan refugees. When I walked around the town, sometimes I would go into the shops. The shopkeepers guessed that I was a refugee. They were very courteous and hospitable. Like the Afghans, they would offer tea and lumps of sugar and then invite me to come in and sit down in their shops, while they went ahead and did their work selling goods.

New Home, New Life

Finally, the UN Refugee Office informed my wife and me that our casework had been completed and that they were going to issue our airplane tickets. However, they issued the tickets for my wife and daughters first; my tickets would be issued a week or so later.

Fariha and the girls did not have much baggage. We took a taxi to the airport and went into the terminal. Although we were going to be separated again, saying good-bye to them when they were leaving for America, where I had spent my student years, was a very happy occasion for me. My tickets were ready a week later. I went to the office and got my tickets from Pakistan to the United States of America.

On my day of departure, I lugged my old galvanized iron trunk to the airport and the airline's ticket counter. The chap who was checking me in could not stop smiling when he weighed my old trunk. It was big and beat up, but not heavy. There wasn't much in it.

My wife and daughters had arrived in the United States on September 4, 1981, and had been met at the airport by Fariha's brother's family. Tamim had already reached the States. I came exactly a week later and arrived in California on September 11, 1981. Everyone was there to greet me.

It was quite a reunion. The Miskinyar kids and my kids were about the same age; I'm sure that they were contemplating a lot of mischief when they got home.

341

We stayed with my brother-in-law and his gracious wife and their beautiful kids for about five months.

It was one of the happiest times of our lives. Our relatives took us to see Big Bear Lake, Newport Beach, and Laguna Beach. As far as I'm concerned, these are the loveliest beaches in the world. For our hosts, it was probably a bit inconvenient having us stay there, but for us, it was a chance to come to a heaven on earth.

The contrast between escaping from the slavery and subjugation imposed on us by the Soviet Russians and their Afghan Communist protégés—from the confines of Prison Kabul to the land of the free, where all of us could have equal rights to liberty and justice—was something that we could not have dreamed of. Even though I had lived in America before, and even with my very rich imagination, it simply was not imaginable.

We had been afforded a chance for a new life! And that is what we enjoyed taking, step by step. While we were staying with the Miskinyars, I prepared several kinds of resumes and sent them to about forty places that had job openings. Ten of them sent me application forms. I applied to all of them, and three asked me to come in for an interview. Finally, I was hired by the Irvine Ranch Water District (IRWD) to work as an engineer planner.

When I got the job, my wife and I found an apartment and moved out of my brother-in-law's house. The first thing I did when I got my paycheck was reimburse the Catholic Community Churches for the cost of our airplane tickets. I paid all that we owed them and wrote them a letter of thanks for the loan they had extended to us.

After the legal waiting time for refugees, each one in my family passed the examination for citizenship and became a citizen of the United States of America.

My parents managed to join us in 1986, and my mother lived to the age of a hundred. She became an American citizen, proudly waving an American flag and proclaiming, "I'm American!"

I began working for the engineering department of the Irvine Ranch Water District on February 2, 1982. After several years, I was promoted to principal engineer. I worked there for about twenty-two years.

I retired in 2002 in order to go to Afghanistan, which had been ruined by decades of communism and war, and to help USAID as chief of party for its AARIA (Assist Afghanistan [to] Rehabilitate Irrigation and Agriculture) projects.

I provide full detail of the above events of our lives in part three of these memoirs. Apparently, whether as an Afghan or an American, helping Afghanistan was in my blood.

Note: After my imprisonment in Pul-i-Charkhi, my family spent about a year, from 1980 to 1981, getting out of Afghanistan as refugees bound for to the United States.

PART 3

LIFE IN THE UNITED STATES OF AMERICA

My wife, Fariha, our daughters, Madina (seven years) and Shamila (six years), and I came to the United States of America as refugees in September of 1981. We were sponsored by my brother-in-law Dr. Shir Ali Miskinyar in this process. Ali, his lovely wife, Makai Miskinyar, and their children, Sonya, Eva, and Mustafa, were most gracious in allowing us to live with them for almost five months. They were so kind and hospitable that words cannot do justice or describe it.

Seeking Employment

During this period, I approached the state employment office, which put me in a training program specifically designed for newly arrived refugees for preparing a resume and presenting oneself for a job interview. This program was very useful and helped me to get ready for employment. I began canvassing newspapers and engineering magazines for job openings.

In the end, I sent my resume to about forty-two places. But before mailing the resume to those places, I consulted with my wife's cousin Hasan Nouri, an engineer. His advice was, "On your resume, do not mention the high-level jobs that you have worked, or else you will be seen as overqualified." His advice was good; therefore, on my resume, I mentioned that I had worked as an engineer, which was actually the truth, but not as a president or cabinet-level minister.

Out of the forty-some places, I received application forms from only ten.

I filled these out and sent them back. Out of all this, I received positive results from only three places, which asked me to come for interview. One, to which I did not respond, was on the East Coast.

My Interviews

I had an interview with the International Engineering Company (IECo) in San Francisco. IECo was the engineering firm that had designed the Kajakai Dam in Helmand and the Dahla Dam on the Arghandab River in Kandahar. They had also designed the Boghra and Shamalan Canals and irrigation systems. I went to San Francisco for the interview, as Mr. Shu, who was a vice president, had invited me to IECo's headquarters. He introduced me around and invited me for lunch with several other vice presidents. They offered me the job of filling the VP slot for all their business in east Asia and Southeast Asia. Actually, they knew more about me than I had described in my resume, or else they had exaggerated information. That is why they offered me such a big job! My response was, "Please, give me some time to think about this."

However, the more I thought about this job, the more I came to realize that it was too large for me. Specially, after being a political prisoner of the Communists for twenty-two months and having harrowing experiences while in Afghanistan and when coming out of it, I could not see myself doing a good job for IECo at that particular time.

My next interview was much easier. Philip Eastman, a headhunter for Irvine Ranch Water District (IRWD), called me and invited me to come that next morning for a breakfast interview at a posh restaurant in Irvine. We had breakfast, and then Mr. Eastman told me that Mr. Ron Young, the director of engineering, would himself do the interview the next day. He gave the address of the district. Accordingly, I met with Mr. Young the next day.

The interview went quite well. Mr. Young told me that they had two openings: a supervisory position and an engineer-planner position. He asked me which one I would choose. I told him that I would rather work at the engineer-planner's job. He said that the salary for the supervisor's job was higher.

I said, "At this moment, money is not as important for me as experience is, seeing as I'd like to get back into my engineering profession. I think it would be better for me to work at a 'nuts and bolts' job first, because the jobs that I have done in the last six years were mostly managerial or executive. After working as an engineer-planner, if I do a good job and am qualified, you may promote me to a supervisory position if there is an opening."

He then asked, "When can you start working?"

I said, "Right now."

He said, "We are moving to a new place, and you can begin your job after a week at our new address." He then continued. "By the way, will you get a letter of reference from someone who knows you?"

I said, "Okay."

Letter of Reference

The same night, I called H. E. Theodor Eliot, who was the American ambassador in Kabul when I was the minister of mines and industries in Afghanistan. I asked if he would send a letter about me to the engineering department of IRWD.

He was very gracious to send a very good reference letter. I shall always be grateful for this kindness (in continuance of my report of being hired by the Irvine Ranch Water District).

Note: It has always been a privilege to know good Americans like Pat and Ted Eliot. My family has visited their lofty home in the hills with a view of San Francisco Bay, and they have been kind to visit us in our humble abode in Mission Viejo, which is in southern California.

Pat Eliot is a forest ranger. Every day, she rides her horse all around the groves and vineyards of beautiful Sonoma. I have discussions with her about the issues of water between northern and southern California. My discussions with Ted are, of course, about international and Afghan issues, about which he knows very much. My wife and I cherish our friendship with Pat and Ted. We are thankful to know them.

The same night I spoke with H. E. Theodor Eliot, Mr. Philip Eastman called and congratulated me for getting the job. He then asked, "By the way, why did you tell Mr. Young that money was not that important to you?"

I told him what I had said to the director of engineering. He then proceeded and said, "Mr. Assifi, remember that you are in America now. Money is important here!"

I said, "Thanks, Philip. I shall remember your advice in the future."

He laughed. "Okay. Congratulations again. If ever you need my services in the future, please, do not hesitate to call on me," he said.

Irvine Ranch Water District

I started working for IRWD on February 2, 1982. From 1982 to 2003, I worked in the engineering department of IRWD in Irvine, California. During this period, I held the following positions: engineer-planner, principal engineer, field operations engineer, and engineering manager. At the job, I did the following things:

- Prepared an emergency response preparedness manual for IRWD
- Performed economic and facility life-cycle studies, recommending and established a new cathodic protection system for all IRWD metallic pipelines

- Planned and designed projects, and prepared plans, specifications, and contract documents for the construction of domestic-water, reclaimed-water, and wastewater systems in Foothill Ranch, the Irvine Spectrum Center, and the Newport Coast Drive areas, all of which are part of the district
- Managed project bidding, contracts, construction, and inspection of these projects

As field operations engineer, I recommended improvements to operational and maintenance methods, and introduced preventive measures and cathodic protection against the corrosion and deterioration of existing district facilities.

All of these functions are related to water resource development and supply, including groundwater development and the supply, storage, pumping, and transmission of potable water, reclaimed water, and wastewater.

Consultancy and a Leave of Absence

On several occasions, I was asked by two firms, Volunteers in Technical Assistance (VITA) and Development Alternatives, Incorporated (DAI), which were working on cross-border projects for USAID, to travel to their offices in Peshawar, a city in Pakistan close to the border of Afghanistan. Specifically, I was asked to assist, organize, and train the engineering and technical staff to rebuild irrigation systems, water systems, roads, bridges, and other structures in Afghan communities and villages that had been damaged or destroyed by the Soviet Russian military attacks and war machinery.

Two of my former colleagues, Dr. Wakil (with whom I had worked at Helmand) and engineer Sediq (with whom I had worked at the Rural Development Department of Afghanistan [RDDA]), who both knew me from my previous work with those organizations, had recommended me to USAID and were instrumental in giving me an opportunity to participate in this important work. I held great regard for both of them. They were known for their integrity and their capability and love for helping the Afghan people rebuild Afghanistan.

Since rehabilitation and rebuilding process had to be accomplished as fast as possible to counter the Soviet plan of destroying Afghanistan, I introduced the concept of predesign for typical structures that could be finalized without much loss of time. As soon as our field reconnaissance surveyors identified the location, relative size, and purpose of the structure, engineering office personnel would design a replacement structure and prepare plans, specifications, and construction documents for the its construction inside Afghanistan.

In my past work, I had introduced this method to the engineering department of RDDA, which had resulted in a quick turnaround of the construction of projects that people from all over Afghanistan needed and had requested the RDDA to provide.

Trips and Another Leave of Absence from IRWD

On two occasions, I took a two-month leave of absence without pay from IRWD. USAID, through these firms, paid my travel expenses and provided me with a per diem for the period when I worked for this objective in Peshawar.

On one occasion, I even went inside Afghanistan to Kunar Province, to inspect the structures and facilities that were built under this program. The people and freedom fighters were very grateful for the fast rehabilitation work that we had done.

Asmar Village, Kunar Valley

On the same trip, I visited the Asmar village and military base that is situated, strategically, on top of a steep hill in the middle of Kunar Valley. I was fascinated by the accounts of the Afghan freedom fighters (mujahideen) detailing how they had accomplished this feat and captured the military base that the Soviets had heavily fortified, believing that no one could move them from that location.

The commander of the freedom fighters told me that a mule road built under this program was important in that it had helped them to liberate the fortifications at Asmar from the Soviet Russian forces.

I asked the freedom fighters' commander, Khan Jonn, who was a tall, handsome fellow, one who could get an acting job in Hollywood anytime, "Seeing as you have accomplished a miraculous job here, why don't you capture the town of Khost in the Paktia Province from the Soviets?"

His candid answer surprised me. He said, "Sir, we can take Khost very easily from the Soviet forces any day, but what concerns us is that whenever we take a town, following behind our freedom fighters are a bunch of looters, who follow us with trucks, camels, and mules. They loot the town, and the people living there fall at their mercy. We are organized to fight the Soviet forces but do not have police forces with us to protect the people who are living in the liberated towns from these looters after we move out from that location."

That is when I realized the enormity and tragedies of war—and the fight for freedom in a country that has been invaded by a foreign power. Wars and invasions result in disruption of peace and the destruction of people and their living facilities. Great effort has to be made to rebuild the destroyed facilities and bring peace and normalcy back to people's lives.

Floods Destroy Lower Helmand

The 1991 floods dealt a knockout blow to river diversion structures, irrigation systems, villages, and the people living in the Lower Helmand Valley area. The severity of these floods, which I estimated to be of hundred-year-flood magnitude, was much more devastating after the bombardment and destruction inflicted by the Soviet Russian invading forces and their war machinery.

United Nations contacts inside Afghanistan had informed USAID that the services of an Afghan engineer familiar with the Helmand water control system were needed to assess the system's current status and identify actions needed to remedy existing and/or damaged facilities and water control systems. Specific reference was made to Boghra Canal's head works and water control and irrigation systems below it, all the way down to Charburjak Canal.

In May 1991, I was asked to go inside the affected area with a mission sent by the United Nations, make an assessment of the damages, and recommend measures for rehabilitation.

At this time, the central government of Afghanistan was still in the hands of the Soviet-installed Communists. The area that I was requested to go to was a "war zone" between the Communist government forces and freedom fighters. I requested USAID to do the following:

1) Send a letter requesting that IRWD allow me do this job as a consultant.
2) Provide a life insurance policy for me, in case I was killed during the job.

For the first item, USAID requested that IRWD allow me to do this job. However, for the second item, life insurance, USAID informed me that they could not provide life insurance for those who went inside Afghanistan. However, they said that I would be able to do this job under a separate special services agreement, as a consultant to the United Nations, under which my compensation for services would not exceed $1.00.

By the way, the UN still owes me the $1.00 for the services that I performed in this assignment!

Since I had been asked, if it was possible, to visit Kajakai Dam, I went briefly to IECo headquarters in San Francisco, got a full set of as-built drawings for Kajakai and Dahla Dams, and took the drawings with me to Islamabad.

In Islamabad, I met Mr. Curt Wolters of USAID, and Mrs. Martin Barber, Jan Haugland, and Bayisa Wak-Woya of the United Nations

Regional Office for Central Africa (UNOCA). During this meeting, the details of the mission's trip to Quetta and the Helmand area were discussed.

Before the trip, I went briefly to Peshawar, where I met Dr. Wakil and David Garner of DAI and engineer Sediq of VITA. I also studied the Landsat photos for the Helmand area and made necessary recommendations for improving the structures in question.

I then returned to Islamabad. During my stay in Islamabad, I was a guest in the rented apartment of my cousin Wali Ahmad Sherzoy and his gracious wife, Sahira Jon.

I Develop a Gallbladder Problem

Unfortunately, the first night I felt very sick with severe abdominal pain. The next morning, I went to see a specialist. She told me that I should have gallbladder surgery. Since all arrangements had already been made for the trip to go inside Afghanistan, any delay of the mission's trip to Helmand would have caused many problems.

Upon my insistence, the doctor gave me antibiotics and some other medications for a time before the surgery, which allowed me make the scheduled trip.

The medications worked, and the pain subsided. But I would get sick upon smelling foodstuffs. I became nauseated and could not eat anything during the trip to Lower Helmand, nothing except bread, tea, and *doogh* (diluted yogurt).

To Quetta

On the basis of the trip schedule, I went first to Quetta, where I met Zia Mujadedi of USAID. Zia told me that I was once his twelfth-grade science teacher at Lashkargah High School. The school principal sometimes asked the professional cadres of the Helmand Valley Project to fill in for the teachers who were not there due to unforeseen reasons. When I went to Zia's office, his office was full of mujahideen commanders—members of Ustad Sayyaf's party. They said that they had demonstrated against and then resigned from the party, objecting to the misuse of jihadi funds. They said that they had told Sayyaf many times not to spend war money for personal purposes, but he did not listen. So, all of them sitting here, about twenty in the room, had resigned from Ustad Sayyaf's party. The oldest one of the commanders was wounded, having lost one eye and a leg in the fight against the Soviets.

Speaking in Pashto, this commander told his son to go and get his bag from the pickup. After a while, the son came back lugging a midsize bag, which he put in front of his father. The commander opened the bag, which was full of paper documents, envelopes, and copies of letters from Sayyaf to his assistant in the war zone (Quetta). He went ahead and showed me some of the papers that instructed Sayyaf's assistant to give the money that he had sent to this person or that person for the purchase of property, land, etc. I told the commander that I had great respect for what his group was doing, sacrificing themselves in a freedom fight against the Soviets and Afghan Communists. However, I had not come there to investigate that matter.

During my stay in Quetta, I also met Marilee Kane of UNOCA/ Quetta; engineer Nadir Waziri of the United Nations Development Program (UNDP); some other engineers and officers from VITA, UNDP, MCI, and ARR; and Commandant Abdul Ghani, who was to escort our mission, with twenty armed freedom fighters, to the Lower Helmand areas.

Qala-i-Afzal Khan, Lower Helmand

From Quetta, I went with the mission to Chaman, and from there to Dalbandin. From there, we passed near the alabaster mines in Afghanistan and moved on to Qala-i-Afzal Khan in Helmand, the headquarters of our escort commander, Ghani.

On the way to Qala-i-Afzal Khan, we could see the Khan Nishin Mountain in the distance. I told the driver of our Land Cruiser to go toward Khan Nishin first, saying that afterward we could go to our destination in Qala-i-Afzal. I became familiar with these routes when I was working in Helmand and lower Nimroz. However, after going some distance, we were accosted by armed soldiers who appeared to belong to the Communist government in Kabul. They told us that we were not allowed to go any further toward Khan Nishin. This was a surprising event, since all surrounding areas were under the control of freedom fighters. Why, then, were they preventing us from going toward Khan Nishin?

When arrived at Qala-i-Afzal Khan, I talked to some local people there and told them what had happened. They said that the Kabul government and Soviets were saying that they were excavating canals to pass water around the mountain and did not want to be bothered. They had heavy fortifications and strong mechanized military units in that location.

Russians Mining Uranium at Khan Nishin

Note: I was familiar with the geologic formation of the mountain at Khan Nishin and had previously surveyed it when I was the minister of mines and industries during President Daoud's time. At that time, we had identified the existence of rich uranium ore in Khan Nishin Mountain.

So, I thought, *the Soviets are doing now what they wanted to do before. They installed a puppet government, invaded Afghanistan militarily, and are extracting uranium from this location.*

In 1983, I wrote an article called "The Russian Rope," which was published in *World Affairs Quarterly.* In the article, I explained that the acquisition of natural resources was one of the important motives for the Soviets to invade Afghanistan. It looked like I wasn't wrong after all!

From Qala-i-Afzal Khan, we went all the way down the river to Charburjak and the Band-i-Kamal Khan area. We surveyed all washed-out canal diversions, canals, and villages. The head works and Lashkari Canal's intake were not washed out. This showed that earlier, during the design phase of the canal, I had picked a very good location for the Lashkari Canal intake.

Then, we retraced our route, went back to Qala-i-Afzal Khan, and then traveled up to Darweshan. Darweshan Canal head works and river bridge crossing abutments had been washed out by the floods. Most of the villages near the river channel that we visited had been washed out, and the population in those villages had migrated to other areas. Those who were left behind had relocated themselves to higher, safer ground.

We were clearly witnessing a disaster-stricken area of the Helmand River Valley.

I Meet a UN Delegation in Hazarasp

On the way to Marja and the Nad-i-Ali area, I and my fellow travelers met the UN delegation at the half-finished Swedish clinic at Hazar Asp, near Shamalan Canal. This was an historic meeting. The UN delegation was headed by Mr. Anthony Donini, chief of the UNOCA office in Kabul.

I briefed the UN delegation on my assessment of the critical situation of the water control systems and of the destruction to villages in those areas that we had visited. A quick method was necessary for repairing what had been damaged.

For this job, I recommended the use of gabions; available resources, such as agricultural tractors and trailers; and the participation of people of the affected local communities on the basis of a food-for-work program.

The local population was familiar with the use of rock-filled tree-branch (*Kaela*) baskets and tree-trunk tripods for controlling river erosion and diverting canals. They have used this method throughout the ages.

According to my proposal, males and females would take part in weaving the galvanized iron baskets, and local masons could easily learn to place the gabion baskets and fill them with larger-size rocks picked up and transported to the job site by tractor-trailers. The entire cost of weaving the baskets, picking larger-size rocks and transporting them to the site in tractor-trailers, and filling the gabion baskets with transported rock would be covered by the food-for-work program.

This method allowed the gabion baskets—which are flexible to begin with and which settle further when eroded by the river—to be repaired in the following season by placing new gabion baskets on top of the old ones that are settled. This way, by annual repair of the eroded dikes, the local population would have a continuous method of preventing river erosion from destroying their canal diversions and villages with its destructive forces.

The method that I recommended did not require sophisticated engineering staff for its implementation. I told the delegation that I would, for each affected location, provide the necessary sketches and maps showing the location of the dikes as well as describe the method of laying gabion baskets. Local masons and mirabs could very easily learn, and then help other people learn, how to make the baskets and then lay them according to what was indicated on the maps and sketches that I provided.

Food Import and Gabion Repair

I recommended that the United Nations import foodstuff to the area as soon as possible. This was very important and necessary to curb incipient famine, as was providing food for labor and also hiring tractor-trailers to do the reconstruction and repair work.

The main cost for this work entailed the purchase and transport of galvanized iron wire, tie wires, and tools for weaving the gabion baskets. The cost of food-for-work would be for humanitarian purposes, for the prevention of forced migration of the population to other areas. Importing foodstuff to the areas would curb this migration to other areas, including to neighboring countries.

The UN delegation and Mr. Donini were very impressed by my recommendations, which, a rough estimate indicated, would cost about a million dollars. They mentioned that after talking to other engineering firms, they were worried that these repairs could cost something in the range of a hundred million dollars.

The Mission Is Attacked by Government Forces in Sayedabad

Our mission then went to Marja and the Nadi-Ali area to meet with people there. We stayed at Sayedabad village in Nadi-Ali one night. As our escorts and the area commandants had guessed, the place where we rested for the night was attacked by government forces. The fighting lasted from 9:30 at night to about 3:30 in the morning. Freedom fighters and their commander, who was the son of Sayed Tajdaar, valiantly defended us and the village of Sayedabad.

In the morning, we had a late breakfast, seeing as the nearby farm was unable to deliver milk at the regular, earlier time. A number of old acquaintances had gathered to welcome us in the middle of war. They looked at me and my haggard face. I then looked at an old dragline operator named Barat and said, "You have grown terribly old and have a gray beard on your face. What has happened to you?"

He responded, "Why don't you look at your own face in the mirror? You are not very young yourself anymore." Then he laughed! "They were saying that they thought that you were killed by the Communists. We are so glad that you are alive and came back to help us rebuild what was damaged! We are confident now that the Helmand Valley Project will be built again." I admired his optimism, but doing what he was hoping for was not easy!

However, one should not give up hope in any difficult or even impossible situation. Hope is one of the pillars that sustains life!

In Nadi-ali, I met the area commander of the freedom fighters. He would not allow me to go to Baghra diversion and Kajakai Dam. He said that in both areas, heavy fighting was going on between us and the government forces. I told him, "I am familiar with these areas. I can go to Kajakai from the back roads in Musa Qala."

He said, "Sir, in Musa Qala and Sangin areas, there is heavy fighting between two mujahideen factions, Hizb-i-Islami and Harakat." I asked him why these two mujahideen factions were fighting among each other. He said, "It is all because each one wants to get hold of liquefied-chars-making laboratories. They fired two thousand rockets against each other in one day. Sir, we are responsible for your safety and will not allow any harm to come to you and your group."

The Mission Is Not Allowed in Kajakai because of Fighting

The fighting was the reason that the mission decided to cancel our trip to Kajakai Dam. We were forced to go back the way we had used to come into the Helmand Valley area in the first place.

At night on my laptop, I was made notes about the reconnaissance surveys we did during the day. A draft of my detailed report was submitted to the USAID offices in Islamabad before I returned to the United States. The same night that I came home, I had another gallbladder attack. My wife took me to the emergency department at the hospital. They performed surgery and removed my gallbladder for good! It looks like I am a lucky guy after all!

Repairing Damage: Recommendations and Submittal of Report

My recommendations regarding the *fastest and least costly repair* of the washed-out diversions, canals, and villages were as follows:

1) As a matter of urgency, bring foodstuff and wheat into the area to stave off the impending famine and prevent further dislocation of the people whose canals, villages, and wheat and other food supplies had washed away in the floods.
2) Use galvanized wire, which could be imported at a fast rate, for making gabions in the washed-out sections.
3) Local people, men and women, would work for food when weaving the gabion sheets and baskets.
4) Local agricultural tractor-trailers would be hired (and their drives be paid in food) haul in large-size rocks to fill in the gabions.

5) I would provide sketches and specifications for the making and laying of the gabions for river protection and making canal diversions.

6) Note that rock-filled gabion baskets are flexible and allow subsequent ones to be stacked, which, when the baskets are put in place, staves off further erosion of the canals and diversion dams.

Later on, when I was working in my office of the Irvine Ranch Water District, someone called me from one of the big firms that manufacture galvanized iron sheets for making gabion baskets. He said, "Sir, do you know what is going on? The UN and USAID offices have ordered rolls of galvanized iron wire."

I answered, "Sir, don't you think that it is much less costly than purchasing galvanized iron gabion sheets and then transporting them to a foreign location?"

He said, "Oh yes, I understand!"

He may also have guessed who might have been the real culprit.

Post-Taliban DAI/USAID Mission to Afghanistan

After the US forces kicked the Taliban out of Afghanistan in 2002 and a legitimate government had been established, USAID hired DAI to organize a mission composed of professional team members who would survey all the provinces in Afghanistan and make recommendations for how to rehabilitate the country.

Afghanistan had been destroyed by Soviet Russians during their occupation, and later on in the war against the Taliban carried out by the United States of America. And, finally, the city of Kabul was almost half ruined during the infighting between the competing mujahideen groups.

DAI asked me to participate as a member of the professional team and travel to Afghanistan.

Once again, I requested a leave of absence of two months from IRWD so I could take part in this mission and visit Afghanistan with the team.

Our mission was to assess the irrigation sector in Afghanistan and recommend strategy for its rehabilitation. We submitted our final report to USAID in September 2002. *A copy of this report was also presented to the president of Afghanistan.*

USAID approved our recommendations and the budget for doing the work. Subsequently, DAI/USAID eventually asked me to take part as chief of party (COP) for this job.

I Leave IRWD to Go to Afghanistan for Recommending Rehabilitative Work

Accepting this COP job meant that I would have to retire from my principal engineering position at IRWD. IRWD graciously accepted my request and threw a going-away party in my honor. It included all the frills, even the roasting of the guest of honor.

From 2003 to 2004, I worked for DAI as the COP for this job, which was part of DAI's and USAID's Assisting Afghanistan to Revitalize Irrigated Agriculture (AARIA), the water IQC (indefinite quantity contract) program in Afghanistan.

DAI had already rented two large houses in the Wazir Akbar Khan sector of Kabul, one for offices and the other for use as a guesthouse.

To set up this new office in Kabul, engineer Sediq and David Garner had transferred DAI's office and personnel from Peshawar, Pakistan, to Kabul, Afghanistan. When I accepted this job, the Kabul office was up and running.

This program accomplished the following things.

Phase 1: I organized and managed a team of engineers, agriculturists, economists, and GIS specialists to plan, design, contract, and construct the rehabilitation of major irrigation canals and drains in Konar (Salar Canal diversion and structures), Puli Khumri (Gawhargan Canal flood structures, bridges, and canal turnouts, and the two large retaining walls of Puli Khurmri Canal), Baghlan (Darqad Canal river diversion dam, intake gates, spillway flood structure, bridges, and turnouts), and Helmand Valley provinces, with the help and active participation of local communities.

Phase 2: From 2004 to 2006, I was a COP for phase 2, which entailed the rehabilitation of irrigation and drainage systems and the construction of farm roads in Kunduz (Chardara Canal diversion intake, flood structures, and turnouts) and Baghlan (Dandi Ghori canals and farm roads).

I led the team of engineers and agricultural specialists that I had prior helped organize at DAI.

Rehabilitation Needs Assessment for the Middle Helmand Irrigated Agriculture System

My job here was to make an inventory of rehabilitation needs assessment for the Middle Helmand irrigated agriculture system, from January to March 2004, under a contract for Rebuilding Afghanistan's Agricultural Markets Program (RAMP) of USAID.

We submitted our detailed findings of the needed repair work and its costs, and a feasibility report, on April 19 of the same year. The following things were found:

1) All downstream areas of the project and the canal and drainage systems had silted up and suffered from water deficiency, waterlogging and accumulation of salt on the farmland, and low agricultural productivity.
2) The Helmand Valley Authority (HVA) had lost most of its trained staff and was in need of reorganization.

Implementation of My Recommendations

Subsequently, on the basis of these findings and recommendations, USAID awarded another contract to DAI, under RAMP, for the implementation of my recommendations.

I organized a DAI contract management team to begin the rehabilitation work in Middle Helmand. Under this work, the following things occurred:

1) Ten to eleven thousand laborers from these areas were hired to do manual desilting of mid- to small-size canals and drains.
2) Local contractors were contracted to bring heavy equipment for the desilting of large canals and drains. The rehab work done under this contract was received with great appreciation and enthusiasm by farmers and settlers living in the Middle Helmand area.

On this basis, desilting (taking the mud and silt out of the channel) of Boghra, Shamalan, and Darweshan Canals, and drains in Nad-i-Ali, Marja, and Darweshan, was completed, achieving about 90 percent of the levels estimated in the report.

We Told the Local Population that these Projects Were a Gift to Them from the American People

For all the works mentioned above, our team prepared big signboards and placed them at the entrance to each project, announcing the purpose of the project and telling the people of the local communities that the projects were funded by, and were a gift from, the America people to help the local people living in the communities of that area of Afghanistan.

The people loved what we did for them and cooperated in keeping order and peace in the area. As a result, the local governors and staff in charge of security told us, "Your projects have reduced crime and quarrels in the area." The Taliban no longer dared to come and inflict their plans on these communities. In a way, the people who benefited from these projects kept security in their areas.

Terrorist Attacks

We curtailed our work on the desilting program of drains ten days after terrorists, in broad daylight, killed five agriculture workers, who were employed under another RAMP contract, in the Babajee area, close to Lashkargah.

Following that, when the dead were being transported to their families, six more people were killed on the road between Kandahar and Qalat.

The Governor of Helmand Refuses to Provide Security

After the governor of Helmand Province did not meet engineer Shakir, DAI's area manager, on three occasions and was not able to provide protection and security for DAI's construction field crews, and after I consulted with USAID, I directed Shakir to stop work on the project and make the necessary arrangements for safe transport of the staff to Kabul.

Subsequently, I informed USAID and RAMP about a *force majeure* situation, which forced us to pull our crews out of the area.

An Unholy Alliance: Drug-Lords, Warlords, and the Taliban

When I was asked by the USAID mission director in Kabul about this incident and my opinion of it, I analyzed the situation for him as follows: "This was a declaration of war by an unholy alliance between drug-lords, warlords, and the Taliban," who all wanted to stop the good work and increasing popularity of USAID in the area.

Institution Building

I was a team leader for the Institution Building and Advisory Services under a DAI/Chemonics and RAMP/USAID program in

Afghanistan. During this period, to do this work, we reorganized and strengthened our original team, adding sociologists and lawyers, and then proceeded to accomplish the following:

1) Recommended to the Ministry of Water Resources and Environment (MIWRE) the adoption of a water policy in Afghanistan to empower farmers, mirabs, and water users to take over the operation and maintenance of irrigation water and drainage systems in their service area.
2) Prepared model charters, bylaws, and regulations for the organization of the Water Users Association (WUA) for the Nadi-Ali and Marja areas in Helmand Valley, on the basis of studies and consultation with water users, local farmers, and landowners.
3) Helped water users elect representatives to the board of their WUA.
4) Helped the MIWRE to prepare a revised water law to accommodate the above objectives.
5) Prepared model charters, bylaws, and regulations for the organization of a Water Users Association for the Enjil Canal water command area in Herat Province.

All this work was based on studies and consultations with local farmers and landowners in the respective provinces. We then trained water user representative members and helped them conduct their general assembly meeting for the election of board members and the president of the WUA for the Enjil Canal in Herat Province.

Note: Earlier, after I had announced my retirement from Irvine Ranch Water District and before I went to Afghanistan to rebuild the country and its water and irrigation systems, the engineering department of IRWD threw a going-away and retirement party for me, as mentioned previously.

As is customary, the party attendees each took a turn in saying good words about me, including some exaggerated compliments. There were also some comments that made me feel like a real toast.

However, one of the comments that I didn't forget was made by the director of engineering, Greg Hiertz. Later on, I thought that his comment was quite prophetic. Greg had said, "Maybe Tawab, with his experience at IRWD, could someday set up a water district in Afghanistan."

Surely enough, the charters that the water users, with some help from our team, came up with in the Marja and Nad-i-Ali districts of Helmand, and then later in the Enjil district of Herat, resembled the charter of the Irvine Ranch Water District. So, we had helped the water users come up with a simplified charter for a mini water district.

Our team helped seal this concept by putting special provisions in the new Water Law of Afghanistan.

Technical Advisory Services to the President and Government Ministries

I helped the Afghan president and government ministries on related matters, under RAMP/USAID, on an as-needed basis. Examples are as follows:

1) I assisted MIWRE in revising the Afghanistan Water Law.
2) I prepared and submitted a concept paper on emergency drought response to the government of Afghanistan in August 2004. The concept paper presented hydrologic data, records of previous droughts, historic accounts of the devastating consequences of past droughts, and recommendations for an emergency drought response program in Afghanistan. Copies were submitted to several ministers and included recommendations for organizing a ministerial council and details of the action necessary to help drought-stricken people in the country.

Concept Paper on Emergency Drought Response

A copy of my concept paper on emergency drought response was also submitted to the president of Afghanistan.

The government took immediate action, organizing the Steering Committee of Ministers (SCM). As an advisor, I participated in the Steering Committee of Ministers for emergency drought response. I also participated in program meetings and helped the international donor organization representatives in a countrywide emergency drought-response program.

Technical Advisor to the President of Afghanistan

The president of Afghanistan requested that I assist the presidency as a technical advisor. After consulting with USAID, I accepted this position.

From August 2007 to 2009, I was a technical advisor to the president of Afghanistan, during which time I advised the president and cabinet ministers on an as-needed basis.

Long-Duration Drought Response in Afghanistan

My earlier studies, and further investigation by interdepartmental missions that went to all provinces of Afghanistan, showed that the country was at the beginning of famine brought on by a long-duration drought.

As the technical advisor to the president, I brought the criticality of this situation to the attention of the president and his cabinet. I recommended specific emergency measures, such as importing large quantities of wheat into Afghanistan, to save the country from widespread famine.

A long-duration famine would have forced the affected people to migrate to other places in the country. These migrations would have resulted in conflicts between the people who moved into an area and those who were already there, which would have brought dire social and political consequences to the nation.

President's Action to Stave Off Famine

President Karzai took my recommendations quite seriously. He ordered the relevant ministers to act, importing wheat to Afghanistan and filling all the silos and wheat storage facilities in Kabul and the affected provinces.

At the beginning of each cabinet meeting, the president heard a progress report from the ministers and stressed further action for importing wheat into the country and the provinces.

I believe that my recommendations and the president's affirmative and decisive action spared Afghanistan from the consequences of the long-duration drought, impending famine, and any adverse effects on the war-torn population of the country.

President's Question Re: Difference between Past and Present Government Ethics

After I had attended a couple of cabinet meetings, the president, at the beginning of a cabinet meeting, asked me an unusual question. He said, "Mr. Assifi, could you tell us the difference between the way work was done in the past, when you held a position as minister, and the way things are done now?"

Since I had observed many problems in the way things were being done during that period, I asked the president to clarify his question. I wanted to see if he meant what he had said. He said, "Yes, Mr. Assifi, go ahead."

I stood up, came close to the table where the ministers were sitting, and addressed those who were present. I said, "Regarding the way things were done before—I am talking about the period of King Zahir Shah and later, during the presidency of Daoud Khan—the motto that I frequently heard in the government, from people both above and below me, was, 'Serve the people!' This was the motto stated by the king, and then by President Daoud, at the end of speeches or proclamations.

"Now, sir, I have worked for several years with DAI/USAID. I have taken trips to different parts and provinces of Afghanistan, and I have met with a lot of people, contractors included, who worked in nongovernmental organizations (NGOs), firms, companies, and government offices." At this point, I moved my hand, palm down, in a semicircular sweep.

I continued. "Sir, I think I am the oldest person in this room. Most probably, I am more experienced, and possibly more knowledgeable, in many subjects than some who are present here today. Sir, I was raised in a system wherein there was a difference between right and wrong. God Almighty made a heaven for the people who do good and a hell for the sinners. There is a difference between black and white. Sir, in Afghanistan, there is no difference between honest people and those who are corrupt. Everything in Afghanistan is gray! When one mixes black paint and white paint, the result is gray.

"Unfortunately, the people of Afghanistan are in a state of confusion. But, sir, I have been hearing another saying or motto now. Everyone frequently asks, 'What is in it for me?' or 'What is my take in it?'" Again, I moved my hand in a semicircular sweep.

Sensing that I was giving a speech that sounded more like a sermon, I started to talk about the day when Communists made a coup, Saur 7. Then, I mentioned the next day, *Saur 8, when President Daoud and his family, women and children included, were murdered by the Communists.* I very briefly spoke about that event's gory details.

I then added, "Sir, the dates of 7 and 8 Saur are a time when Afghans should mourn the tragic events that set a ruinous path for this country. But I have heard that some in this country have set this date for celebration. Sir, I vehemently protest this celebration, and I have told your people who are in charge of such events that I will not participate in them, so as to protest against this tragic celebration."

I could hear no sound of paper shuffling in the meeting. The ministers had confused looks on their faces. I had been counting on the Afghan tradition of respecting one's elders. At this meeting, I was an old man

369

among young men. So, up and going, I gave it to them, as an old man talking to his young ones.

After the meeting, some came to me, thanked me, and shook my hand for what I had said. But the hand-shakers were in the minority.

The president, on his way out of the room, came toward me and shook his head in acknowledgment. I could not guess whether he had expected me to say what I had. But one thing is like a law of Newton: one never knows what politicians really believe.

Policies and Laws for Natural Resource Development

In my capacity as technical advisor, I also helped prepare and enact policies and laws for natural resource development and evaluation, and for monitoring projects in the following sectors:

1) Mines, including gas and oil
2) Power and energy
3) Water, agriculture, and environment

In addition, I assisted in establishing the Department for Evaluation, which monitored and inspected infrastructure projects.

The president asked me to sit in during his cabinet meetings and attend the meetings of the Council of Ministers on Economy.

Dahla Dam Rehabilitation Project

The president also asked me to oversee and ensure the proper execution of the Arghandab Irrigation Rehabilitation Project (Dahla Dam) in Kandahar.

Accordingly, I assisted the Canadian embassy, the Canadian International Development Agency (CIDA), their consultants, and the Ministry of Energy and Water (MEW) in the formulation and implementation of the Arghandab River Dahla Dam project.

New Water Law: Preparation and Enactment

The president asked me to continue and make sure that the new water law was enacted. He requested that I help resolve the issues that had delayed the cabinet in passing the water law.

Note: I had earlier helped draft the new water law while I and my team were working for USAID. I helped resolve the problem by conducting several meetings between water professionals and related ministers. Minor revisions to the water law were made. Then, I helped the Ministry of Justice prepare the final draft for its submittal to the cabinet for approval.

Consequently, the water law, after being approved by Parliament, was printed in the *Official Gazette* on April 26, 2009.

Periodically, during cabinet or other meetings attended by the president, the need for further study and expert opinion became apparent. On these items, I submitted my recommendations to the president on an as-needed basis.

Discontinuance of Technical Advisory Services to the President

After a year and half, because I had health problems, I could not continue my advisory services to the president of Afghanistan.

Professional Work

I established an engineering consulting firm called ATA Group, Inc., and was the principal and president of this corporation. I was not successful at marketing my expertise.

Recommendation to US President

On the basis of my extensive work in Afghanistan and the United States and the experiences gained therefrom, I wrote a recommendation on how to succeed in Afghanistan and reduce American troop casualties.

I sent it to the US president's secretary by way of certified mail. However, to date, I have not received any response.

Maybe someone threw it inadvertently into the wastebasket and no one even read it. As I have repeated on many occasions in my writings, the leadership of a such a large bureaucratic office may have been overloaded!

My Memoirs

I have written about the work I did in the past and about that of my early years, when I worked for Afghanistan. I wrote about the tragic events of the Communist coup and the ill-fated period of my imprisonment. I described my coming out of Afghanistan, working in California, and again working in Afghanistan, up to my current period of retirement. I live in beautiful America. Needless to say, I call myself a patriotic Afghan American.

My Current Status

I reside with my family in Mission Viejo, California, USA.

When we came to America, my wife, Fariha Assifi, worked at small jobs here and there. At first, she did alterations work with a tailoring shop. Later, she worked with a wedding gown tailor in Fashion Island in Newport Beach. Later on, Fariha got a job as a secretary with the Orange County Community Development Council (CDC). Given her good performance at her job, she was later promoted to executive secretary and administrative coordinator at CDC.

After I was hired by the Irvine Ranch Water District as an engineer-planner, my family's financial situation greatly improved. We immediately rented an apartment, thereby lightening the burden on my brother-in-law and his lovely family.

When searching for means of transportation, I became familiar with secondhand car dealers. I decided to buy an old secondhand

Honda Civic. It appears that Hondas are the best alternative when one considers cost, performance, durability, and resale value.

At IRWD, I had a very good engineer as my supervisor. His name was Ergun Bakall. He hailed from Turkey and behaved quite like a young pasha. I learned many things about pipeline design from him.

One day, he asked me, "How much do you pay to rent your apartment?" After I answered him, he said, "Look, that is almost as much as paying for a house. If you buy a house, you will pay the same amount monthly, and the house will become yours. But with the rent that you pay monthly, the apartment will not be yours. So, why don't you guys buy a house?" The young Turkish pasha was right, but I had no down payment or other money for a house.

When I went home that evening, I discussed this with Fariha. She was very happy to hear about it and reminded me that we had sent Giselle, our daughter, some money earned from the things we had sold in Kabul. I called Giselle and asked her if she had any left of the money that I had sent her from Kabul. She said, "Yes, Dad, I have ten thousand dollars of your money with me, and I will send it if you need it."

I said, "Thanks, my love."

As you know, such things as buying a home don't happen overnight. Fariha and I, after searching, finally found a nice French Canadian by the name of Mike Dionne who was in real estate business. With his help, we started looking at housing possibilities. The criteria that I had given Mike were as follows: the house should be in a good residential area, of single-story construction, and close to a grade school. It should not have a swimming pool. The down payment should be no more than ten thousand dollars.

As is usual, we looked at many houses until we found one in the city of Orange. It met all our criteria, and the final price was $117, 500, requiring a down payment of $11,000. Mike said that he would pay the $1,000 more than we were able to pay. But, as it is obvious, we needed some more money for additional expenses and escrow costs. It was a dilemma, but we were not doing so bad. I still had some money from my monthly payroll check, but everything was rather tight.

One evening, Fariha and I were visiting her brother Abdullah and his wife, Seema jon. My wife and I had been discussing the matter of the house. I noticed that Seema jon's mother was about to leave the room. All who were present stood up in her honor. After about five minutes, she returned to the living room and placed an envelope in front of me. She said, "There is a thousand dollars in the envelope. It is yours to spend. You do not have to pay me back."

I said, "No, Auntie, we cannot accept this money. You are a refugee like us and do not have much money. We cannot accept the money." But Seema jon's mother was firm. She would not take the money back. Finally, I stood up, went to her, kissed her hand, and said, "I will accept it on one condition: that we pay you back when I get some money later."

She said, "Okay, my dear, we will see that later. God help us all!"

I had to put this event in my memoir. It is the good deeds we do that matter. The deeds and gestures of the beautiful people on earth are the things that strengthen our belief in humanity and make life a thing of beauty, something worth living. Our auntie has passed away, but I am certain, as certain that I can be, that *her place is in heaven.*

Although the price on the house in Orange was good, the interest rate on the loan was high (13.25 percent). Later on, my wife and I refinanced the house several times and took some money out of it for our kids' education costs as they went through college.

My Kids' Education

Madina and Shamila both attended the grade school, the intermediate school, and Al Modena High School, in the city of Orange. Neither of them knew English when we came from the old country. But they graduated from these schools with honors.

Like many American kids, both of them worked to pay their expenses through high school and university. It was especially good when they were working at Disneyland, because we could get free tickets to go there when a guest visited us from another place.

After graduating from Cal Poly Pomona, Madina took a master's degree in computer graphics. Shamila, after getting her degree from UC Fullerton, went for a master's degree to become a science teacher. She taught sixth-grade science at a school in Long Beach.

Our Family

Shamila has a daughter, Laila (ten years), a bright and advanced student in her school, and a son, Alexander (eight years), who is an equally bright student. Shamila's husband, Sulaiman Hamidi, is an environmentalist working with the Allergan pharmaceutical firm. He is a wonderful person.

Shamila and Sulaiman bought the house in Orange that Fariha and I had remodeled. However, they have added more features to and beautified the house that we once lived in.

Madina and her husband, Charlie Ostergren, have a house in Laguna Niguel. Madina's husband studied geology at the university level, but he has been working in charge of a computer networking firm that is spread over several continents.

Although Madina has had difficulty with an ailment called fibromyalgia, which requires frequent visits to the doctor, her husband has always been at her side and has taken care of our dear Madina throughout this difficult period. May God be with them and bless Madina and Charlie.

My wife and I are very fortunate to have such intelligent and nice sons-in-law. They are very compassionate and kind. They advise us on many issues and even help us whenever they come to our home.

Giselle, our oldest daughter, lived in Scotland and England. She married an Englishman, and they have a beautiful daughter, Somaya. Giselle and her daughter joined my wife and I after we came to the United States.

Our granddaughter Somaya was married to Masih Ishaq, a computer expert and businessman. Recently, they had a beautiful daughter named Sophia. So now Fariha and I have a great-granddaughter. Can you imagine how old I am getting? For several years, Giselle has been working with the US Navy in Afghanistan.

Both Giselle and our granddaughter Somaya are very considerate and kind people. Giselle is always here to help my wife and me with whatever problem we have.

Our son, Tamim, is the oldest of our children. Both Tamim and Giselle were born in our bedroom in Lashkargah. At that time, there was no hospital in Lashkargah.

Tamim was a very bright student in his classes. His IQ is in the higher range, and he went through several classes in high school and was the youngest when he entered the College of Engineering at Kabul University. He studied architecture and was in the fifth year when the bloody, Soviet-assisted coup broke in Kabul, Afghanistan. At that time, the Communists closed Kabul University's College of Engineering, because it was based on an American system of education and was assisted by the United States of America.

During the time when I was in Pul-i-Charkhi Prison, Tamim helped take care of his mother and sisters and my father and mother, which was quite a heavy burden for a boy of his age. Since Communists could not get him to join any of their organizations or committees, he was in grave danger of being imprisoned or killed. One of my greatest worries when I was in prison was the thought of his being brought to the prison as well.

The night when I was lucky enough to be released from the prison, Tamim said good-bye to me and then left with a friend and relative of our family, Mr. Sherjon Baha (Said Ibrahim Baha). Together, Tamim and Mr. Baha managed to walk out of Afghanistan by crossing mountains and deserts, and by making it past other seemingly insurmountable features and obstacles, such as the Communist government and the Russian Soviet soldiers and security forces. They were lucky to make it to Europe and then to the United States of America. Later, Tamim worked in architecture with several firms.

My father, true to his promise, came to be with us in America. For our family, this was like a gift sent from heaven. We were very fortunate to have my mother and father join us here in the United States. Throughout the years they were with us, they rented their own apartment. Giselle and Tamim were the two important people who took care of them when they were living in the apartment.

Some years later, when Tamim was going to a soccer match in New York, someone had to be staying with and taking care of my mother for a few days. Tamim told me, "Father, I have been taking care of your mother for the last ten years. Now it is your turn to take care of your mother for a week."

When I was in Kabul, Tamim asked me to get a copy of his transcript from the College of Engineering. After I got his transcript, he took additional courses in college, here in Orange County.

Since he had become enamored with computers, he then worked very hard to get a master's degree in computer science.

Tamim is the type of person that makes me very proud to be his father. He has been very helpful to and patient with me during my period of writing these memoirs. Although I was a pretty good engineer in my time, I could never have made it through this very important work without Tamim's assistance. God bless him and my lovely family and kids.

Both Fariha and I are retired from our jobs. Currently, we are living in a very good neighborhood in Mission Viejo, southern California. We are fortunate to have very nice people as neighbors in this location, and we enjoy living in this beautiful part of America.

I do not travel as much, going back and forth between the United States and Afghanistan, as I used to do before. Afghanistan is on the other side of the globe from where I now live. Traveling the long distance between the two countries is tiresome. We still have an apartment in Micro Rayan of Kabul City and my father's retirement land in Khanabad, in the northern part of Afghanistan. My father collected all his retirement money and bought a piece of land that did not have any irrigation water. He asked me to survey the land and see if I could design an irrigation system for it.

My Father's Irrigation Project—Design and Feasibility

At that time, I was working in Helmand. I took some time off from my work, surveyed my father's land, designed an irrigation system, and wrote an economic feasibility report for it. On that basis, he applied for a loan from the Agricultural Development Bank. He ultimately received a loan for developing that piece of nonproductive property. After the loan was approved, he built the irrigation system himself.

He used to go to his property in Khanabad and live in a farmhouse that he had built there. He paid off the entire loan by using his annual crop revenues. With the invasion of Afghanistan by the Soviets, he could no longer go to Khanabad, but he donated the revenues from his land to the cause of the freedom fighters. The farmhouse was rocketed by the Soviets, after which my father's dream to build a farm on that land was curtailed.

After the Soviets withdrew from Afghanistan, there were many government changes in the country. At one time, a number of refugees had come from Tajikistan, due to some trouble there. The United Nations Office for Refugees had built six hundred houses for these refugees on my father's land. After many years, when I returned to work in Afghanistan, I visited the property and was shocked to see that it was almost ruined. The Tajiks had already gone back to their country, but many transgressors were living in the houses that the UN had built.

I asked some friends who were familiar with the area to let me know the name of a person whom I could trust and assign as a manager to do the things that I planned to do there. After some time, Mr. Akbar Barakzai, whom I knew from the past, introduced me to Haji Ghulam Sakhi (HGS) and said that this person would do what I wanted and that I could trust him to be honest. From then on, Haji became my representative and the manager of the affairs of my father's property.

I made up my mind to rebuild the land and try to make my father's dream come true. From then on, I gradually redeveloped the land, got rid of six hundred houses that had been built on the arable sections, and tried to bring the farm back to a state of semiproduction. My petitions to the UN offices were met with the usual bureaucratic deaf ear, which meant that I had to suffer the extra cost of redevelopment. I went ahead and rebuilt my father's farmhouse and the orchard and tree plantations that he had toiled hard to develop.

However, in my eagerness to help the poor farmers, I allotted parts of the property for their farm shacks. I also went ahead and hired the poor, displaced people to farm parts of the land so they could make a living.

I Build a Grade School and Create a Mini School District

Later on, I discovered that there were no schools near the farmhouse in Khanabad. So, I proceeded to build a village school on our property for the boys and girls who belonged to the farm community.

My son, who is an architect, designed a six-room village school. I went ahead and started its construction using my own money and donations from village people and friends such as Billy O'Connell, who had taken a trip with me to the site and donated some money toward its construction costs.

I then went ahead and held a village meeting, where I told the people that this was their school. I advised them to elect a board of directors, a manager, and a school principal. In this way, I helped to found a mini school district in a village in Khanabad. After the villagers elected their school officers, I requested one favor from them, which concerned the name of the school. I asked them to vote for the name that I was requesting, which was my mother's name: Bibi Hawa ("Lady Eve"). The villagers gladly voted on this name.

Districts are unique in America; however, *I believe that this mini school district was the first of its kind in Afghanistan,* given that schools are part of the government's responsibility in my native country.

Later on, once the school was built, the villagers asked me to come to the site and take part in its opening ceremony. I asked some friends to travel with me to Khanabad. Mr. Elias and his brother Daoud Miskinyar went there with me. During the opening, the school principal said that the school needed a well for drinking water for the students. I asked our manager how much it would cost. He said that it would cost $1,000 to dig a deep well. I told the manager that I did not have the money at that time but that I would try to find some later. At that moment, the Miskinyar brothers said that they would contribute the money for this purpose. Later on, Haji said that he dug two deep wells with the money that was donated on that day.

When the Education Department asked Haji if he needed anything for the school, he asked them if they would support the two teachers' monthly salaries. So, the salary of Bibi Hawa School's teachers is now paid by the Education Department.

The Bibi Hawa School is functioning well, and it is run by the mini school district. My friend Billy asks me, "Why don't you build an intermediate school in that location?" He says that he will go with me and help build that school. I have not yet answered him on this call. I am waiting for the security situation to calm down before I venture back to that area.

Appendix

Additional Information About the Author

Since 1983, Tawab Assifi has been a registered professional engineer in civil engineering. His registration, RCE # 36093, was issued by the state of California.

Memberships

American Society of Civil Engineers (ASCE), member ID #282962

American Water Works Association (AWWA), California/Nevada, member ID #00189639

National Association of Corrosion Engineers (NACE), member ID #016978-00

Mr. Assifi was trained by the World Bank, receiving an Economic Development Institute (EDI) fellowship in economics and financial analysis in 1972.

Publications

Master's thesis accepted by Colorado State University, Fort Collins, Colorado, as a PhD dissertation. One thousand copies were printed as a book in 1966.

Helmand Valley Shamalan land development project plans were printed as a report titled "A Concept for Ownership Consolidation and Land Development" and submitted to the Eighth NESA Regional Irrigation Seminar, September 1970, Kabul.

Tawab Assifi, "The Russian Rope: Soviet Economic Motives and the Subversion of Afghanistan" *World Affairs* 145 (Winter 1982): 253–66.

Tawab Assifi and J. F. Shroder, "Afghan Mineral Resources and Soviet Exploitation," in *Afghanistan: The Great Game Revisited,* ed. Rosanne Klass (Washington, DC: Freedom House, 1987), 97–134.

Author with mother 1933

Author with parents 1935

Author a student at Cornell University

Author with wife in Lashkargah 1957

Author giving speech as
governor of Herat 1973

Author & wife at Agra
India state visit

Minister of Mines & Industries

عبدالتواب آصفی
وزیر معادن و صنایع

Author with other
political prisoners, a
month before release
from Pul-e-Charkhi

Author with other political prisoners,
a month before release from
Pul-e-Charkhi

With Anthony Donini
and UNOCA mission
meeting at Hazar Asp
Shamalan

With Anthony Donini and UNOCA mission meeting
at Hazar Asp Shamalan.

With Anthony Donini
and UNOCA mission
meeting at Hazar Asp
Shamalan

With Anthony Donini and UNOCA mission meeting
at Hazar Asp Shamalan.

Author at Darqad Intake
site during project
opening, with engineers
John Priest and Ed Stains

Author as Eng at IRWD

Author's parents

Author with family

Author with family and grandkids

Author & son Tamim at Tashqurghan pass,
going north to Balkh Mazar-i-shareef

Author's father holding grandson Tamim 1957,
above Helmand river at Kajakai

INDEX

Part 2

393

Part 3